That Went By Fast

That Went By Fast

MY FIRST HUNDRED YEARS

Frank White

HARBOUR PUBLISHING

Harbour Publishing Co. Ltd.
P.O. Box 219, Madeira Park, BC, V0N 2H0
www.harbourpublishing.com

Edited by Howard White
Photographs courtesy the White family unless otherwise noted
Text design by Mary White
Dust jacket painting by Kim LaFave
Dust jacket design by Shed Simas
Indexed by Nicola Goshulak
Printed and bound in Canada

Cataloguing data available from Library and Archives Canada
ISBN 978-1-55017-668-1 (cloth)
ISBN 978-1-55017-669-8 (e-book)

We gratefully acknowledge financial support from the Government of Canada
through the Book Publishing Industry Development Program and the Canada
Council for the Arts, and from the Province of British Columbia through the
BC Arts Council and the Book Publishing Tax Credit.

Contents

Preface

I Become an Artifact

Getting old isn't all it's cracked up to be but it has some plusses. When I trundle down to the shopping centre in Madeira Park people I don't know greet me like a long-lost friend. I've lived in Pender Harbour sixty years and never did feel part of the place before, but now they treat me like a local hero. When I put out the book about my early years in 2013 they put on a do for me in the old ranger station and half the town turned out—the good half at that. I guess what has happened is that at a hundred I have outlived all my enemies. Everybody that's left always seems to be glad to see I've lived another day. I guess that's good, I don't know. It's something.

When I was fifty and still had most of my marbles, all people wanted me to tell them was why their car stalled at the intersection. Now that everything is starting to get hazy, they're not satisfied unless I can tell them the meaning of life. Luckily that has become easier. I just look wise and say no matter what happens, the girls are just as pretty as they ever were. If I'd said that back when I was only seventy, they would have called me a dirty old man, but at a hundred it goes over big.

The next thing, they want to know all the changes you've seen. The biggest one. I say, "Oh, girls are harder to fool now." They laugh like I'd cracked the joke of the century. But the truth is, I was never able to fool any girls then or now.

When I was a young fellow I was pretty sure I was going to be a great man and go down in history. Then when I saw how tough that was I decided to settle for just making a lot of money. Then when I saw how hard that was I settled for just earning a living and keeping my wife and kids fed and clothed, and even that was touch and go at times. I'd got used to thinking my life hadn't amounted to much and it seemed most people agreed with me on that. Now it's, "Oh, you rode in a horse and buggy? You worked on a steam donkey show? Your girlfriend was a flapper? You ran a cable shovel? You hunted basking sharks? You sold gas at forty cents a gallon? You should write a book!"

For a good part of my life I had the sense of being a little behind the times, then completely out of date, but by hanging on as long as I have it seems I've gone right off the scale and become an object of historical interest. And, you know? It was the easiest thing I ever did. All I had to do was wait.

To tell the truth, when I try to think what's changed not all that much seems different from when I started. I feel lucky. It seems to me I have lived in one of history's good stretches where nothing too bad or too crazy happened. I have to remind myself I've lived through the two greatest wars in history, the deadliest plague in history, the worst depression in history, and I've seen them go from the horse and buggy to the Mars rover. But you have to stop to think about that. You don't really notice history when you're living it. You don't really remember that most homes had outdoor plumbing or that women wore skirts down to the ground back then. Looking back, it's not the wars and the plagues and the revolutions in taste and technology you remember but the personal things. Dumb things.

You still feel bad you never kissed the cute girl from down the road when you were five. I still feel a rush of fresh panic thinking about that stupid damn stunt I pulled as a kid that almost killed a man, ninety years later. You remember your first daughter taking her first step, all the promise that seemed to represent, promise you somehow feel you missed out on because you were too busy chasing your tail. Now that daughter's children have children and it all seems just the blink of an eye. I see people's faces crumpling with age like scraps of paper in a fire. Where did the time go? All my life I've been putting things off, especially the good things, the things I knew were most important but I thought could wait. Now at a hundred the hardest thing to get used to is—there's just no time left. You're forced to look at all these dumb damn things you've done and say, well I guess that was it. I guess that was my life. There is nothing like an ending to make things fall into place.

Frank White
Madeira Park, BC, May 10, 2014

Part 1

THE MAKING
OF A
GYPPO

1

Valley Boy

Before I get into the meat of this book, which covers the stumbling around I did between the ages of thirty-five and a hundred, I'm going to take a quick spin through my first thirty-five years even though I wrote about it at excessive length in my first book, *Milk Spills and One-Log Loads*. I don't like to repeat myself but since only .00005 percent of the Canadian population read that other book, I guess I can't assume everybody knows what was said. Luckily my recollections are inconsistent enough that the second telling might seem like entirely new stories, but those who can't stand the thought of hearing them again are free to start at Chapter Two.

I was born in Sumas, Washington, in 1914, just as the First World War was about to begin. My parents had a farm in Aldergrove, BC, and Sumas had the nearest hospital, so I became an American of convenience. People have told me I could claim US citizenship and double up on my old age pension but I never got around to it. My Canadian one creates enough paperwork to drive me nuts as it is. For years now they have been claiming I owe them $40,000 because I got married without asking their permission or something, but I hope to die before they show up at my door to collect. Then they can have anything they find, I won't care.

In 1919 my father moved to Abbotsford, BC, and that is where I grew up. He himself had grown up in Ottawa. In the first book I freely admitted I hadn't paid proper attention to family history lessons as a kid and really didn't know much about my father's family background, but was prepared

There I am ninety-nine years ago with about the same attention span, motor skills and bladder control as I have right now.

to make some wild guesses. But one of the good things about publishing a book is you get to find out how wrong you are about all sorts of things. My younger second cousins, Gregg and Irene Carmichael, undertook a little research and found out that my father was born in Upper Canada in 1864 and not on a refugee ship coming over from Ireland as I had been told. The romantic family myth that his father had got to Canada by eloping with his boss's daughter was also cruelly debunked. According to apparently irrefutable records my grandfather George White was born in "Canada West" in 1841 and married a Canadian-born woman, Martha Kelly, with whom he had five children in rapid succession whereupon she perhaps understandably expired. My grandfather then married a local spinster named Emma Ferrand, who learned from her predecessor's example and had no children. So my father's brothers and sisters were actually full-blooded siblings and not stepbrothers and sisters

Abbotsford about the time we moved there, with truck parked in front of my father's meat market. THE REACH P12983

as I had unblushingly informed the world. It's amazing what little knowledge of your own history it takes to get by in this life.

Once in Abbotsford, Father started a butcher shop and I became an apprentice butcher by the time I was eight. I used to like to startle the neighbourhood ladies by getting up on my butter box so I could see over the counter and steel a butcher knife half as long as I was, while I politely asked them what I could get them. I hoped they would go home and tell their daughters that, contrary to popular opinion, I was a pretty cool guy.

My father was a pretty cool guy, but none of it rubbed off on me. He was one of the most popular guys in town. He had a smooth, round face that when he laughed it just lit up like the full moon, and he laughed a lot. He had been the Canadian welterweight boxing champion when he was eighteen but professional boxing wasn't really organized then, so the only way to make a living at it was to go on tour fighting local tough guys. He had spent a good part of his life touring Canada and the US as a prizefighter with carnivals and vaudeville shows, and he had a big streak of entertainer in him. He loved telling jokes and giving recitations of Shakespeare and Omar Khayyám and people just liked to be around him.

He kept his fighting skills all his life. Even as an old man he would challenge tough guys to try and hit him—"C'mon, hit me, I won't hurt you, c'mon, give me your best shot." So they'd start out with a feeble little swat that didn't come close and he'd say, "You can do better than that, c'mon . . . " and pretty soon they'd be going at him like a windmill, sweating and grunting but still not coming close to touching him. Sometimes after one of their wild haymakers had them off balance, he'd give them a little tap and sit them on their butt, not to hurt them but just for laughs.

To him, boxing was one of the great arts every bit as skilled as fencing or ballet. Wherever he lived he'd set up boxing clubs and train all the young fellas around—except me. He wouldn't teach me the first thing. He said it was because I didn't have the right touch and it would only get me into trouble, but looking back I think the trouble he was thinking about was the trouble he'd get into with my mother. She was a straightlaced Presbyterian and she disapproved of his boxing activities, which she associated with sport and rowdyism and smoking and drinking and most of the things in life that were any fun, which she was firmly against.

My family about 1918, just before we moved to Abbotsford. My dad Silas F. White holding my sister Beryl; me and my mother Jean White (née Carmichael) holding my sister Hazel.

It was pretty tough for a kid when your father was teaching all the other boys the manly art of self-defence and leaving you out in the cold, so I did the only natural thing and set out to prove him wrong. Anytime one of the boys who thought he could box started trying to push me around, I'd pop him a good one in the nose. To my great surprise and delight I found that usually ended the session right there. When it didn't, I would keep whaling away until somebody was out of commission, and usually it wasn't me. I had the advantage of having something to prove, although it was never enough to convince my father I might have any promise as a boxer after all.

He called what I did brawling and he had nothing but contempt for brawlers. That just made me try all the harder, and I became known around Abbotsford back alleys as something small and nasty that was better avoided. My father was a pretty good psychologist on most days but his plan for keeping me out of trouble wasn't one of his better moves. After all his years in the ring, his features were still clean and sharp but by the time I was twenty-five my nose looked like it had been through our old sausage grinder.

Apart from our disagreement over my fighting ability, I revered my father. He showed me everything else he knew except boxing and from about the age of eight onward I was his chief assistant in the meat business. By the age of twelve he had me going out to butcher pigs with only my sidekick Rendell McKinnon for help. He also taught me to drive, or taught me as much as he knew, which wasn't much. He'd bought one of the first Model T Ford trucks in Abbotsford and used it to make deliveries but he was never comfortable with horseless carriages.

He'd grown up driving the non-horseless kind and when he needed to stop, he'd roar, "Whoa, ya bastard" and yard back on the steering wheel like reins. I could see this was the wrong approach and set about demonstrating the right way as soon as I was tall enough to reach the pedals. This was okay with him and he would let me drive him around town sitting on his lap. Of course, in a small place like Abbotsford very little escaped the attention of the local provincial policeman. Corporal Greenwood eventually took Father aside and told him it might be better if they conspired together to fix me up with a proper licence. I was only thirteen at the time but that didn't seem to matter. After that there was no holding me back and the old Model T and I became a fixture on the roads of the central Fraser Valley.

So by the age of thirteen I already had two professions: butcher and truck driver.

Before settling down, my father had used up a good part of his life chasing around the country beating up local tough guys and operating fitness centres (they were called gymnasiums then). By the time I was helping him in the butcher shop, he was in his sixties, which made him an old man by 1920s standards. On top of that, he had chronic asthma, which grew steadily worse. In 1929 his coughing fits were getting so bad the doctor recommended he take a break in the BC Interior, thinking the dry air might help his lungs. I was assigned to drive him up to visit his cousins in Oliver and we spent what seemed to me an idyllic summer there camping out in a rented cabin and working in the fruit packing plant, where my uncle George trained me in the gentlemanly art of box-making.

I thought we were doing fine, but one day toward summer's end, Father told me he was dying and wanted to get home. This caught me completely off guard. I knew he was sick but up to that time we had always treated it as a passing thing and I actually thought he was getting better. I refused to believe him at first and didn't know how to handle it. He was my buddy. I didn't have many friends my own age because I spent all my time with him. During the summer we had become closer than ever before. When I thought of facing life without him, I just felt lost. But there was no getting around it and we drove back home, where he went straight to bed and wasted away until November when he died.

So here we were, five fatherless kids ranging in age from nine to fifteen with a mother who was completely unsuited to fending for herself, with no money saved, no income and the Great Depression just beginning. Mother was the eldest of thirteen in her family, the Carmichaels, and you'd think there would be some support there but it didn't amount to much. One of my many uncles, Fred Carmichael, took over our meat business and grudgingly hired me as assistant but he got his revenge by driving me like a slave.

I had to go down and help open up before school, then go back at lunchtime, then again after school. Sometimes he kept me so late in the mornings I'd have to run to school and still be late for class. I'd been a good student and wanted to become a doctor but with all the classes I was missing and no time to do homework, my grades started slipping. I passed all my finals except for one English course that required a lot of reading, and that was the end of my hopes for higher education. With Mother struggling to get along on the widow's pension of $30 a month there was no way we could afford it anyway.

Safeway began moving into BC in the early thirties and when they set up a branch in Abbotsford, Uncle Fred took over the meat department and took me with him, so I spent four years working at Safeway. I didn't mind the work and became a pretty sharp young butcher but I was never going to be more than a go-fer in Fred's mind so I started looking for other things. I loved driving so I started driving a delivery truck for a man named Milton Nelles, who had a small creamery in town. Nelles had a son-in-law named Les McGarva who was his main driver and in about 1931, McGarva struck out on his own with a three-ton Ford hauling bulk milk into Vancouver for dairy farmers on Sumas Prairie. Les had a wild reputation as a hard drinker so it didn't look promising at first glance, but it was a matter of doing the right thing in the right place at the right time and Les' business took off.

Farmers up to that time had been dependent on the BC Electric milk train to take their cans to market and it was up to the farmer to get the cans to the train, which meant getting up extra early to milk the cows, hitch up the wagon, load it up, drive to the nearest station and move the load once more onto the train platform. It was a lot of extra work added to the farmer's already hard-working morning. With his truck, Les McGarva could come right to the barn and whisk the milk away, which not only saved the farmer all that extra work, it allowed him to get up a little later. But all the work the farmer saved was loaded onto the shoulders of the truck driver, who had to load his entire truck with 125-lb milk cans stacked two decks high, stop at the end of the route to switch them all around in the right order for delivery, then drive them into Vancouver and unload them all. McGarva was not a very big guy and liked to spend as much time as possible sitting in the beer parlour getting drunk each day, so it wasn't long before he went looking for somebody dumb and strong to drive his truck for him. His father-in-law said, "I know just the guy," and that is how I became a full-time milk truck driver.

It was a crazy job. Les ran the company out of the Atangard beer parlour in Abbotsford. His chief competitor, Irving Parberry, ran a rival

Irv Parberry and Les McGarva went head-to-head in a Wild West–style battle for the Abbotsford trucking business.

milk-hauling outfit from an opposite corner of the same beer parlour. They didn't have any actual offices. McGarva and Parberry schemed endlessly to steal each other's customers and at one point, Parberry's gang even hijacked one of McGarva's trucks, and would have hijacked the one I was driving if I hadn't fended them off with a jack handle. They spent a lot of time and money suing each other. Both of them were heavy boozers and when they weren't brawling, spent a lot of time partying together.

Coming from a strict Presbyterian home where drinking was verboten and you weren't even allowed to go fishing on Sunday, I didn't know what to make of this scene at first, but I soon learned how to sock back beer as good as anyone and got into the spirit of the thing. We would drink in Abbotsford before we started out, we would drink in Vancouver while we waited for the dairies to give back our cans, then we would finish off the day drinking at Les' table in the Atangard. I remember once in the mid-thirties realizing I had not parked the truck sober for an entire month.

I moved out of my mother's home and began boarding with Les McGarva and his wife Florence. Their place was full of life with people coming and going all day long, and kind of a hub for a lot of the stuff that was happening in and around Abbotsford. It was quite thrilling for me with my sheltered upbringing and I couldn't get enough of it. Les had a big streak of what today they'd call charisma and he became like a second father to me, although he was only seven years older.

He was a complete alcoholic. He could hardly talk until he'd had a few beers in the morning. Being drunk was his normal state, but he was one of these people who could think when he was drunk. He did his best work drunk. This was a big part of his success. He would get everybody else drunk then talk business and have them at his mercy. He used that method to build up a successful trucking business, to build a nice new house without going a penny into debt, to grab two failing dairy farms and build them into good producers. He became one of Abbotsford's most successful businessmen—right in the middle of the Great Depression. I tried to copy him, and it took me way too long to figure it out, but I was definitely the other kind of drunk.

I stuck with McGarva and the milk route for most of the Depression. It gave me steady work and a lot of adventures but I didn't make enough money to get ahead. Les kept hinting he'd make me a partner but instead he took in his brother John, who defaulted on the truck payments and gas bill, then tried to sell out to Parberry behind Les' back. That pretty much finished things between me and Les but the thing that really tore it was a pretty lady.

Being on the road every day and forming one of the only regular links between the isolated valley town and the big city put a young guy in a pretty good position with just about everybody, but especially with the local womenfolk. Everybody in town was dying to get away and see the sights of Vancouver, and us truck drivers had a reputation for knowing where the action was. Most girls didn't have any money for a train fare in the Depression and they'd do just about anything to get a free day in the Big Smoke. Les had places along the route where he'd pull off into the bushes to collect the fare.

There was a farmer on Sumas Prairie named Howard Boley who had four beautiful daughters. The eldest, Kathleen or Kay, was probably the prettiest girl in the Fraser Valley, but she was very aloof and had been giving me the cold shoulder for years. But being shut up on her parents' farm with her battleaxe of a mother got even to her after a while, and I was pleasantly surprised one day when she hit me up for lift to town. Naturally I made it clear she could come any time she wanted, even though there was no question of any monkey business with her. It was months before I got to hold her hand and months more before I managed a kiss. But things did slowly progress and in 1939 we got married.

Kay was wonderful. In spite of being movie-star beautiful, she was as down to earth as they come. She knew I didn't have ten cents in the bank and a fairly iffy reputation for fighting and drinking, but she seemed thrilled out of her skull to move into a little shack with me. To get a little money ahead, she spent the first year of married life raising a herd of pigs in the backyard.

There was one thing she wasn't easygoing about however, and that was my drinking and my drinking friends. This was a major crisis for me because that was my life. I had been a nerdy kid with few friends and it was only when I had fallen in with the drinking crowd I had ever felt part of the group. The drinking was tied in with trucking and my life ambition was to become a successful truck owner myself. I figured if an illiterate drunk like McGarva could do it, it should be a lead-pipe cinch for a smart, hard-working young guy like me. In the meantime, driving trucks gave me a place in a group of people I looked up to and I was still getting a lot of satisfaction from that. But Kay made it clear right away that she wasn't going to be a part of it and she wasn't going to sit home and be left out of it either. It came to where I had to decide between my life on the trucks and her, so after a lot of soul-searching I quit McGarva and went to work at the Buckerfield's feed store. That was seasonal and petered out, so I went back driving at an entirely new kind of trucking job: hauling logs.

Trucks had been used to haul logs in a minor way up to the late 1930s but hadn't seriously challenged the dominant method, which was rail. Logging on the coast had started in the great flat valley bottoms where the heaviest timber grew and this encouraged the development of large operations that could afford to build railways down the length of the valley. But by 1935, those valleys were getting used up and loggers started looking for ways to get at the timber growing higher up on the side hills. Trains can't climb steep grades but trucks can, so the time was right for trucks. At the same time, Detroit came out with affordable mass-produced trucks mounted on pneumatic tires that could handle rough dirt roads. Previous to that logging trucks had used solid rubber tires that needed roads laboriously constructed out of wooden timbers. The new balloon-tired trucks created the opportunity for a new kind of logging, although this wasn't obvious to everybody at once.

When an industry gets in the habit of doing a thing one way, it will go on trying to do it that way even after new technology has made it obsolete, sometimes for decades. This often creates an opening for some young sharpie educated in the new ways to move in and take over. Only in the case of logging, it wasn't a young whiz kid, it was an old deaf mechanic named Bill Schnare (we said it "Snar") who ran a haywire gas station on Abbotsford's main drag.

I was there and watched it all happen. Old Schnare was a know-it-all kind of guy who was always fiddling around with bright ideas that didn't quite work out. He made the first radio in Abbotsford, a scratchy little crystal set my father and I listened to the famous Firpo–Dempsey heavyweight fight on. He was always buying and selling old wrecks out of the back of his shop and this one time he got stuck with a Ford truck. He'd sold it to a couple of guys to haul poles with but they ran it into the ground then skipped town without paying. Schnare fixed it and put it back up for sale but was having a hard time moving it. If it had a flat deck or a cargo box on it, he probably could have sold it, but these guys had rigged it up with a haywire trailer for hauling poles. Finally Schnare took his own kid out of school and sent him out driving this truck. Stan hadn't been going anywhere in school anyway.

Well, by god, it turned out there was quite a demand for a truck that could move poles and logs from farmers who were clearing land and small patches of timber usually cleared by horse teams, so Schnare got a few more trucks and rigged them up with trailers. There were other guys trying this here and there but the difference with Schnare was that he had this inventive streak so he got fiddling around trying to make things work better. These old single-axle three-tons really couldn't handle much rough-going the way they came from the factory so he put a second axle on them and lowered the gear ratio so they could climb steeper grades. Then he was able to lengthen out the trailer and beef it up with a second axle so it could haul bigger and heavier logs. The brakes on those early trucks were useless, so he beefed them up and added water cooling so they wouldn't burn up coming down the long hills, and pretty soon he had those old beaters humping wood like there was no tomorrow.

At this time, some of the best timber left in BC was growing on top of Vedder Mountain, between Abbotsford and Chilliwack. A big railroad outfit named Brown and Kirkland (B&K) had logged the lower levels but the mountain itself had been too steep for them. Now a group of local contractors put their heads together and undertook to log it for B&K using Schnare and his new-look logging trucks. The old-time loggers used elaborate cable systems powered by huge steam donkeys to reach far back from the rail end or "trackside" and drag or "yard" the logs into the railcars but the Vedder contractors used a bulldozer to punch roads in close to the standing timber where it could be loaded onto Schnare's trucks using lighter, more portable equipment. It was a whole new kind of logging, small and mobile. And cheap. Schnare rode his drivers hard to get the wood out and spent nights and weekends changing burnt-out engines and doing repairs needed to keep the wheels turning.

They finished the Vedder Mountain claim in record time and made nothing but money for everyone involved. It was the talk of the logging world. Everybody was coming around to see how the modern way of logging worked. Schnare kept pushing his advantage, expanding and upgrading his fleet until by the late 1940s he was the biggest hauling contractor in BC and a very wealthy man.

I seem to have told this story too often but it was the one time in my life I saw history in the making and actually took part in it myself. This one show changed logging, and set the stage for the next part of my story. Before Vedder, logging was largely a big company industry. After Vedder, every chokerman and rigging slinger on the BC coast was getting his hands on an old truck and looking for a little patch of timber to log as boss of his own show. Over the next twenty-five years, a new kind of logger came into being—the truck logger—and for that period logging became something an ordinary guy could jump into on his own. Soon there were hundreds of small "gyppo" operators like a plague of termites munching away in every inlet and bay up and down the BC coast. It was the heyday of the little guy, and I was right in there munching with the rest of them.

In 1939 I got started driving logging trucks on Vedder Mountain where the logs were huge and the trucks were tiny.

Just as the Vedder operation was starting, Schnare got hold of me and said, "Why don't you come driving for me and make some real dough?" I was getting frustrated with my shrinking hours at Buckerfield's and missing truck driving, so I jumped at the chance. It was a very different kind of trucking from highway hauling and at first I didn't think I was going to make the grade but I got the hang of it eventually. When the Vedder job finished up, Schnare took a contract at Nanoose Bay on Vancouver Island so I took several of his trucks over there. Schnare was okay and I was making good money but I still had ambitions to get into trucking on my own and even though I was making decent money, I began to chafe at working for wages.

About this time my old boss Les McGarva came back into my life. His milk-hauling business was still limping along but he'd pretty much handed it over to his brother, who was busily running it into the ground. Les himself was in bad shape. He looked all bloated and yellow and his doctor had warned him he would die within the year if he didn't kick the booze—but for Les life without booze wasn't worth living. One day I was surprised as hell when he just turned up on our door at Nanoose Bay, unannounced. He was at loose ends trying to figure out whether to shoot himself or go on living and he decided to come over and have a talk to me. Kay was horrified—she had hoped we'd left him and the whole drinking nightmare behind us forever—but I was actually kind of glad to see him and touched that he would turn to me at a time like this. I didn't know what the hell to tell him and we couldn't go on a drunk so I took him out on the truck to show him what logging looked like up close. He had never seen active logging before and was all eyes.

"Jesus, this is real trucking!" he said. "You and I ought to buy a truck and get in on this!" So by Christ if we didn't go back to Vancouver together and buy a truck, a real dandy 1936 Dodge Heavy Duty with low hours. For Kay, it was her worst fears realized, but for me it was my dream come true. My old pal Les had come through and I was a truck owner at last, or at least a part owner.

Well, you can probably guess the next part. Being a successful truck owner wasn't as easy as it had looked to a young guy doing all the work and watching his boss bank all the money. Since I was now an owner-operator,

I had to work all day driving the truck, then stay up all night doing the repairs. I took a contract on Salt Spring Island on a road up Mount Maxwell so steep it beat the hell out of the truck, then the loggers went broke and I didn't get paid. I got a good job hauling for a logger on northern Vancouver Island who did pay but Les got up to his old tricks and cleaned out our bank account, leaving us with nothing to pay our gas bill. When I finally got a job that was clear sailing over at Garibaldi Station and started to get ahead, I gave in to the temptation to go big and traded my good Dodge in on three beat-up old Macks so I could take a contract back on Vancouver Island for the forest giant, H.R. MacMillan Co.

This was the company Schnare had made his fortune with and I thought I was on my way but I was unprepared for big company politics and they put me on all the tough, low-paying hauls and loaded my trucks with the crappiest wood so I couldn't get any scale. The harder I worked the more I fell behind. An underage driver named Gordie Cochrane ran one of my Macks over a cliff and totalled it. By 1948 I was so far behind I could see I was never going to make it, so I turned the two remaining Macks back to the dealer I'd bought them from, Charlie Philp.

Philp was a former car salesman who had left his job to set up BC's first Mack truck dealership and he had made a fortune supplying trucks to Bill Schnare. He let me off the hook for the rest of what was owed on the trucks but he kept everything I'd paid on them, which was quite a bit. Charlie was sharp. He'd give a guy just enough rope to keep going but he would make damn sure that every time a nickel came in, it went into his pocket. He was not unlike Les McGarva in that. Keep your eye on the money. It's a simple credo but one I didn't figure out till way too late in life. I had the idea that if I worked harder and did a better job than anyone else, it would pay off. Guys like Philp must have loved to see me coming.

There, I've covered my first thirty-five years in only one chapter. I have no idea why it took me a whole book the first time.

2

Out of the Woods—Briefly

n my mid-thirties I was still thinking I could become rich, although my sights were lowering. I had helped other guys make fortunes in the trucking business and tried my damndest to copy them—with poor results. I had spent twenty years working my ass off and had nothing to show for it, except a bunch of other rich bastards who gave no sign they were the least bit thankful for my efforts. So the conclusion I came to was that I would be better off in a business where I was my own boss and not depending on the favour of corrupt higher-ups who wouldn't give a guy a break unless he kissed their ass in just the right place.

One of the things that got me thinking this was my sister Beryl. All this time she'd been birling away in the dress store I'd helped her start when she was still a teenager and she'd been getting ahead all the time. She hadn't made a fortune exactly, but she had paid off her house and been putting money in the bank every year. It got me thinking a small business like that where you had a chance to write your own ticket would be a better way to go. I got talking it over with her and she was full of encouragement. She steered me to the dry cleaning business. She said more and more people were wearing store-bought fabrics you couldn't launder or press at home and there was a crying need for good dry cleaning businesses in just about any town you could name, including Abbotsford.

I liked the idea of moving back to Abbotsford and setting Kay up in a proper house in a good neighbourhood after dragging her around to all those godawful shacks in the bush. Not that she'd ever said a word. She was game for anything I threw at her, except being left by herself. That was the thing about Kay. She always bought right in on any lunatic scheme I was pursuing and put her full support behind it. None of this harping stuff about "you should do this, you should do that, I want a fancy house and a fur coat." We now had two children, Marilyn, born in 1942 and Howard in 1945 and she worried about the kids having proper friends and schools when they got older but even that she didn't push too hard because she always figured we should do whatever it took to get ahead. We were young and resourceful and she wanted to do more to help.

The funny thing was, she wasn't all that fussy about the idea of moving back to Abbotsford. She liked the idea of having a nice house and being close to schools rightly enough, but she never did feel comfortable living in Abbotsford. I don't know why this was. It could have been to do with my drinking and banging around with the old bunch, but they were all scattered now, or dead.

One of the old bunch I'd kept in touch with was Dutch Parberry, who stayed driving trucks and had always been a kind of a decent guy and not too much on the booze. I looked him up, but I found he had picked up a worse habit than booze. He was using heroin. Nowadays, heroin has such a bad reputation you have to be a fairly committed outlaw to mess with it, but in those days it wasn't quite so far out. It had originally been marketed as an over-the-counter cough medicine from the same people who made Aspirin. They labelled it Heroin because it was supposed to be the hero of medicines, a safe kind of morphine. It had an aura of acceptance that clung to it for many years and a lot of ordinary guys like Dutch took it for innocent kicks and got hooked before they knew what hit them. He thought it was just the greatest thing ever and put a lot of pressure on me to try it. So I let him give me some one time but I couldn't see the point of it. I didn't like the idea of it at all. I was over at his place one time when he got back from town and it seemed everybody in the house was jumping around: "Did you get it? Did you get it?" Even one of the kids. That was the end of Dutch for me.

We were living with Beryl in her house up on the Old Yale Road and I was anxious to get in a place of our own, so I made a down payment on a double lot out in a new development on what they were calling McCrimmon Drive, on the Matsqui side of Abbotsford. When I was up in Garibaldi I had built a nice little cottage for Kay and the kids and I couldn't get it out of my head that it was just abandoned there—the logging company had gone broke and pulled out—so I cooked up the idea of going up there and bringing it out. I broke it all down and loaded it on a flat car and moved it up to Lytton, then took it down to Abbotsford by truck.

It was a hell of a lot of work by the time I had the house back together and sitting up on a foundation all wired and plumbed and ready to move into. Stan Grigg, a local guy who was supposed to know something about carpentry but turned out to know less than me, swore I would have saved time and money starting from scratch and he was probably right. But we ended up with a house—the first house we had built with our own hands. Kay got involved in everything, from planning to buying materials to nailing up shingles and painting. We were very happy in it and finished it off in a way more suitable to its new location in a suburban subdivision. I sided it with asphalt siding in a red-brick design and rebuilt the roof in a pyramid style with rounded eaves and thought it looked quite smart. The only problem was it was too small for a family of four going on five.

I began making plans to build another house on the other half of the lot, this time a three-bedroom one with a basement. This was my first go at a real serious house and I was determined to do a first-class job of it. We got a plan of what seemed a very elegant 1940s bungalow with an L-shaped floor plan and finished it over the next two years. It was our dream house, a fine handsome thing I was as proud of as anything I ever did but it was never the happy home that the little one was. The little one was something we tossed up without too much thought and since we had no expectations, it easily exceeded them. But the big one was our dream home and like most dream homes it never quite lived up to the dream. For one thing, it stretched our resources to the limit and like a lot of self-built homes, we didn't get around to finishing it until I was getting ready to sell it to someone else. But it did serve one purpose: it proved to me that I could build a house as good as anybody else. Both those houses are still in use as of 2014.

You couldn't stop Kay from picking up a shovel.

I don't know why I didn't just keep building houses. There's been about a million of them built around the Valley since that one and it was something I could have stayed busy at from that time to this. But somehow it never occurred to me as something a guy could do for a living. Instead I decided to pursue Beryl's idea of dry cleaning. I didn't have the money to set up a complete cleaning plant of my own, so I started by getting a garment press. Beryl had it figured out that pressing was the labour-intensive part, and if we did that ourselves we could make a pretty good deal with Kingsway Cleaners to do just the cleaning at bulk rates. She was always thinking, and it probably would have worked out for the right kind of guy. But I wasn't that guy. When I tell people I once tried to make a living cleaning and pressing clothes they inevitably burst out laughing. I am not exactly known for my razor-sharp creases. I am more known for wearing Red Strap jeans hemmed with a dull falling axe and fuzzy sweaters decorated with samples of my last week's lunches.

Of all the things I ever tried to do, this was the most unlikely. But I had this dream of providing my family a nice civilized life in a pleasant suburban setting with dancing classes and sports teams and honour rolls and college, just like the vision of the post-war American dream in *Life* magazine. That was the right thing to do for your family if you were a good 1940s man, so I believed. I worked my butt off chasing dirty laundry all over Abbotsford in my old van. I took Marilyn with me often and had her running around making deliveries. It was great fun for both of us. Beryl acted as my storefront, taking deliveries and drumming up business but the money just wasn't there. I couldn't get used to the nickel and dime stuff again.

I really wanted to make it work because I had this idea of coming home to my family at nights, but Trethewey's sawmill, the town's main employer during my childhood, had long since closed down and I didn't want to spend my days earning a pitiful wage in some service job like I'd had when I worked as a butcher's helper at the local Safeway. I wanted to play for bigger stakes and I knew where to find them so I started looking up my trucking friends to see what was happening on the logging front. As usual, there was quite a bit.

Charlie Philp, the Mack truck dealer in Vancouver who had sold, then taken back, my last two logging trucks, was one of these nonstop hustlers who, when he got supplying equipment to the logging industry, couldn't resist dabbling in a little logging himself. He had financed a small operation up in Estero Basin thirty miles north of Campbell River and the man he had running it had walked out on him after getting half-started. He needed somebody to go in and get the thing producing so he offered me the job. I hadn't run a whole logging show before, just the trucking part, and I was kind of surprised Charlie thought I could handle it. I didn't know if that was a credit to his perspicacity as a successful businessman or a sign of his inexperience as a logging boss but I was pretty tickled and jumped at the chance. They had a crew of about ten guys already in there including a couple I'd worked with on Vancouver Island, a kind of bull-shitter named Eddy Barnes, who had a lot more logging experience than I did and thought he should have the job, and a young greenhorn named Jack Spence who was married to Charlie's sister Eve.

It was a pretty strange place. Estero Basin is a big tidal lagoon at the head of a small inlet called Frederick Arm and it was separated from the main inlet by a narrow rocky channel called the Gut that could only be navigated at high tide. So here you were so far up into the nether reaches of the coast you might as well be on the back side of the moon, then you had a further barrier in that you could only get the camp boat out when the tide was high. It was the gloomiest goddamn place I ever saw with big high mountains around most of it, except the mouth on the north side and the head end, where a valley opened into Bute Inlet. It had a strange silence to it when we shut the equipment down, like some kind of a dead zone where no life survived. It gave you goosebumps. The top layer of the water in the basin was mostly fresh and froze up on us in the winter, which made life miserable.

They had set up a beach camp inside the lagoon and punched a road into the timber but ran into a roadblock where it crossed a small river. They'd managed to drag their yarder across the riverbed and fall a bunch of timber but before they could haul logs they needed to get their truck across the river, and that would take a bridge. Usually when loggers needed to cross a creek they got a bunch of logs, placed them side by side across

My real fancy logging bridge at Estero Basin.

the creek bed, bound them together with cable and spread gravel on top to make a road. The trouble here was the span was too wide. Even if you found some really long logs, they would sag in the middle and never carry a loaded truck. It needed some engineering and this is where they were stuck. I could see the answer was to use long logs, but get some kind of support under the middle of the span to stiffen them up. I cut a bunch of smaller logs and stood them up in the creek bed to form a series of props which we braced diagonally with smaller poles, then laid our big stringers on top. There was nothing much to it once you realized what you needed, but it looked pretty elaborate for a logging bridge and I used to see people taking pictures of it. With that last hurdle cleared we got busy logging and had logs hitting the water pretty steady by freeze-up.

The most excitement we had that winter was nothing to do with logging. One of the guys we had on the crew had his own boat in there and he lived on it with his wife, who was in the late stages of pregnancy. I remember asking him if he didn't think he should get her out of there to someplace where she was close to a hospital, but she didn't have any place to stay and anyway they figured they had plenty of time. Well, they didn't, and one day at the worst possible time she goes into labour. We don't have a radio phone to call in a plane, the tide is not going to be high enough to get a boat out of Estero for six hours and even if we did, it would be another four hours to get to the nearest hospital in Campbell River. The closest other people are at Shoal Bay, an hour away once you're out the Gut, but there's no medical help there either. There's nobody in our camp who knows any more what to do than I do. It's just the one screaming woman and ten scared loggers, the husband the most scared of all.

I figure there's no way out of this, I'm going to have to deliver this baby and I might as well face it. I try to remember everything I ever heard about having babies, from Kay or anybody else. I hadn't been around for any of our kids' deliveries, that wasn't the style in those days, and Kay's descriptions of it didn't give me much comfort. She hated the whole process and had said un-encouraging things like "it rips you right apart." And she was about to go through it again. She was expecting our third child in October 1948, which was one reason I hadn't tried to bring her up to Estero. But I wished she was there with me then. I wished any woman I ever knew was. I could have killed these fools for not planning things better.

We had a first-aid manual but it didn't have a thing in it about childbirth. I knew, I looked ten times. Working loggers weren't expected to have babies. I tried to remember the doctor books I had found as a kid—I had paid particular attention to the obstetrical section too, but not for the purpose of increasing my medical knowledge, unfortunately. I comforted myself by thinking that women had been successfully having babies for thousands of years before doctors came along, but then I discomforted myself by thinking how many of them died in terrible agonies, from eclampsia, breech births, tangled cords, excessive bleeding and a hundred other quite common problems only a doctor could fix.

The goddamn boat was a dirty, cramped little thing so between contractions I had her husband bring her up to one of the bunkhouses where we had a little more room. I couldn't think of much else to do so I told the cook to boil up lots of hot water. I had no idea what it would be used for, I just remembered they always did this in the childbirth scenes I'd seen in movies. I still don't know what it was for, although it turned out to be handy during the clean-up.

It seemed to take a week for her to finally get down to business. I lost track of the time. She was yelling and cursing her husband and me and God and finally she just kind of flamed out, but once the baby started to come, it came fast. I knew about catching it, cutting the cord, and getting it breathing from helping my butcher father deliver calves and it turned out that's all I needed to know. The husband was oh so thankful and even Eddy Barnes had to ask, "How the hell did you know all that?" I didn't think it sounded good saying it was from being a butcher, so I just acted mysterious. Mother and baby made it down to Campbell River eventually and everything checked out just fine.

I forget how I came to leave Estero. We closed down when the lagoon froze up and I think maybe Charlie sold it or took in a partner or something. Anyway, he didn't need me to come back so that was that. I had tried my hand at running a logging camp, building a bridge and being a midwife and had gotten away with it.

North Bend

'm damned if I can remember, either, how I got started on this next escapade. Bob Hallgren, a kid I taught how to head load when I was logging at Garibaldi during the war, was in on it. So was his brother, Len. I was back in Abbotsford knocking around with nothing to do and somehow we heard about a guy named Hashie who had a little bush mill near North Bend and needed somebody to come in and take some timber out for him. This was the opposite extreme of Estero Basin, a completely landlocked place up the Fraser Canyon right on the border of the Interior drybelt. I figured at least the weather would be better, which shows how much I knew. It should have been a tip-off when I discovered you could only get across the river by taking what was known as the "Aerial Ferry," a heart-stopping cage suspended by cables a hundred feet above the churning Fraser that took one car at a time. It bounced up and down and swung around in the wind but was actually kind of pleasant once you got over the terror of being suspended above one of the world's most turbulent large rivers. Kay hated it but the kids loved it and would have ridden back and forth all day if you'd let them.

Hashie's camp was actually about seven miles east of North Bend in an area loosely referred to as Chaumox. I think there was an Indian reserve by that name there one time but by this time, the band members were all across the Fraser at Boothroyd. There were a few small ranches, a few bush mills like this Hashie's and a larger mill owned by a man named Dr.

Dumont. I really wanted to get Kay and the kids up there but Hashie's camp was the bare minimum with no place for a family so Bob and I rolled up our sleeves and built a place in a matter of days. This was the worst house I ever built but by far the fastest, a real, honest-to-goodness tarpaper shack with doors, windows and wood cookstove scrounged from an abandoned Japanese mill nearby and, of course, an outhouse.

It was quite a comedown from our nice suburban home in Abbotsford but Kay moved in with the two kids and the new toddler, Cynthia, and never breathed a word of complaint. Cindy was just walking and one day Kay opened the oven door to take out a loaf of bread and while her back was turned, Cindy came toddling along with her bottom bare and sat down on the smoking-hot oven door. Her poor little bottom just kind of bubbled up like pork crackling, my god it was a mess. Fortunately we were in road contact with a doctor, and we got her looked at right away but there wasn't much to be done except keep her clean and coated with butter for a couple months.

During the summer we treated it kind of like a camp-out and even had visitors—my mother came up for a while and Kay's sister Jean also stayed for a bit. They hiked and swam and had a great time and it was a real treat to have them. A Japanese group had been operating a little mill up the road until they were rounded up in the internment of 1942 and had left everything they owned hidden around the property. It had been pretty well picked over by the time we got there but it was still a fascinating place to visit. There was an air of mystery and tragedy about it. The kids had great fun roaming around Chaumox and Marilyn even found a friend, a girl her own age whose parents, the Carholmes, had quite a decent farm on one of the benches up the road from Hashie's camp. Howie was about four then and he developed quite a liking for visiting these Carholmes, too. I thought it was because of the girl, although he insists it was Mrs. Carholme's cookies. Anyway, he was always at me to take him over there so one day I said, "Why don't you go yourself?"

It was a mile or so by road because the road looped up and back, but it was only about a thousand feet straight through the bush. I don't know exactly what came over me, but I pointed at the bush and said, "See that

Cindy and Howie at the swimming pool in Boston Bar about the time Cindy planked her bare bottom on the hot oven door.

pointed mountain over there? If you just head into that bush and keep walking straight toward that mountain, you'll be at the Carholmes in ten minutes." The little bugger looks at me to see if I'm joking, figures I'm not, says, "Okay, Daddy," and before I can say another word he disappears into the trees. Well, now I start to get worried. He's only four. As long as he does what I told him, I'm sure he will be okay. On the other hand, if he got turned around, he could end up at the snarly Nahatlatch River, now a favourite site for whitewater rafting. Or he could fall and twist an ankle. I decided to give him a chance and see what happened. It's what my father would have done. He was a believer in giving a kid challenges. This Carholme had a little two-wheel walking tractor he'd hooked up to a wagon so he could ride on it and maybe forty minutes later I hear this putta-putta-putta coming down the road. Here's Carholme with Howie bouncing along in the trailer.

"You better keep an eye on this young fella," Carholme says. "He just cut through those trees right through to my place. I couldn't believe my eyes!"

"Tell 'im Dad, tell 'im you told me to do it!" said Howie, jumping up and down. Carholme had been sure he'd run away and nothing Howie could say would convince him we wouldn't all be desperately searching for him.

I was in a spot. Carholme was a pretty humourless old stick and I hated to admit I'd put Howie up to it. At the same time, Howie had performed so admirably I didn't want to let him down.

"Well, he was busting to go visit, so I just pointed the direction and told him that's where it was," I said. Carholme looked at me strangely and I did feel a little guilty. But inside I was rooting for Howie. I was glad he pulled it off.

Of course we had no electricity and all lighting was by kerosene and gas lamps. I was always worried about the kids tipping over one of the lamps and setting the shack on fire so I spent a lot of time warning them to be careful. The damn things would act just like Molotov cocktails if you tipped them over, but we lived with them for years and never had a mishap, at least not one of our own making.

One night Len Hallgren was over for a visit and we had one of these old two-mantle gas lamps hissing away on the table. I was especially wary of gas lamps because they ran on high-test gas, which was a lot more explosive than kerosene, especially since you had to keep it pressurized. Kay was terrified of them but they gave such a bright light they were hard to resist. This particular lamp had a little lick of orange flame that would pop out of the stem every so often and flare harmlessly for a few seconds then go out. The wooden handgrip was a little charred from it. I had tried tightening the stem but it was as tight as I dared make it and the leak persisted. We were used to it and knew it didn't get any worse, so it had ceased to bother us but it did look very alarming the first time you saw it.

Len was one of these bull-in-a-china-shop types who just did things without thinking and after watching the flame lick out a couple times he reached out and picked up the lamp, saying, "Here, I can fix that." Before I could open my mouth to say a word, he gave the lamp a hard twist and broke the stem off so he had raw gas spurting out of the tank in one hand onto the flaming mantles in the other hand. I will say this for the dumb bastard: he ran to the door and threw the flaming mess out into the yard. If he'd just dropped it like most people, the shack would have gone up like a pile of kindling. He was so foolish and heroic at the same time you couldn't be mad at him. His hands were so badly burned he had to get skin grafts.

Hashie was pretty haywire and we ended up wasting a lot of time waiting for him to get things running, so we came to freeze-up and he hadn't filled the lumber order we were working on. He thought he could postpone it until spring so he shut down but the customer played tough and demanded he complete the contract. He had to scramble to get the mill going again and begged me to stay and help. We worked for another three weeks but it got so cold the logs froze solid and wouldn't go through the saw—it was like sawing stone—and he had to give it up. The poor bugger had to buy lumber in Vancouver to fill this contract, and he had no money left over to pay wages.

That left us short so I decided we might as well stay put until spring when I could find work. We had a renter in our Abbotsford place and Hashie gave us access to all the food left in the cookhouse so it seemed like the easiest solution. The first thing that went wrong was that his cookhouse, which was supposed to be loaded with supplies, froze up and spoiled all the canned goods. The dry foods were ravaged by mice and rats. For some reason he had great leftover stores of something called Sunny Boy cereal, we speculated because nobody would eat it, even the rats, and we ended up having it morning, noon and night until it became so full of weevils it just about jumped out of the box under its own power.

The next thing that happened was the bottom fell out of the thermometer. This was the winter of 1949–50, which turned out to be one of the coldest ever recorded. It started out fairly mild, in fact November was unseasonably warm, but by December it was getting pretty damn cold and we were struggling to keep the shack liveable. The walls were just rough mill-run boards with a thin skin of tarpaper over the outside and I could see it just wasn't going to get us through—not even after I went up to Lytton and bought the largest tin heater I could find and not even after I stoked it until it was cherry red and chuffing like a steam engine. Our fronts would be searing while our backs were freezing. It was a major excursion for the kids to get out to the outhouse so we let them use potties. During the night the contents would freeze into a yellow block Kay would get rid of by putting them on the stove and heating just enough to get it loose in the pot, then she would stand in the doorway and heave the toxic block over the snowbank. "We better be sure to be out of here before it all thaws in the spring," she said.

It got too cold even for the skunks. I never saw such a place for skunks. The big striped ones, not the little spotted ones we have on the coast. They were all over the place. One time in the fall the kids found a little one that seemed to be lost so they got playing with it and the damn thing was as tame as a cat. We had a cat and they introduced it to the skunk and—nothing happened. They got along. The skunk became an honoured member of the household. It had soft long fur like a Persian cat and would writhe with pleasure when petted, making a sound not unlike purring. It was clean, ate anything you put in front of it, and put up with endless molesting by the kids without making a stink. It didn't like me though. If I came too close, it would raise its tail at me and do a little dance with its back feet, which I found very convincing. I backed off. But it was such a great pet I've often wondered why they're not

Howie with the pet skunk, which got along fine with Marilyn's cat.

more popular. Maybe they don't thrive in captivity—ours got something like distemper and died after a few months.

Once the temperature started plunging north of 20 below they somehow figured out that our little cabin was the one building in the whole neighbourhood that had some heat coming down through the floor, so they started congregating in the crawlspace, which was cosily closed in on all sides by the deep snow. Pretty soon we had a veritable parliament of skunks down there. I don't think skunks are designed to live together in a confined space because these guys didn't get along worth a damn. They were constantly fighting and chittering at each other in their weird birdlike way, so it sounded like a monkey house day and night. Occasionally they would blow off at each other and the fumes would come up through the floor so strongly it was like breathing tear gas. We'd be running outside to get fresh air until we started to freeze, then we'd run inside where it was warm but asphyxiating. This only happened a few times, but all of the time there was some amount of stink, as if they had the ability to give small warning shots at each other.

We got used to that, but the thing that finally broke our patience was the phantom knocking sound. One night, we began to hear a distinct tapping sound on the floor. Tap tap-tap-tap tap. It would move around from one corner to the other, growing louder and fainter but never stopping. We were going nuts trying to figure out what the hell it was. We knew it was something to do with the skunks, but it was unlike any of their other innumerable sounds and the mystery of it bothered us just about as much as the racket itself.

I don't suppose I would have put up with them as long as I did if it hadn't been for our pet skunk making us a lot more kindly disposed toward skunk-kind than normal, but finally I'd had enough. I knocked together a box trap out of an old apple crate and placed it strategically along their path. Skunks are not very cautious and in no time at all we had one in the trap. It wasn't very happy so I shot it from a safe distance and chucked the body out behind the snowbank with all the frozen pee. By the time I was done, I'd shot twenty-two skunks. The answer to the phantom knocking noise came with the last one I trapped. Skunks have quite small, wedge-shaped heads and this one had obviously been rooting around in the garbage where it found a jam jar just big enough to get its head into, but too tight to wiggle out of. It had spent a week banging this bottle on our floor trying to knock it off.

Things were getting serious. We had no food, no money, the roads were plugged with snow, I was running out of firewood and we had three little kids to keep alive. Wood was a major problem. There was some scrap lumber and slabs around but it was frozen hard as rock. You couldn't saw it or chop it, you could only break it and you had to get the fire damned hot with dry wood before it would burn. The goddamned shack wasn't built for weather like this and was really impossible to heat no matter how hot you got the heater.

I checked over all the cabins in camp and found one that was lined with beaverboard and had an oil heater, so we moved into it. It was cramped as hell but that meant less space to heat and we could at least keep it frost-free. Through January the temperatures just kept falling—20 below, 30 below, 40 below—and the snow kept piling up. By the time it was done, it was the worst winter storm in BC history. If you check, you'll find the record lows for many parts of BC were set in January of 1950, right when I happened to be spending my one year away from the coast in one of the coldest parts of the province. I find a way to blame myself for most of the jams I've gotten into, but that was just plain bad luck.

I kept waiting for a break in the weather so I could hike out for supplies, but it only kept getting colder and windier. Finally I decided I was going to have to strike out regardless and bundled up in every piece of clothing I owned. Hashie was supposed to be sending my back wages, but we had to go into North Bend to get the mail.

Everybody who could had cleared out by this time. I didn't know about Carholme, he didn't seem like the type who would leave his place but for some reason I never thought of turning to him for help, maybe I just didn't think he would give any. He had his own little corner of the world tidily in hand and disapproved of anyone who didn't have their shit together as good as he did. We were a bit under ten miles from North Bend but only about three miles from the flag stop at Chaumox, where you could flag down the passenger train.

There was another family, the Hatelys, wintering over in a small ranch about halfway between us and Chaumox and I was figuring I could duck in there for a break if it got too much for me. I filled up the oil tank, piled up the wood box, showed Howie and Marilyn how to go down to the well with an axe to break the ice that grew four inches thick every morning so they could have water for the day, and rather nervously set out, kind of swimming through the deep snow. It was slow going and as the wind rose, I began to wonder if I had maybe bit off a bit more than I could chew, but I had to try or we might all starve to death. It was that desperate. It took me until noon to get to the Hatelys so I decided to stop in, really hoping for a hot coffee and maybe even a stopover for the night if it looked like the wind was going to keep rising.

The Hatelys weren't a whole lot better off than we were. They were also low on money and food and had three small children—a girl about Howie's age and twin boys about Cindy's age, even smaller maybe. Still, they couldn't have been more welcoming. Sam, the man, was a specimen to behold. Big, gristly and rough spoken, he was fresh home from serving as a commando in Italy and France, where he had specialized in reconnaissance behind enemy lines and had lost track of the number of men he had killed with his bare hands. Like a lot of guys who'd been through that sort of experience, he had a kind of wild look in his eye that put you on your guard and a lot of people gave him a wide berth but I found him pretty damn good.

He had been trying to hack out a living with a haywire little tie mill, doing the work of a five-man crew all himself, but the tie market had gone flat, their livestock had died in the extreme cold and they were having a real tough time of it. His wife Merle was a wonderful woman, amazingly cheerful and steady amid the chaos Sam always had swirling around him. She fed me a hot lunch and gave me a better parka and a thermos of coffee to take with me.

The bad news was the trains weren't running. The line was blocked downriver from North Bend where a freight train had run into an avalanche then backed up into a tunnel where it ran out of fuel and froze up. The boiler burst and the crews were at work cutting the locomotive up and throwing the pieces down the bank into the Fraser River. I had to get food somehow and I was weighing the possibilities of walking into town following the railroad, which was partially ploughed, but Sam insisted I take their precious horse which he had been using to make his own supply runs. That probably saved my life and the life of my wife and kids, but it was still no stroll in the park.

That was the longest horse ride I ever went on, and by far the coldest. Walking I had put out enough body heat to keep warm, but sitting up on the horse in that brutal wind funnelling down the Fraser canyon was the coldest thing I ever did in my life. I was numb from head to toe, and would never have made it without the parka and extra clothing Merle forced me to take.

The blowing snow made it almost impossible to follow the road, which dropped straight down a two-hundred-foot bank into the river on the low side, so I over-corrected toward the high side and kept steering the horse into the ditch. He wasn't enjoying it one bit more than I was. It was quite a sight passing Washtock's ranch where you could see the humps under the snow that had been their livestock. In a blizzard an animal will turn its back and walk slowly before the wind until they come up against a fence, so there were all these frozen corpses jammed up against the fences, some of them still standing like frozen statues with snow piled up on their backs and gaping holes in the midsection where the coyotes had eaten their guts. Some of their tails were sticking out sideways, showing how hard the wind had been blowing when they froze.

I had to stay in town for the night. I was so damn cold I couldn't bloody well talk but managed to negotiate myself a room in the hotel, a rambling wooden affair that looked like a CPR station. I had to spend the first couple hours thawing out in a tub of hot water—which, by the way, I have since learned is the worst thing you can do for hypothermia as far along as I must have had. It causes all the blood to rush to the skin and lowers your core temperature or some such thing. You're supposed to drink hot liquids and reheat yourself from the core out. I was lucky I didn't have a heart attack in that rusty little bathtub. Once I was back on my feet I couldn't see much else to do but spend a long session in the beverage room, which was full of all these CPR lifers who acted like you were intruding on their personal property. North Bend was a major division point on the CPR in those days and had a couple hundred men stationed in town.

They had lots to talk about. Two trains had got trapped out on the lines, one a passenger train and the other the freight train that froze up. The passenger train they'd somehow rescued and the freight train engine was almost all cut up and heaved over the bank and they figured to have the line open as soon as they got the big rotary plough down from Rogers Pass to clear the track. As if they weren't having enough trouble dealing with the weather, they'd somehow managed to run a locomotive off the rails in the roundhouse where it was sitting nose down in the grease pit, also in danger of freezing up.

They were going kind of crazy with everything that was happening and throwing their well-ordered lives into chaos, which is the railroader's worst nightmare. Normally the railroader lives to make the trains run on time and has a hard time dealing with any situation not covered in the company rule book. One of the things that was giving them grief was the snow around North Bend's large switching yard. They had been blowing it off the tracks with small yard blowers but it had got piled up so high their blowers couldn't throw it high enough anymore, it just fell back down on top of them. They were talking about getting a bulldozer to push back the thirty-foot-high windrows of snow. They had one up the line, but nobody to run it. It doesn't take much brains to push snow with a cat but a railroader doesn't do anything he's not classified for in the company organizational chart.

"You guys looking for a cat skinner?" I asked.

"Yeah, you know one?"

"I'm a cat skinner," I said. I wasn't but I had been around cats enough I figured I could push snow. So they tell me where I should go apply and there's all this rigamarole you have to go through even to be a casual worker offering to save their asses—sign this sign that, company not responsible if this happens or that happens, blah blah blah, but I tell all the right lies and by god, before I know it I've got work and at pretty damn good rate.

They still have to bring this cat down the line from wherever it is so I have time to get home with the supplies and take Sam's horse back. I stocked up with as much as I could carry including a bottle for Sam and a ham for Merle and got back to North Bend in time to meet that cat coming in on the train. They had a pretty nice RD8 and once I figured out how to start it, I didn't get off it except to fuel up for three solid days. It was tricky because you were working in and around the tracks all the time and you had to try not to hook any rails or knock over any switches. Once I noticed a dark line in the load of snow I was pushing and realized it was a rail, curling up like a shaving of wood. I hadn't even felt the blade catch it, it must have been loose and sticking up or something.

I wasn't all that experienced driving a cat at that time and probably did a little more damage than I should have, but the way I looked at it, dealing with a natural disaster, that was the risk they had to take. The way they looked at it, I should be court-martialled and thrown in the brig or something. They would all be out there with tape measures and cameras and report forms for me to sign. They were the damndest bunch of men I ever saw. All they cared about was brownie points. They actually called them brownie points. There was some system of merits and demerits they lived by and any time anything happened, it was looked at in terms of who stood to make brownies and who stood to lose. It overrode any concern for the actual work to be done.

My crowning achievement as a servant of the CPR came when they brought in their big rotary snow plough. This was a huge iron propeller mounted on the front of a steam locomotive. It must have been twelve feet high and it was the pride of the fleet. It was a weird-looking beast like something out of Jules Verne and normally lived in the Rocky Mountains but they had moved it out to the coast to try and keep the lines open during this terrific storm. The town of North Bend was all abuzz with excitement that they had finally rated an appearance by this legendary apparatus, which flung the snow so high it looked like a blizzard all of its own when it was coming down the track. That is, when it was running.

They no sooner landed the thing in town than it stopped working. In the extreme cold, the heavy casting contracted and clamped down on the shaft so firmly it couldn't turn the big propeller. The solution was to heat it up so the housing would expand and let go its death grip on the shaft. The railroad guys with their shrunken brownie-obsessed brains vaguely understood this and went at it with blowtorches but blowtorches with their tiny jets of intense heat were not up to the job of heating this fifty-ton iron monster, which conducted away the heat much faster than they could apply it with their little torches.

What they needed was to park the whole engine in one of their heated barns for twenty-four hours so the whole mass could thaw. But these guys were in their own world beyond the reach of common sense. It's an article of faith with railroaders that the physics and mechanics of railroads are entirely different from that of the outside world and can be understood only by other railroad men with lots of seniority. They blowtorched and pounded with sledges for days without getting the snowblower to budge.

Finally they came to me. Some bright egg had got the idea of having me hook a line on one of the blades of the big rotor and give it a yank with the cat. I could see this was stupid and said the only thing to do was put it in the barn but that had about as much impact as you'd think, so I got the cat firmly planted at right angles to the big plough and paid out the winch line, which they hooked over one of the big blades of this twelve-foot-high rotor. I made it clear I would only pull on a signal from the guy who was giving all the orders because if things went like I thought they would I didn't want any ashes on my head.

I figured the blade, brittle with the cold, might snap off, but it did better than that. I took up the slack and looked at the head honcho, waiting for a signal. He signalled for full power. The line tensed, the whole locomotive shuddered on the track, there was a loud bang and the entire ten-ton rotor, the pride of the CPR, tumbled forward and crashed onto the ground. The six-inch steel driveshaft had snapped off like a dry twig.

The roadmaster or yard boss or whatever he was looked like he just shat himself, which he might well have done. I imagined he was visualizing the demerits thundering down on him like an avalanche, burying his entire career in the CPR. The lesser lights, quite a number of whom had found reasons to be sweeping and polishing and oiling in that area surreptitiously watching the action, vanished like smoke. The head man retired to his office, no doubt to begin writing his report blaming it all on me. I freed my line from where it was pinned under the fallen rotor and went back to my ploughing.

Nobody said anything and the decapitated rotor lay there on the tracks like an elephant in the living room until I left on my days off, when the whole shebang mysteriously vanished. It was never mentioned by anyone the rest of the time I was there. They'd found another cat operator to spell me off, which was good because with the cushy double time they were paying me I probably would have kept working until I froze in position like one of Washtock's cows. As it was, the worst storm in BC history hadn't brought me all bad luck: I took home a bigger paycheque for that month than I'd ever earned in my life up to that time.

About mid-February the weather went back to normal and by March things had eased up enough to think about getting out. Hashie wanted me to stay but we'd all had enough of living like Eskimos and were dying to get back into our nice comfortable house in Abbotsford. I started working on the old grey 1936 Pontiac I had then, a great-looking car that didn't run worth a damn. I'd forgotten I'd ever owned it until I was in Cuba with Cindy in 1998 and by god, there in Revolutionary Square was one exactly like it, which had played some heroic part in the Castro revolution and had bullet holes to prove it. Mine didn't want to start after being in a deep freeze all winter but finally one morning we launched ourselves onto the Aerial Ferry one last time, the car so overloaded with kids and toys and blankets you could hardly get the doors closed.

Things went fine until we got just far enough down the canyon highway to be too far to turn around, and here was a line of cars a mile long, stopped dead. There'd been a hell of a rockslide nobody had told us about and they were taking forever to clear a path through. I couldn't believe the way they were just picking at it. I went storming out ready to give somebody hell but got talking to some of the other strandees and learned there was a truck buried under the rockfall with the driver in it, and that was why they were being so careful. What good they thought this was going to do the poor bastard I don't know and eventually after wasting most of the day with kids getting hungry and having to go potty and a couple hundred drivers getting fighting mad they punched through a tote road and we drove over top of the buried truck. They never did find the driver.

4

The Suez Crisis

Back in Abbotsford it didn't take long to run through the small savings we had left and I was back feeling the pinch to get some money coming in. I decided to go drop in on Charlie Philp. I figured I'd done a pretty good job for him at Estero and knew he was always mixed up in some side action in the woods. When I walked into his office, he was on the phone listening to quite a tale of woe by the sound of it. "That bad eh? That's tough. Well, I wish there was something I could do . . . " Then he looks up at me and it's like a light bulb went on. "Well, just a minute, somebody just walked into my office—let me call you back."

So he sits me down and pours me a drink and treats me like a long-lost friend and eventually he gets around to talking about this pretty decent little camp on Nelson Island sitting on some damn fine timber but the guys just aren't cutting the mustard—they're a couple of moonlighting teachers and they're screwing everything up. Charlie's got some money tied up in the operation and he needs somebody up there who knows how to get logs in the water. It sounds a lot like the Estero deal, except this time Charlie is talking about a partnership deal with me right from the start. So we agree I will go up and size things up, get the camp on its feet, and decide whether I want to get in any deeper. I found the idea attractive.

The truck logging boom that had started back on Vedder Mountain in 1939 was still flooding the BC woods with small operators and a lot of guys I'd worked with were running their own shows and making good dough. Well actually, it turns out most of them were *not* making good dough, or any dough, but that was not the story they told when you met them in the beverage room of the Rainier Hotel. It looked good to me and I wanted to get in on it.

I'd proved I could run a camp at Estero and logging was the one place I could see where a man could still make it if he played his cards right and worked hard. I had all the tools, I knew that—I knew every part of logging, except the business part of selling the logs, but Charlie could help me learn the ropes there. I was wary of Charlie, he was another Les McGarva in that if there was a dollar to be had, his idea was not to split it with you but to take all of it, but I should be getting to where I could deal with that by now. If this was any kind of a camp, and Charlie assured me it was a great location with plenty of untouched timber, this might just be the opening I'd been looking for.

I had never heard of Nelson Island before and had to get a map to look it up, figuring it would be one of these little islands you could spit across, of which the BC coast has too many to remember. I was quite surprised to find Nelson Island was actually one of the larger islands in the Gulf of Georgia, bigger than Gabriola, Denman or Lasqueti and only a little smaller than Salt Spring. It had hardly any people living on it and no villages, only a few gyppo logging camps and a couple small resorts. It was on the mainland side of the gulf about sixty miles north of Vancouver, kind of blocking the mouth of Jervis Inlet.

It had a lot of bays, lagoons, basins and lakes and Charlie's camp was tucked into a little nook on the south side called Green Bay. The timber was pretty much untouched except for a little hand logging in the early days, but it was nothing like the first growth I'd seen on Vedder Mountain. It was very stunted and scrubby around the edges where it was exposed to the ocean winds but the interior had some heavy stands that would make for nice logging once you worked your way into it.

The nearest settlement to Green Bay was the fishing village of Pender Harbour, seven miles down Agamemnon Channel, which had several stores, a post office, schools and a hospital. This would make Green Bay a little less isolated than Palmer Bay and Estero Basin, but not a whole lot. It was too far from Pender Harbour to get the kids to the schools, which would be a problem since Marilyn was going into grade three and Howie would be starting grade one in a year. Kay was game as usual—she was always ready to move on to the next thing, especially if it looked like it might finally work into a decent opportunity. She was in top form and ready to do her part, whatever that might be.

There was a steamer service to Pender Harbour, not Union Steamships, the famous pioneer steamboat company that settled the BC coast, which was already cutting back on its routes by this time, but a newer outfit called the Gulf Lines that had three war surplus ships all called the *Gulf* something—*Mariner*, *Wing* and one they'd already lost when it slammed into Dinner Rock off Powell River a few years before, the *Gulf Stream*. The *Gulf Mariner* and the *Gulf Stream* were minesweepers and the *Gulf Wing*, which we would get to know all too well, was a Fairmile, a smaller, wooden class of sub-chaser around a hundred feet long and narrow, maybe twenty feet wide. For a while, the war surplus Fairmiles were all over the place but you seldom see one now.

For this first trip Charlie said I wouldn't have to worry about the Gulf Lines because they had a new camp boat I could run from Vancouver up to the camp. As a Fraser Valley boy, boats were not my thing and I had

Gulf Lines' converted fairmile *Gulf Wing* loading freight and passengers at Irvines Landing, still the throbbing heart of Pender Harbour in 1950.

never run a boat that far before so this was a bit of a challenge. Still, I'd run boats for short distances here and there and was at home with motors so I thought that was fine. I packed my bag, picked up the usual collection of machinery parts and logging supplies around town, drove down to Granville Island where Charlie's truck yard was and where this boat was tied up at a place called Clay's Wharf, a grimy False Creek institution that persisted into recent times.

It wasn't hard to spot my command, even among the peeling derelicts that populated Clay's Wharf. It looked like a typical gyppo logging camp boat, a sad-looking thirty-two-foot hulk on its last stop before the boneyard. It was a long, narrow-gutted, low-slung thing with a drooping bow, long passenger cabin with big square windows—several of which had lost their glass—and a V-to-flat bottom with the chines built out to form little sponson-wings toward the stern. This was an unusual feature I later found made handy shock absorbers for knocking against logs, although I'm sure the designer had some higher purpose in mind. There was no name or numbers painted on it, though I learned it had been one of a pair of quite famous sister ships, one called the *White Hawk* and the other the *Black Hawk*. I never did know which one this was, because for reasons I could never imagine somebody had renamed it the *Suez*. I should have expected trouble from a boat named after an Egyptian ditch.

What the *Hawk* boats had been famous for was speed. The *Suez* had originally been powered by a V-12 Allison airplane engine that was said to push it forty knots, making it the fastest boat in Vancouver Harbour. It was supposedly built to serve as a water taxi for running log scalers back and forth between Vancouver and the big log sort grounds in Howe Sound, although I met people who insisted that had only been a cover story for its real purpose, which was running booze into Puget Sound during Prohibition. Certainly it had the classic design of a lot of rumrunners—their idea back then was to get speed by making the hull long and narrow so it would cut through the water, they hadn't come up with the idea of the planing hull yet.

The big Allison had long since been replaced by the standard cheap boat power of the day, a six-cylinder Chrysler Crown salvaged from a wrecked car, which drove it at a plodding seven knots. The engine conversion was

Once the pride of Vancouver's water taxi fleet, the MV *Suez* was a typical sad-sack camp boat by the time I took charge of her.

typically haywire with straight sea-water cooling and a dry manifold that used to get so hot it glowed red, which proved handy for brewing coffee. We even used to fry eggs and make toast on it. There was no motor cover—it ran too hot to be shut up and I wondered how they kept spray from coming in through the missing windows and killing the engine.

I didn't know much about boats at that point but I knew enough to see this was a boat best used in calm water and I had a little twinge of concern thinking about the kind of long crossing through open water I was about to attempt in it. The marina-owner's son, a smartass kid who manned the gas pump, didn't do anything to ease my nerves.

"You're not taking this thing out today, are you?" he chirped. "Where you taking it? Nelson Island? You're nuts. I wouldn't go across the harbour in this floating coffin today. Have you even checked the weather?"

He jabbered away like a squeaky young crow without waiting for answers. As a matter of fact, I hadn't thought to check the weather beyond the farmer's forecast, which consisted of a quick glance at the sky, but I wasn't about to give this sawed-off little shit the satisfaction and made like I knew what I was doing. He just shook his head and said, "So long, buddy. It's been nice knowing ya. Any last words for your wife and kids? I'll keep this space open in case you come to your senses and turn around."

This was Harold Clay Jr., aka Squeak, who in later years would move to Pender Harbour and carry on where he'd left off getting under my skin. He was honestly one of the most annoying individuals I ever had the misfortune to know, and the most annoying thing about him was that he was just about as smart as he thought he was, at least around anything to do with boats.

I wasn't out under the Lions Gate Bridge before I realized there was no way I should be out there in that punky old wreck. There was a pretty good southeaster blowing up and the clouds were black and menacing. I only had a sketch map that Charlie'd pencilled on the back of a letter because the route was supposed to be so simple, but the vista of low grey humps I saw before me now bore no resemblance to the map. There was an unreliable-looking little car compass mounted on the dash that seemed to be working and checking it against the map I picked out what I thought must be the left side of Bowen Island and the mountains of the Sunshine Coast beyond.

It looked like a thousand miles of ugly cross-seas I had to survive before I got to the next shelter and I think I would have turned around and gone back if it hadn't meant having to face the taunts of that smartass kid. The old *Suez* was no good in a beam sea—it was no good in a following sea or a head sea either—and all the cargo I'd packed was soon flying around and falling into the bilge and spray was pouring into the cockpit, which was open and had no self-bailers. I couldn't let go of the wheel to run back and save anything or check the bilge, which I could tell was getting full by the sloshing sounds. I had to keep ploughing grimly ahead until I was past Bowen and coming up on those little islands off Gibsons where I could get some shelter and stow things a little better and bail the bilge.

I'd been pinning my hopes on reaching Gibsons where I could wait out the blow but it was still early in the day by the time I got there and I hated to quit. I got things nice and shipshape and figured what the hell, I might as well keep going and at least get a little closer to my destination. The trouble with this plan was that I was about to enter what towboaters call "The Stretch" which is the thirty miles of exposed shoreline between Gibsons and Secret Cove where there is no sheltered moorage. I had a vague idea about this from what some towboaters had told me in the pub but I figured I had a good six hours of daylight, which would be plenty of time to get me to Secret Cove or Pender Harbour where there would be good shelter for the night.

I might even make it all the way to Green Bay if things went well. What did vaguely bother me was this was all lee shore, meaning if the motor conked out the wind would blow you up on the beach but so far the old Chrysler Crown was purring along like a champ so I figured I might as well keep pushing. I've never been good at resisting the temptation to squeeze in an extra mile before dark.

The weather had all been coming at me from the port side which was the boat's good side—there were no missing windows. What I discovered as I turned up past Gower Point and started along toward Roberts Creek was that the seas were now behind me. The *Suez* had a full stern and a narrow bow which made it hell to handle in a following sea and not only that, the cabin was completely open at the back and now the spray was funnelling into the boat and hissing where it hit the hot motor. Again I was in the position where I couldn't take my hands off the wheel, the way the boat was wallowing around. That bleak, menacing shore seemed to go on forever. The boat seemed to be dead in the water, even though the motor was grinding away as normal.

I was discovering what a lot of unhappy mariners discovered about The Stretch—it's only thirty miles but in a southeaster with an ebbing tide it can seem like three hundred. The current runs two knots against you on an ebb tide, reducing the old *Suez*'s net speed over bottom to five knots, and less than that once you subtracted all the zigzags it was making in the following sea. I cut in close to the steamer dock at Roberts Creek but there was no safe tie-up there that I could see. There was a bit of a haywire breakwater around the Jackson Brothers booming ground at Wilson Creek but the tide was out and it looked too shallow so I kept chugging. I don't know what gets into a guy that makes you want to keep pushing, keep heading into a worsening situation rather than pulling back when you have the chance. There's something so tempting about sticking to your plan even after it's gone all to hell, the momentum of the trip that is so hard to resist.

The three hours had stretched into four and the afternoon light was draining away. As I came up to a couple of wave-washed rocks called White Islets feeling very lonely and exposed with nothing but open sea before me as far as the eye could see and foaming shore on my starboard side, the motor developed a miss. I dashed back to give it a ten-second check, saw nothing, then dashed back to grab the wheel as the boat began to yaw. The miss got worse. The motor was now only running on four cylinders.

I crawled along the coast in the fading light, desperately checking the map and the shore for a place to get a little shelter where I could throw out an anchor—I did have a rusty little thing with hardly any chain and rotten-looking rope—and like so many a sailor before me, I pinned my hopes on reaching the Trail Islands off Sechelt, where it looked like a guy might get a little shelter. If I'd been doing it now, I would have swung way out and got as far from shore as possible, but the greenhorn's first impulse when he's in trouble is to hug in close to shore, not realizing that is your worst enemy if you lose power. Too late I saw breakers ahead and realized I was running into some kind of shallows way out in the strait where there should have been deep water. I swung to port and took seas hard on the beam, holding my breath with every sputter and miss of the motor.

I wasn't a praying man, even in a spot like that so I had to make do with yelling, "Come on you son of a bitch, hang in there, don't quit now . . ." But quit is exactly what it did. I hit the starter and got it going and it went a few hundred feet then quit again. I birled the starter till it started to run out of battery then went out into the stern. I had almost got clear of the spit, which I learned later was Mission Point, the gravel bar formed by the region's largest watershed, but the tide was pulling me right back into it. I searched around madly in the wallowing boat and found a broken pike pole about six feet long. I was able to hold the boat off for a while but it was a losing battle.

Finally just as the boat was about to start crunching on the gravel bar, I jumped overboard and stood on the spit trying to hold it off. That worked better than the pole but it took a brutal effort with the boat surging and twisting, as if madly wanting to wreck itself. It was now completely dark. I hadn't passed another boat in hours, though there were house lights twinkling along the shore. I don't know how many hours I stood there in that freezing water. I don't know what I thought I was trying to accomplish. I was just trying to save the punky old wreck of a boat, which Charlie had probably traded for a couple truck tires.

I don't know why a man does things like this. If I'd been thinking straight I would have realized I was risking my health if not my life, risking leaving my wife and kids without a breadwinner—and for what? Just to complete a mission, just to not have to phone Charlie—a man who'd cut your throat in a minute if you stood between him and a buck—and tell him I'd lost his junk heap of a boat. But you don't think in a spot like that, at least I didn't. I was always ready to sacrifice myself for the worst broken-down hunk of equipment in the most hopeless goddamn situation.

I don't think I actually hatched a plan so much as my feet found it. Luckily Mission Point is a gravel bar with few large boulders, or the boat would have been kindling. But as I kept pushing the boat out, the waves kept shoving it up-coast, the tide was coming in now, and the water started to get deeper. I somehow managed to drag my half-dead carcass back in and went back to the pike pole. I was now around the point and going down the windward side of the spit, which wasn't so rough. I'd been noticing some kind of structure further up the shore, and as I got closer I could make out another big steamer dock like the one at Roberts Creek, jutting out into the water. After another hour or so I had worked the boat around to the dock where I got it tied off to a piling.

I was just about done for. I didn't know what hypothermia was then but I'm sure I had it to the nth degree. I couldn't feel myself. My feet were like pieces of wood. My skin was dead, like canvas. My brain felt like I'd been on a week-long drunk. I was shaking so bad I couldn't close my hands on a knife to cut bread, so I just grabbed handfuls. I felt different than I had ever felt before. I felt like I'd broken something inside myself. I was used to asking a lot of my body and it had always delivered, but it felt like this time I had just asked too much. I was scared. I wondered if I would be found in the morning dead from exposure.

Then I got my eyes focused on shore and realized there was something there called Davis Bay Inn, or something along those lines. A warm bed. Hot food. I had no idea what time it was but I figured I better make an effort to get ashore because I might not make it through the night otherwise. There was nothing to do but swim for it, which wasn't as bad as it seemed because it's shallow there and my feet hit bottom before I got halfway in. The door to the inn was locked so I pounded and shouted till I got somebody up. A guy stuck his head out of a window.

"We're closed," he says.

"Look, I'm in bad shape," I stammered, my tongue so thick I could hardly talk. "I just about lost my boat and I need to get warm . . ."

"We're closed," he says again. "If you want a room, go up to the lodge. They'll take you."

"Where's . . . the lodge?" I said.

"Top of the hill. Can't miss it." Slam.

So I drag my shivering ass up Davis Bay hill, which seemed like Mount Everest and I get into this little flophouse where they're not too overly thrilled to see me either, but they give me a bed and I eventually stop shaking enough to sleep.

The next day it's sunny and calm. The boat is sitting innocently alongside the wharf still as a picture. I find a skiff on the beach and paddle out with a piece of driftwood for an oar. It's easy to see why the motor stopped. It's white with dried salt from the blown spray. Every spark plug is shorted out. It's a wonder it ran as long as it did. I clean up the plugs and wiring real well, knowing I don't have much battery, but it starts right off and purrs like a kitten. For some time, the asshole from the inn has been standing on the shore shouting about his skiff so I grab the stubby pike pole and paddle it in.

"What the hell do you think you're doing?" the guy says. "That dinghy is for inn guests only."

I get up good and close to him and say, "How would you like a punch in the goddamned nose?" I really wanted to give it to him too, and I guess he could tell because he was suddenly a whole bunch more understanding and agreed to row me back out.

It was a beautiful day without a ripple in sight. It was hard to believe this was the same ocean as the day before, and it also made me realize what a damn fool I was to be out on it. All I had to do was listen to Squeak and wait twenty-four hours. I felt good about having survived the ordeal but I had that strange feeling that I had strained something inside that was never going to be 100 percent right again. It was an odd feeling, one I'd never had before.

Looking back, I can admit something that I wouldn't have admitted then, and that is that I was past my peak. I was thirty-five and at a point where a man's physical abilities start to go into decline. A logger in those days was like a professional athlete. Many working trades were. Your work took pretty much a maximum physical effort. You never saw belly fat in the bunkhouse in those days, except maybe an old donkey puncher, but even the machines in those days took a lot of work. The steering clutches on a D8 took a 30-lb pull and you were pulling them thousands of times a day. Trucks had no power steering so truck drivers had arms like wrestlers. All different today of course. Everything's air or hydraulic and you spend all day twiddling computerized solenoids. They have to have gyms so the men can get a little exercise.

From the time I first went out driving truck, I'd always felt I could overcome almost any obstacle with physical effort. Just lift harder, pull stronger, work longer—and always when I asked my body for more, more was there. But a man's body is like a drum of gas. There's only so much in there and you can use it up fast or slow. I had used up a lot by the time I was thirty-five. Up to that time, every time I opened the bung to check the level, it looked as good as full. Now this time I looked and for the first time, I could see a lot was used up. And from that time on, I noticed it more and more.

I'd always been sound as a dollar physically but now I started to have a lot of back trouble. Already I'd lost the ability to sleep, and I was tired a lot. I had stiff joints in the morning. And somewhere around then I started to experience the first twinges of phantom pain in my face, a tic that would become more familiar over the years. I still had forty years of working life in me as it turned out, but it worries a young guy when he encounters his first whiff of mortality. It wasn't an auspicious start to this new phase in our lives.

5

Green Bay

I was pleasantly surprised by the camp. It was in a small bay about a quarter mile deep completely protected from wind with a big waterfall on your left side as you went in. This was where the camp was, on an eighty-acre piece of private land leased from a family named Yates who had briefly tried to homestead there during the war. I was quite buoyed by my first sight of the place and began imagining improvements I could make as its lord and master. A person could put a turbine to generate electricity below the falls, since the place currently had no electric lights. (I did eventually get around to trying a small four-bladed water wheel hooked to a car generator and it lit one light bulb but the flow went down to practically nothing all summer then came up so high in the rainy season it washed the whole thing away.)

There were three old skid-mounted bunkhouses that had obviously been dragged in from some other camp propped up on posts just above the tideline, two more up the hill and a permanent house that had been built by the Yates family over beside the waterfall, which was the one assigned to us. The log dump was over by the waterfall where a steep, mean-looking road twisted down the hill. I could tell just by looking the hill was going to be a bitch to get up with anything but a Jeep and the dump looked too high—it would be hard on the cedar, which was prone to breakage. As I would find out, there wasn't much water at the bottom of the dump so the logs just piled up, forming godawful jackpots that had to be tediously pulled apart by the gutless little boom winch or a passing tugboat if you could catch one.

One of the first things I did was to start planning a better dump lower down the hill where the water was deeper, which I began but never finished. There was a standing boom running from the dump about halfway across the bay where it was anchored to a reef that only showed at low tide and used to fool lots of unwary yachters, much to the amusement of our crew. Why we never stuck a marker on it I couldn't tell you right now, maybe because the men enjoyed rescuing the yachters and reaping liquid rewards. It was a good booming ground for the size of camp it was—in deep enough water to float logs at the lowest tide and perfectly protected from all winds.

There was no sign of the guys who had been running the camp. I guess when they heard Charlie had found another sucker, they made good their escape. I never met them and can't remember all their names now. One was Cam Prior. Ian Blaker was involved somehow. Harold Pearson, a local guy with a good logging pedigree was in there somewhere too, he must have

Green Bay camp looked best under cover of a little snow. L to R: big bunkhouse, cookhouse, storeroom/toolshed, little bunkhouse. There were two more bunkhouses up the hill and the Yates house was off to the right. Thanks to the snow you can see the radio aerial later shot down by trigger-happy chokermen. The *Suez* is at the wharf, leaking.

been pretty young then. Every time I start naming names from my past, I first of all think, "Who could I phone up to check with?" And then I go through a list of prospects and it's always the same thing—they're all dead, every one of them. Which leaves me wondering—do these names matter to anyone but me? And when I'm gone will they matter to anybody at all?

Sometimes it just kind of takes your breath away at how completely all our tracks disappear behind us, like footprints in drifting snow, or in sand on the beach. And yet something in me refuses to just let go and say, it's all gone, all the people, all the things we worried about and fought over—I want to name as many names as I can, not just because it's a way of marking their lives, but mine. Because when you look back and ask yourself just what it was that makes a life a life, it's the people more than anything, the people you bumped up against along the way.

One of the guys from the earlier crew in Green Bay who was still on the scene was a guy named Charley Trebett. He was older than me, probably in his mid to late forties, with sandy hair and a face that always struck me as simian. He affected the manner of the wise old logger who'd seen it all and knew all the answers. I'm not sure right now whether he had been an official partner in the earlier company but he had a firm grip on the proceedings owing to the fact he owned—or claimed to own—the yarder the camp was using. It was a good machine, a converted steam yarder with a good-sized truck motor bolted down across the hole formerly occupied by the steam boiler. This was the main item of equipment in camp and it seemed that however the operation was reorganized, this Trebett fully expected to be included in the management group using his machine as equity. This was a surprise and a disappointment to me. I was primed to be my own boss and run the show with Charlie Philp silently supplying the credit. I didn't want a stranger in the mix, especially one who was assuming the position of senior partner, the guy who had been on the scene longer and knew what needed to be done.

I wasn't sold on this guy. According to Charlie Philp, all Green Bay needed was one good man to turn it around. But Charley Trebett had been there all the time and if he was half the man he claimed, why hadn't he turned it around? Nevertheless there seemed to be no way to avoid having Charley Trebett as a partner.

The previous company was called Arbutus Logging, which told you all you needed to know about it. Arbutus is the favourite tree of poets and Sunday painters because of its eye-catching appearance but it has no commercial value and no self-respecting logger would ever name his company after it. Might as well call it Daffodil Logging. Philp's accountants, Briggs and Young, formed a new company and wanted to know what to name it. They suggested White and Trebett but Charley said no bloody way was he going to play second fiddle to anybody and by Jesus, once he put it that way, I wasn't keen to play second fiddle to him either. Names based on Green Bay and Nelson Island weren't available so I said they could call it the Cordova Street Cathouse for all I cared. We were located on Agamemnon Channel but everybody agreed that was too hard for loggers to say so we took the next nearest body of water and Jervis Logging it was. We were miles from Jervis Inlet, but that didn't matter.

Charley Trebett, my erstwhile partner in Jervis Log who taught me one of life's most important lessons: avoid partnerships.

Looking over the operation, I could see signs of bad management everywhere. They didn't have a decent power saw in camp so I convinced Charlie Philp to buy us a new Titan two-man falling saw and one of the good little one-man bucking saws that had just come out from a Vancouver company called IEL. In those days a lot of the equipment used in logging was made right here in BC—the Hayes truck that was a favourite in many camps was made in Vancouver, the Easthope motor on our boom winch was made in Coal Harbour and the Madill plant in Nanaimo made all manner of yarders and yarding gear. Now of course everything is imported from Asia.

They had an ancient D8 cat with a cracked frame, good only for parts, but we could get by without a cat for a while. For a truck they had a terrible old White with a wooden cab that looked like it came from the days of hard rubber tires so I asked Philp if he didn't have something a little better he could send up. One day a barge appeared with the Clark truck on it. You had to see this truck to believe it. A resourceful mechanic named Archie McKone had built it out of spare parts during the war when you couldn't buy a real truck and when gas was rationed. He built it for a logger on Pitt Lake named Clark so we always called it the Clark truck. It had a big ugly square cab welded out of a quarter-inch steel plate with two Chrysler Crown engines sitting side by side. It had tandem axles on the tractor and one motor drove the forward axle and one the rear.

McKone's cute idea was that going up hills you'd use both motors but on the level you'd turn one off to save gas, which of course was rationed and scarce. It didn't work worth a damn. If one motor was pulling a little harder than the other, that axle would spin out. One motor did always run better than the other, so that axle just ate up tires. You had two transmissions to shift and if you didn't time it just right you'd never get the second one into gear. Then you'd have the two axles in different gears and the thing would buck like a bronco, and like as not break an axle. It only

The homemade Clark truck undergoing major surgery at the log dump with our empty booming ground below. The half-pint dump-winch operator poses on the bumper.

had three-ton rear ends and went though axles like toothpicks. Oh, it was a nightmare.

Charley Trebett was supposed to be the rigging genius who was going to take care of all the yarding issues involved in pulling the logs from the woods to where they could be loaded onto the truck but one look told me the spar tree was located in the wrong spot. At least half the "setting" (the area to be logged) was down over a hump and impossible to yard without constant hang-ups. I asked him if they weren't having some trouble and he went into a big long story of hard luck and grief.

"Why didn't you put the tree over on that rise where you'd have a clear pull in all directions?" I asked him, figuring there must be a good reason I wasn't aware of.

"Wasn't a tree there," he said.

"Couldn't you have raised one?" I said.

"Too much work. You never raise a tree unless you have to." Well, this was complete bullshit. If there wasn't a tree suitable for a spar growing where you needed it, you fell one, moved it over, guyed it on the ground and stood it up with the yarder. It was standard procedure. Half the trees I'd ever worked under were raised trees. Besides, I could see a good enough tree still standing in a better location.

"Without a cat we're never going to get at that setting behind the hump," I said. "We should rig that tree over on that knob."

"That bloody thing? The top's out of it!" I wasn't a bit sure it did have a broken top, but in any case it didn't matter.

"Looks sound enough."

"Can't make a spar tree out of a broken top. Compensation rules."

Well, I'd never heard of that rule before. I'd seen trees with broken tops used many a time. A lot of the old-growth firs that were big enough to be spars had missing tops. The man was talking complete nonsense.

"If we don't move the tree higher, how in hell are we going to yard the low side of the claim?"

"You just leave that to me. I know some tricks you probably never even heard of. A little side-pull is all you need." Well, I couldn't believe my ears. He'd just spent half an hour telling me how much grief he'd had already, and they hadn't even gotten to the hardest part. So we got in the crew and started in yarding but Charley couldn't get the logs in. They were fighting hang-ups all day and the truck would just sit in the landing waiting. We were getting about one load every two days. It was crazy. We had a full loading crew standing around picking their ass while the rigging crew beat their brains out trying to pull logs through solid rock. By the time we got a turn into the landing half the logs were broken. Charley was beside himself, cursing the goddamn useless chokerman, the goddamn useless rigging slinger, the goddamn haywire outfit—even though all these guys were only trying to do what he had ordered them to do. Finally I couldn't bear it anymore.

"We can't stand any more of this," I said. "We're losing our shirts here. Philp will shut us down if we don't start getting some wood."

"Philp doesn't have a clue."

Well, this was just nuts. I told him we had to move the tree and if he didn't want to do it, I would.

"Well, you just go right ahead. I won't have anything to do with it," he said. I was no high rigger but any goddamn chump can put on spurs and work his way up a tree if he's got enough time. I told them to strip the old tree while I was limbing and topping the new one but when I looked down from up the tree I could see nothing was happening. They were just rolling smokes and bullshitting and Charley was right in the middle of it. I had to strip all the blocks and lines off the old tree and move it over to the new tree, hang the blocks, tighten the guylines, everything. Charley sulked the whole time and muttered and swore under his breath as if it was all pure foolishness but as soon as we had the new tree working, it made all the difference. We got two loads the first day and then three. On the third day I was down at the dump with the third load at 2:30 so I hightailed it back to the tree figuring to get a fourth load. I knew we had to get four loads a day if we were going to make a go of it. But as soon as I got up the hill, here was Charley and the crew walking down the road toward the crummy. Goddammit, I think, just when we get going good something breaks down.

"What's up?" I ask. "Breakdown?"

"Naw," Charley says. "We're just knocking off early. We got our three loads."

I'd never used climbing spurs in my life but somebody had to rig a new spar and I was boss, so up I went.

"I was hoping to get four. We got time," I said.

"If we get four once, then we'll have to get four every day," he said, looking around at the crew for approval. I couldn't believe my goddamn ears. This is my partner? This is a co-owner of the company? I should have had it out with him right there. It would have saved a lot of goddamn trouble. Instead I let it drag on, trying to run a good operation with this clown trying to trip me up at every turn.

The fact is, I had a weakness there. I wasn't confident enough to go on my own. I was looking for a partner who could be the things I wasn't. I always was. In this case I had Charlie Philp handling the business side because I didn't feel competent to handle that myself. Now I can see I was beat from the start because any money we made, he would have found a way to grab it. And with Charley Trebett I was looking for a guy who knew the logging side.

It's painful looking back because it's so obvious to see the mistakes I was making. It's like watching an old Marx Brothers movie where the hero wanders innocently under the safe being lifted on its fraying rope and you're saying "No! No! . . . " but he keeps right on walking. I felt inadequate facing the logging problems, god knows why. Logging is the simplest thing in the world . . . get that wood into the water with as little waste motion as you can, any way you can. But there was a mystique the old loggers cultivated, they thought of themselves as a breed apart. Rigging was their art. Everything had to be done with lines and blocks. They say it came from sailing. You look at a picture of some of those old skidder settings, there were more lines doing more things than on a windjammer. The old-time logger took pride in not knowing who was prime minister but would stay up all night explaining the complex geometry of a skyline.

I really knew better, all that fancy rigging stuff was pretty much over by the time trucks and cats reached the woods, but I still had the feeling that I was an interloper on the real loggers and needed a guy like Charley claimed to be, to make up what I didn't know. But he cured me of the partner disease. Partnerships almost never work out. They always lead to trouble. Then the work suffers, because the guys are spending more energy trying to foul each other up than they are trying to make the company succeed. I always told my kids, stay away from partnerships at all costs. It's like making a deal with the devil. You know you're going to have to pay somewhere down the line.

The four-load issue didn't come up again for a long time because so many other screw-ups got in the way. I wanted to get away from driving the truck so I could spend time on other things that needed attention so I tried one of the other young fellows. He couldn't handle the double trouble of the Clark truck so I got the old White running and put him on that. It was simpler to run but it was small and slow. It had poor brakes and no doors and none of the modern safety equipment like a steel bulkhead to stop the logs from sliding forward and flattening the driver, it just had a low stack of six-by-six timbers bolted on behind the cab. It was completely worn out in every way and had trouble getting two loads, let alone four.

Finally the compensation inspector put an end to it. "I don't want to see that truck with a log on it ever again," he said. His name was Lehman. He wasn't a bad guy. I knew him from the Valley. He asked why we weren't using the Clark Truck. "I know that truck. It's a good truck. Archie McKone built it." He was right, it was a modern truck. It had vacuum brakes, steel bulkhead, doors, all the modern conveniences. The only trouble was you needed eight arms and two brains to run it. Eventually I was able to hire a real driver named Tommy Gray, and he learned how to drive it as good as anyone could, but the truck itself was such an abortion of a thing it couldn't keep running. We snuck the old White back in service quite often but didn't solve our truck problems until we leased a decent International from a Pender Harbour gyppo named Henry Harris.

Crews were quite a problem. Loggers then were almost all short-stake artists. They were with you until they had enough money to go on a good drunk, then they were on the next boat south. You might see them again and you might not, depending on whether or not they got another offer. In the old-time logger's mind, different was better. Six weeks was a long time to be in any one camp. There were hiring agencies in those days—Black's was the one we used mostly—and you'd phone in and tell him what you wanted and what you were paying, and a few days later some guy you'd never laid eyes on would jump off the boat and announce he was the new rigging slinger. We had some dillies. There was George Peacock, who lived up to his name by spending fifteen minutes greasing and combing his hair every morning. He was a very indifferent logger but a very expert poker player. After he left we discovered a card-marking kit in his trash. "Imagine, not just bringing a thing like that, but leaving it for everybody to see!" Kay fumed.

One rummy old geezer whose name I forget won Kay's eternal gratitude by getting her aside one day and confiding to her that she was wasting her time working for chump change up there in the bush. With her looks, he said, she could be earning real money down on Cordova Street. He even offered to take her down there and introduce her to the right people. She had to act offended but in private she was highly amused and used to remind me of it from time to time.

As soon as we got Jervis Logging up and running we began to have local men from Pender Harbour dropping around. One thing that had been passed down from the previous owners through Charlie Philp was not to use local talent, it was supposed to be no good, but these were young, strong-looking lads who I thought ought to be able to master the fine art of setting chokers—something you could teach to an averagely intelligent baboon.

I soon found out why the Pender boys had the reputation they had. They worked hard enough but they had all grown up together and behaved like a gang. Their constant horsing around on and off the job was annoying to everyone else in camp. You never knew what they were going to do next. They all had .22 rifles and were constantly popping them off. No seagull or loon was safe in Green Bay once they got there.

We had great difficulty getting radio reception in the bay so we had a very long aerial strung high above the cookhouse, anchored in two tall trees on each side of the bay. It had taken most of a weekend and fifteen hundred feet of pricey copper wire to set it up. I heard a bunch of hallooing one evening and when I went out for a look, here was our precious aerial lying on the ground. The idiots had been using it for target practice and one of them had hit it. He was strutting around feeling very proud of himself.

This was just the latest in a long list of stupid things this particular galoot had done so I fired him. The next morning the whole damn works of them were in the cookhouse asking for their time. It turned out they were all cousins—the ones that weren't brothers—and it was all for one and one for all. I was tempted to say to hell with them but it would have put us out of business for a week or more while I rebuilt the crew so I had to back down and let the goof off with a warning. I could have saved myself the trouble because a few weeks later they were all gone anyway. Fishing season had opened and they all bolted in unison like a school of herring. They all went crewing on the Warnock brothers' seine boats.

Just the same, there were a few exceptions who stayed on and in time became first-class loggers like Neil Newick, Gerry Bilcik and . . . there must have been more than two. I guess Frank Campbell would qualify since he worked for me for years. Clary Nichols was a fine logger and a fine man, but left us after a short stay to go to work for another local gyppo— where he drowned in a boating accident. Young Peter Dubois also became a career logger later, but didn't show much promise when he first came to us as a clumsy, overweight teenager.

I can't remember them all now. When the gang rented the old decommissioned forestry station in Madeira Park for my hundredth birthday, I was greatly moved to have a distinguished-looking elder named Harry

Brown come up and thank me for giving him his first logging job, sixty years earlier. I knew Harry from his later career as a stalwart of Pender Harbour's salmon fishing fleet but forgot he had also put in a stint at Green Bay. I guess damn near every young guy in the Harbour did at one time or another.

One useful thing about the local guys was that many of them had their own boats—Bill Salvey had a nice little gillnetter with a Redwing engine that just purred; Parky Higgins had some awful old thing that was always breaking down or threatening to blow up from gas in the bilge; and Archie Nichols, who I trained to run the loading donkey, had the sweetest little work boat that sailed through the water like a seagull, making barely a ripple. It was good to have a few extra boats in camp to make emergency runs into Pender Harbour to get parts or dispose of a quitting chokerman or pick up a new one. The local guys were amusing to watch in action but frustrating from a management point of view.

Parky Higgins was one of a big family of boys and one of the most high-spirited individuals I ever met, whose constant hyena laugh and machine-gun chatter could be heard above the noise of the loudest engine. He was as strong as an ox and hyperactive but you couldn't turn your back on him or he would hook a battery up backward, run out of gas, saw into a boulder with the bucking saw, chop his foot with an axe, etc. I'll never forget the sight of him standing on a stump playing air guitar with such abandon he tore the buttons off his shirt front, throwing in a few wolf howls and laughing his wild laugh. You had to smile, even though he was supposed to be down on the ground helping his brothers set chokers.

His brothers by contrast were all quiet and slow-moving. Willy was the family wit. He didn't speak often but when he did, he came out with some of the most clever one-liners this side of Will Rogers, while Herb and Lorne were practically mute. Speaking of that, there was one of the Pender boys who *was* actually mute—Sonny Scoular. I was reluctant to hire him for safety reasons but the other guys insisted he was as good as any one of them and actually he was better than most of them—he had taught them all sign language and could communicate so well you had to keep reminding yourself he had a handicap. He had the best fishboat of all and of course disappeared with the rest of them at the first hint of a summer salmon run. They said he was the most fearless man in the fleet and liked to set his net off Cape Caution, one of the most dangerous spots on the coast.

Gradually we began to assemble a permanent crew of older men from outside the area. Slim Read was an old Swede faller who brought in a young college kid named Ivan Purdy as his partner (fallers always worked with partners in those days of heavy two-man power saws) and he stayed with us for a number of years, taking care of all our falling needs. Louis LePage, the Quebecer, was a complete ball of fire who looked like he was going to be the next H.R. MacMillan and he did become a pretty successful contractor after he left us. Tommy Gray was a short, good-natured guy who was a good truck driver and he roomed with a tall, gaunt guy whose name, believe it or not, was also Tom Gray. They travelled around together hiring out as a team and as long as you called the long one Tom and the short one Tommy there was no confusion.

Mike Poschner was a great moose of a man who lived on a houseboat with his tough-talking wife Lil, and he was first class all around but Lil was a bit of a troublemaker. She knew we had a rule against booze in camp but figured she could do what she liked in her own floating home and always had a batch of homebrew bubbling away, which made her little kitchen the most popular hangout in camp and led to more mid-week hangovers than enough. I dropped a few hints but Lil wasn't one to take a hint. Mike was a quiet, pious guy and I don't think he exactly approved but he wasn't giving the orders on that houseboat.

We pretty well had to hire Jack Spence because he was Charlie Philp's brother-in-law and he was irritating because he was such a smartass and didn't figure he had to show the boss any respect because of his family connections but that also gave him a certain sense of responsibility and I came to appreciate him more as time went on. He was also quite amusing when you weren't the victim of his acid tongue. He invented nicknames for everybody.

Jack dismissed the entire Pender bunch as "gumboot loggers" (some of them did actually show up wearing rubber gumboots instead of caulked leather logging boots) and for reasons I couldn't quite get, he called young

Pete Dubois "that pimple-face Magellan." I could better understand why
he called our boom-man "Cousin Weak-eyes" after the stumblebum character in the L'il Abner comic strip. I forget that boom-man's real name
now, but he was a definite bumbler. Like a lot of boom-men, he was a
freelancer who had his own boat and travelled around from camp to camp,
offering his services to gyppos like us for the short period when we had
enough logs bobbing around in the bullpen to start organizing them into
a seaworthy boom capable of being towed down to the mill in Vancouver.

Most of the time we didn't have a steady boom-man and would assign
one of the youngsters from the rigging crew to spend the occasional day
stowing logs in various bullpens so the cedar was separated from the fir
and the boomsticks were separated from the sawlogs, etc. You wanted to
be careful who you picked because although it was pretty simple work it
involved running around on floating logs all day and if you weren't nimble
you could end up spending a lot of time doing the dog-paddle. I hated
it every time I heard a splash because invariably every time some tangle-
foot took a dive he'd be carrying a peavey or a stamping hammer or some
irreplaceable part off the boom winch. I spent a lot of time dragging the
bottom with my grappling hook, seldom with any luck. After a while I
began to picture the bottom of Green Bay as completely blanketed with
boomchains, wrenches, batteries, dog lines, axes and other expensive tools
that ate up all our profits.

A more serious concern was that one of the young guys would drown
himself. Despite living all their lives on the water a surprising number of
the Pender kids couldn't swim, and it was hard enough for even a good
swimmer to stay up for long with caulk boots on. We came close to losing
one young fellow. He stepped on a log that was a real roller—you didn't
have to watch out for the small ones so much as the straight, high-floating
ones—and he rolled off into the space between it and the next log. As soon
as he went under, the two logs squeezed back together and he couldn't get
his head up between them to take a breath. He tried to grab the log and
pull himself up but it just spun in the water and shoved him back under.
Nobody had noticed him go down but the camp dog, Lassie, dashed over
and started barking right where he was and I was able to yank him out in

time—just. I always told the guys, don't try to crawl up onto a log from the side—go around to the end.

The regular logs intended for sawing up for lumber were generally around thirty feet long but anytime we found a nice straight tree that wasn't too thick, we'd cut it off at sixty feet to make a boomstick. This would then have four-inch diameter holes bored in each end so that a boomchain could be linked through it to form a kind of log fence to corral the other logs.

We would just dump logs in the water for a few months and keep increasing the size of the big bag holding all the logs. Then at the right time we'd send part of the crew down to the booming ground to work with the boom-man to make up a proper boom. They would pack the logs tightly into square rafts made up of sections sixty feet square. Each section would be marked off with a boomstick laying crossways on top of the other logs called a swifter. Everything was chained together with heavy chains called boomchains and the boomchains were laced through the auger holes in the ends of the boomsticks, pulled tight and held fast with wooden wedges. The final act in getting the boom ready to go to town was to chop a six-foot blaze in the head swifter and letter the name of your camp and the number of the claim the logs were from. Then it was time to call the tug.

In the 1950s there were quite a number of gyppo towing companies serving the hordes of gyppo loggers—Straddiotti Brothers, Coyle Towing, Maritime Towing, Texada Towing, Nanaimo Towing, Blue Band Navigation—and the various tugs would drop around from time to time to see if you had anything ready and try to talk you into buying their services. One that used to come in a lot was a funny-looking tug with a high pilothouse named the *Louise Idaho*. The skipper was a character who might have also been the owner—the kids called him Donald Duck because of his funny high-pitched voice and he tried and tried to get our logs but never seemed to come at the right time.

I tried Maritime, who had a couple boats called the *Green Cove* and the *Hornblower*, and they proved reliable so I stayed with them. Choosing a towing company was a dicey business because you were putting all your logs in its care and you wanted to make sure they got them to the mill safely without having a spill or losing any to log pirates. We used flat booms in those days, meaning each individual log floated on its own, not gathered into big twenty-log bundles like they are today. Flat booms were very frail and the least bit of rough weather would cause them to lose logs or completely break up, so you wanted a towboater who would baby your boom along and not take any chances with bad weather. A boom had a lot of drag in the water and took quite a bit of power to move, but the power had to be gently applied because a tug could pull a boom to pieces if the skipper's hand was too heavy on the throttle. The boomchains would break or pull the ends off the boomsticks and all your precious logs would get away, leaving you bankrupt.

It was common to lose a few logs that were low-floaters or beside a gap in the boomsticks but some towboaters lost more than others. Some disreputable operators worked in concert with the pirates and helped them to steal your logs for a piece of the action. They also were very prone to steal your boomchains. Boomchains cost $60 apiece new and a six-section boom took about fifty of them. The tug was supposed to bring them back after the mill had taken the boom apart but you never got back as many as you sent. They always said the mill guys had dropped some overboard when breaking up the boom, which could account for some loss, but not for the number that were always missing. I learned to judge the honesty of the towboater by the number of chains they stole and it irritated the hell out of me.

The worst thing we had to worry about were the log pirates. That's what we called them. They liked to call themselves beachcombers or log-salvors but that's too good for the ones we had, who were the logging equivalent of cattle rustlers. In later years they made them get licences and cracked down on them but in those years any bottom feeder who wanted to make a buck the easy way could get himself a broken-down boat and go into business stealing logs and selling them to some shady sawmill who didn't care where their wood came from.

Log pirates could find the occasional legitimate log that had gotten free from a boom but those were few and far between so it wasn't long before they gave in to the temptation to sneak up to a boom nobody was watching and "help" some logs get away. It was an easy matter to unhook a boomchain and scoot a few logs out. Usually they would just take a few and do the chains up again but the really criminal ones would open up a boom and leave it open and let all the logs out. Then there would be a feeding frenzy of log pirates grabbing your logs and taking them away, never to be seen again. All our logs were "branded" by stamping the ends with a special hammer that imprinted our claim number into the wood and the mills were supposed to record this number and pay us for them but the pirates would get rid of this brand either by hammering over it with a stamp from some inactive hand-log claim or by sawing the end off the log. The beaches in those days were cluttered with log ends bearing the stamps of luckless gyppos like ourselves. It was bloody cruel.

The worst pirate in our area was a Pender Harbour guy who had his own homemade tug fitted with double mufflers so it couldn't be heard sneaking around booming grounds in the middle of the night. He had a skiff fitted with special muffled oarlocks so that he couldn't be heard silently sneaking up on sleeping logging camps. He was especially annoying in that he called his boat something like *The Rustler* or *The Buzzard* and loved to sit in Gordie Lyons' pub bragging about outsmarting us poor hard-working gyppos. People thought he was quite the dashing hero but to me he was just a lowlife.

One of his sidelines was stealing boomchains. When we sent a boom out, we would double-chain a lot of the stress points, so it had more chains on it than was necessary merely to hold it together. Often a tug wouldn't tow your boom into the mill directly, it would take it to a tie-up, a sheltered place where single booms would be parked while the tug gathered up eight or ten more booms from surrounding camps before towing the whole group down to the Fraser River. While your boom was sitting there unattended, the pirates would have at it and besides stealing actual logs they would steal all the extra chains. This was one of the main reasons we never got all our chains back.

I remember one time this sonofabitch came around and offered to sell me some "salvaged" boomchains he claimed to have bought off a booming ground down in Howe Sound. He said he had a couple dozen and he wanted $75, which was a good price even for old chains. I paid him half down and a few days later, back he comes with these chains. As soon as he brought them in piled on the back deck of his tug and started to pile them on our wharf, I recognized several from a boom of ours which was at that moment anchored just down Agamemnon Channel at a tie-up called Boom Bay. The bugger had filled my order by going around to the tied-up booms and stealing every chain he could get loose, including some of ours! I felt like a damn fool. When he asked for the rest of his $75 I told him to screw himself. He got all irate and said he was going to take the chains back.

He was a big strapping guy well over six feet and used to throwing his weight around so I picked up a pike pole that happened to be lying near and said, "You touch those chains and I'll run this right through you!" He backed off and left, vowing revenge. Howie had been watching, eyes big as saucers. "Were you really gointa stick him with the pike pole, Daddy? Would that of kilt him?" he said. I felt kind of sheepish and muttered I knew he would back off because he was a thief and most thieves are cowards. But I felt bad about losing it and threatening violence in front of my little boy. That is one trouble I've always had with assholes: how do you deal with them without turning into an asshole yourself? But it wasn't over.

It wasn't long after that I was in Pender Harbour for groceries and as usual stopped in for a few beers at Gordie Lyons' beer parlour before heading home. Well, all the talk in the beer parlour was about this log thief and how I had cheated him and threatened him and the beating he was going to lay on me the first time he caught me without a pike pole in my hands. "You better make yourself scarce, Frank. I don't think I've ever seen the big guy so mad," the bartender said to me.

"I'll take my chances," I said.

This caused quite a bit of excitement around the room because, like I say, this guy had about thirty pounds on me and a reputation as a real haywire bastard and it looked like I was in a good way to get my head torn off. That was a prospect that I don't think bothered hardly anybody in that pub. It was home base for the local fishermen, who were not my biggest fans. I was both an outsider and a logger, the two worst strikes against you in their eyes.

I had made the mistake one time of buying a round on the house, which was pretty standard practice in my old watering holes but it was like they'd never heard of it here and thought I was playing the big shot. After that whenever I came in I'd hear mutters about "big tycoon" and "tall timbers" followed by choruses of laughter. The gillnet fishermen in particular were always clumped together carrying on in that special lingo they had from growing up and working together all their lives, it was like they had a shared brain and spent all their time making jokes and laughing at anybody or anything outside their little ingrown group. I had offered to take a few guys outside at different times, which shut them up but didn't help with my popularity rating much. They were laying it on pretty thick about what a beating I was going to get if I didn't skedaddle out of there quick like a bunny.

"If he wants me he knows where to find me," I said. "My boat's tied up at the dock right in front of his shack so he knows I'm here."

They kept on about this and after I'd fortified myself with a few beers I decided to grab the bull by the horns and go have a talk to him. I didn't want to be dealing with this bullshit every time I came into Pender Harbour. He lived a few hundred feet along the beach from where the *Suez* was tied up at Lloyd's Store, in a tiny shack. He had a bunch of small kids and nobody knew how they all fitted into this small cabin, which was still standing and being used as a rental in 2014.

Once I got out in the fresh air and cleared my head a little, I started to have a few second thoughts about what I was walking into. I was depending on my usual rule that guys will back down nine times out of ten, and this applies double to loudmouths, but what if I was wrong? If he stood up to me, my only chance would be to take him out fast before he knew what hit him. You didn't want to get grappling with a long-armed gorilla like that. I would be up against it unless I could get some kind of an edge, but I had an idea. Howie had come down with me on this trip and he was carrying our flashlight, a powerful six-volt lantern we used as a boat searchlight. All the time I'd been in the pub he'd been annoying me by playing its beam at the window where I was sitting and it was blinding when you looked straight into it.

I told him to come with me to this guy's shack and if it came to blows he was to switch on the light and direct it into the guy's eyes. I said I'd take my hat off when we went in but if I put it on before I left, that was his signal to shine the light in the guy's eyes. He took this all very seriously and I was pretty sure I could trust him.

We knocked on the door and the guy's wife let us in. He was sitting at the kitchen table in his undershirt and just about crapped when he saw me, then went all friendly and asked me to sit down and join him in a beer.

I said I'd heard he had a beef with me and I had come over to see what it was. He pretended not to know what I was talking about. "Everybody in Garden Bay has been telling me I owe you money and if I don't pay it you're going to beat it out of me. I don't owe you a goddamn thing and if you think otherwise we can settle it right now."

"Somebody's been feeding you a line, Frank. I don't know nothing about this."

"Well, I don't want to hear any more about it then," I said. "I don't want to have to come looking for you again."

"You won't, Frank," he said. "Jeez, the gossip in this place. Sure you won't have a beer?"

He stayed in his chair and stayed behind the table.

I was relieved, much as I would have liked to have taken a poke at the chump. But it would have been a damn mess with his wife and kids all around him and my own kid there. Still, it went as well as I could have hoped and I knew the guy would have to dream up some real fancy bull-shit to explain to the pub crowd how it was he didn't take me on when I gave him the chance. But fancy bullshit was his specialty.

As soon as we got outside Howie said, "How come you didn't put your hat on, Daddy? I had my finger right on the switch!" I wasn't too proud of that little scheme in retrospect and wished I hadn't thought it up, more proof messing with bottom feeders drags you down to their level often as not. I tried to explain to him that if you make a loudmouth back down, that's as good as thumping him, although I knew in my heart it wasn't that easy to stop a sidewinder like this guy.

I went back to camp and we logged hard all summer. We were getting into better timber and getting good production. We had the bullpen full of logs ready to boom up a good-sized boom that would pay off all the bills and put us in the black for the first time.

The cookhouse at Green Bay, later moved to Pender Harbour. Kay and I slept in a room under the seagull and it was during a high tide like this that escaped logs bumped against the floor, causing her to wake up yelling, "The cows are getting out!" Her nightmare saved the camp.

One night about 2:00 a.m. I woke up with Kay yelling, "Frank! Wake up! The cows are getting out!"

She was having a nightmare, which was unlike her, and it was even more unlike her to yell in her sleep. She knew how much trouble I had sleeping and was embarrassed to have woken me up for nothing.

"I dreamt we had a ranch and all the cows were getting out through a hole in the fence," she said. "It was so vivid, I could just hear them going bump, bump, bump through the hole and getting away."

Then we noticed this sound: bump, bump, bump. It was coming up right through the floor. I got up and looked out the window—the bay was full of logs. Someone had opened the bullpen and let out all our logs. All our year's work was floating away toward the mouth of Green Bay and down Agamemnon Channel into the clutches of the log pirates.

It was high tide and some logs had floated up under the cookhouse where they were bumping up against the floor, and this is what Kay had heard in her sleep. I jumped into my pants and ran down to the bunkhouse and rousted all the men out. Then I fired up the *Suez* and ran out of the bay. Most of the logs were still within the confines of the bay so we grabbed a few boomsticks and chained them across the mouth to stop any more from escaping. Then we began chasing down all the logs that had got away and stowing them back in the boom. By the end of the day we had everything back in place. We'd lost a day's work but that was all. The logs hadn't been counted or scaled so it was hard to tell if we'd lost any, but it didn't seem so. Of course we suspected our log-thieving friend but we never got proof. The incident went down in family history as the time Mum's ESP saved the camp. I hate to spoil a good story but it was probably Kay's sharp ears that deserved most of the credit.

6

Logging Camp Kids

When we first came to Green Bay an Englishwoman was doing the cooking. She lived in the back of the cookhouse, which was one of the long skinny bunkhouses perching on stilts at the water's edge. I wish I could remember her name. It was Mrs. Something, she wouldn't let us use her first name. How a woman like that ended up in a place like that I can't imagine. She was offended by everything about the place and everything about Canada. She wasn't happy cooking and wasn't very good.

Mrs. Something had a little girl about six who she was trying very hard to give a proper British upbringing, a losing battle in that place. One scene that sticks in my mind is the little girl saying, "Mother, it's time for my bath." And Mrs. Something replying, "No, dear, it is time for your *bawth*." The girl was constantly picking up Canadian pronunciations and the mother was constantly correcting her. She left without notice one day and Kay had to pinch-hit and did so well at it we just kept her on. She cooked and cleaned the bunkhouses and did all the camp bedding in a stand-up wringer washing machine for the rest of the time we were there. She also served as timekeeper.

Somewhere along the way she also found time to look after our three children, including providing them with home-schooling, which in those days we called "correspondence school." It was a bit much when we had a full camp of fifteen men and for a brief period we did get a young babysitter

It's pretty clear where the good looks came from in our family. Kay had her hands full working as the camp's cook, timekeeper, bullcook and teacher.

from Egmont to come in. This allowed Kay and I to move into the former cook's bedroom at the back of the cookhouse where we could be more on top of things, while the kids stayed over at the Yates house with the nanny.

That happy arrangement came to an end one day when Howie happened to mention that one of the men—the same one who had shot down our radio aerial in fact—was coming over at night to share the girl's bed—and they sure made a lot of noise. I was afraid of triggering a mass walkout if I fired anybody so I struck on the idea of having Howie stomp out in the middle of their next session and say, "What the hell do you think this is, a whorehouse?" He confessed the next morning he hadn't quite followed the script because he couldn't bring himself to say "hell," and instead said "heck." "Whorehouse" didn't bother him since he had never heard it before and didn't know there was anything bad about it. Either way, his childish display of indignation did the trick. The midnight giggle sessions ended and the girl soon packed her bags.

After that I got my mother to come up. She was at loose ends and needed something to do so I asked her if she wanted to be the kids' nanny and she was all for it. She had been living and working most of this time with my sister Beryl, but Beryl had come to grief. Back in the early forties she had married a returned soldier who was working at Kingsway Cleaners and together they started a dry cleaning business in Mission. Two of my sisters, Beryl and Gladys, fell for guys in uniform during the war and it was a disaster for both of them. Gladys found herself alone with a baby girl but she was better off than Beryl, who was stuck with a drunken party animal who couldn't keep his hands off any female he saw including their own employees. Especially their own employees.

Beryl was a top-notch businesswoman and had a nice bank account plus a house, but this loser drank and stole everything she'd built up and put her through hell. Finally she packed up her two lovely girls and ran away to Ontario where my other sister Hazel was married to an Air Force–trained radio technician and had a good job at a radio station. Gladys was remarried and living in 100 Mile House, so Mother was adrift. I thought bringing her up to Green Bay to help Kay would be the perfect solution. It should have been, but I'd forgotten the kind of person my mother was.

My mother and Marilyn with new arrival Donnie on the camp dock, 1953. The gap between the two buildings behind them is where infant Donnie did his amazing solo swim.

As soon as she landed, she started clucking her tongue at the way we were raising the kids and doing everything she could possibly think of to cross Kay up and make her feel bad. According to her way of thinking we were just neglecting the kids and letting them turn into savages.

Actually she wasn't the only one who thought this. I'd hired old Jim Ross, a former freight truck driver whose truck I'd washed as a kid in Abbotsford and who had been through a rough time with booze, and he was never done lecturing me about how I should send Howie to a good boys' school where he'd learn to stand up straight and speak like a gentleman. He said raising the kids the way I was, they would feel cheated and would have no respect for Kay and I when they got bigger. I didn't agree, but I did worry. They were forced to fend for themselves most of the time and they were behind in their schooling.

We had boarded Marilyn with Mother and Beryl, first in Abbotsford then Mission, so she had got her first two or three grades in regular schools and she was able to keep up her correspondence lessons on her own, but Howie didn't get to first base. He couldn't read well enough to work on his own, and besides, he was more interested in logging. When he was seven I taught him to run the dump winch. We had a little one-drum winch with a Ford flathead and the line led up through a block on a gin pole that leaned out over the dump. There was a bridle anchored to the brow skid that we would lead under the load so we could just drop the starboard bunks and pull up on the bridle to tip the load off the truck into the water. The logs would go thundering down that high spillway and hit the water with a big splash if the tide was in or with a big crash if it was out.

I was always terrified that the kids would be caught playing down there and always double-checked, even though it was highly unlikely. What I was more likely to see was the camp dog Lassie, who couldn't keep away from those falling logs. At the sight of a truck being unloaded she would come tearing across the boom leaping from log to log barking her head off, leaping in the air trying to bite the butts of tumbling logs. It was quite a performance and quite amazing the way she managed to dodge those flying ten-ton missiles for so long. We tried tying her up but it was like tying up Houdini. One day she zigged when she should have zagged and splat! That was the end of Lassie. I felt bad, but at least it brought the suspense to an end.

I could manage dumping the logs by myself since I could do it with the truck parked, but afterward you had to have another person there to hoist the trailer up while the driver backed under it. Logging trucks always carry their trailers piggy-back style when going back empty to get weight on the driving wheels. They have no traction otherwise and in Green Bay you couldn't even have gotten up the first hill leading out of the dump.

When we had a boom-man it was his job to meet trucks and run the dump winch but a lot of the time we didn't have a boom-man and that's when it was really handy to have Howie there to help load the trailer back on the truck. The winch could only lift the trailer straight up, it couldn't swing it, so you had to have one guy running the winch and the other guy backing the truck underneath once the trailer was up in the air. It was funny to watch him. There was a big long brake pedal you were supposed to stand on to hold the trailer up while the truck backed under, but Howie was too light to weigh down the brake and the trailer would slip down. To make up for this, he would add a little holding power by slipping the clutch, which was operated by a long lever. It took a delicate touch, but the little guy figured it out on his own.

I liked to see the kids using their noodle like that. That was my thought when I put them in these situations, so they would learn how to think on their feet. There's two

Kay with Lassie, the incredible life-saving, log-biting dog.

ways to make kids safe from the dangers of the world—protect and shelter them, which is your first impulse and the impulse most parents follow, but you can't keep it up forever and when the day comes that you're not there, they're not prepared to fend for themselves. My father's way was to expose kids to the real world early and often and let them develop their coping mechanism. It takes a leap of faith at first, but it's actually less stressful in the long run because kids love the challenge and learn how to fend for themselves quicker than you'd ever imagine.

Howie wasn't satisfied just to load the trailer, he wanted to have the excitement of dumping the load as well so he would make sure he got up there good and early and got the machine started with the lines laid out and ready. He would have tried driving the truck too if I'd let him. He begged to come along for the ride up the hill and probably too often I'd give in and take him, knowing he was dodging his lessons. I gave both kids plenty to do.

Marilyn helped Kay with the cooking, washing, bullcooking and babysitting, but I also tried to give her some men's work outside. The section of road along the lakeshore was soft and prone to potholes and we didn't have a cat to grade it with at that time so I used to haul bucketfuls of gravel up and fill the worst potholes by hand, which really helped, but I could never persuade anyone else to assist. Finally I got the idea of offering Marilyn and Howie five cents a bucket for digging rotten granite out of the cutbank below the dump and handing them off to the truck driver when he was turning around. The driver had resisted hints to do it on his own, but could hardly refuse to help the kids make some pin money.

Well, the two them pumped out so much material we ran out of buckets and had to start using the fire pails, which were painted red and were supposed to be kept on a rack beside the tool shed strictly for fighting fires. The kids were sending ten bucketfuls up the hill every load, and it started to make a noticeable difference in how fast you could drive along the lake. It became the talk of the camp. At one point Howie came to me and said he might have to go on strike if I didn't stop paying him scab wages and up the rate by a nickel a bucket. I saw Jack Spence's fine Italian hand behind that caper, but raised them to seven cents a bucket.

One morning the yarder broke down and we couldn't log so the crew came down the hill before lunch. I guess I was swearing about having to pay the men for sitting around all day doing nothing and one of the kids said to me, "What else could the men be doing, Daddy?" I couldn't really think of anything, so I said, "Well, they could work on the road. If a couple of kids can do it, there's no reason grown men can't." Well, damned if the two of them didn't set off running across the boom to where the men were standing around hollering, "Grab some shovels, men! We're going to work on the road. Daddy says if a couple kids can do it, there's no reason grown men can't!"

There was some shuffling of feet and muttering about how much a bucket, but the kids wouldn't take no for an answer and started handing out shovels. "C'mon you guys, we'll show ya how! Jack, you drive the truck. Pete, you take a shovel up and spread the stuff we send up. The rest of you help us fill buckets!" Well, be damned if the two of them didn't get that whole crew going for the rest of the day hauling and spreading gravel

Marilyn scraping the *Suez* in preparation for the annual bottom painting. The kids all earned their keep.

until they had that bad section of road looking just like Granville Street. The only problem with that was there was no need for any more gravel and I had to lay my two ace diggers off.

Howie had a regular job carrying oil to the stoves. The cookhouse had an oil range and the bunkhouses all had oil heaters and somebody had to go down to the dock with a five-gallon pail, pump stove oil out of a forty-five-gallon drum, haul it up the ramp and along the trail to the back of the cookhouse, and pour it into the tank, which was a forty-five-gallon drum on its side with a square hole cut in the top. The big bunkhouse had the same arrangement. It was a fair bit of huffing and puffing for a seven-year-old kid and he would spill a lot from rushing the job. You could always tell if he'd done his chores because his pants would be soaked in stove oil.

We didn't have time to watch the kids all day so it was making a virtue of necessity to teach them to be as self-reliant as possible. Instead of trying to keep them off the water, I built them a sturdy little pram-style plywood rowboat of their own and made them vow to keep a lifejacket on the whole time they were on the water. We didn't have kid-sized lifejackets in those days, just these big white ones with a kapok-filled pillow front and back. The kids each had their own and they practically lived in them.

I'd see them out running across the log boom, or sitting out on the front of the *Suez* dangling their legs and it wouldn't worry me because those things were certified for a three-hundred-pound man. Then one day I picked Marilyn's up and it must have weighed twenty pounds. It had become water-logged and it was like lead. It wouldn't have floated a squirrel! Anyway the kids lived on the water and it wasn't long before they learned to swim like otters and were as boat-wise as fishermen. I was happy with the way they were shaping up. They could steer boats, tie knots, chop kindling, keep a fire going, wash dishes, cook meals, climb trees, birl logs, keep out of the bight and amuse themselves without radio, TV or neighbours.

The closest call we had was with the baby, Donnie, who joined us in 1953 and wasn't quite ready to join in the swim, or maybe was a bit too eager, I don't know which. He was at the crawling stage and when nobody

We couldn't keep the kids away from the water so we made them wear lifejackets at all hours. Cindy wears a belt of corks for wading while behind her Howie sports a man-sized Mae West. Meanwhile that booming ground looks pretty empty.

was looking he crawled right out the cookhouse door, right across the big plank deck we had out front, down two steps, along about fifty feet of trail past the tool shed, then off the trail and down through some huckleberries onto the beach. It was quite an epic journey for a rug rat not much bigger than a cat, and he went over some rough ground before he got to the water and fell in. Marilyn was about twelve then and she came walking down the trail from the opposite direction and glanced down at the beach where she spotted the blurry outline of little Donnie lying on a ledge, completely submerged. She tore down and grabbed him and after Kay drained the water out of him, he was okay. We couldn't believe it. Couldn't believe he had crawled all that distance to start with, couldn't believe Marilyn spotted him at the crucial moment, couldn't believe he survived the dunking with noting worse than a few barnacle cuts. We gained some respect for the new kid's talents from the escapade and managed to keep him alive for the rest of his growing up, although he did acquire a fine collection of scars.

We worried about the kids in other ways, too. They had no company other than each other, and they had none of the usual childish entertainments. But they didn't seem to notice. They compensated by using their imagination. You'd hear them chattering away for hours acting out a complicated society of pretend characters they created. It was fascinating and we tried to eavesdrop, but as soon as you got close they would go quiet like frogs in a pond. As well as I could make out the heroes of this daily soap opera were store owners. When we took the *Suez* into Pender Harbour on Saturday shopping trips they would stare saucer-eyed at the shelves of chocolate bars and cookies and comic books in Murdoch's scruffy little general store as if such abundance was almost beyond their comprehension, so I guess for them the country storekeeper represented the highest pinnacle of wealth and power a person could aspire to.

I built them a tree house and they promptly turned it into a make-believe store, with board shelves jammed with bottles and cans they found on the beach. It was fascinating to watch them re-create a childish version of the world they saw around them, complete with broke-down trucks, yarding hang-ups, home-brewing wives, bed-hopping babysitters and booms full of top-grade peelers that made their owners wealthy overnight.

Kay and I would read to them, she the more traditional things like *A Child's Garden of Verses* and *Peter Pan* while I tried them out on adult Book of the Month Club selections like Steinbeck's *Tortilla Flat*. I could see they were getting a warped view of the world being shut away in Green Bay and I thought it might do them good to be exposed to some of the thinking that was going on in the larger world. They really went for the grown-up books and took them to heart. After reading them Edna Ferber's Texas oil patch saga, *Giant*, I was amused to note that their make-believe characters had shifted their economic focus from timber harvesting to oil exploration.

This was three or four years before the Russians put the first Sputnik in orbit but space talk must have been in the air because the kids were big into rocket ships. There was a big old boiler off a steam donkey lying in the weeds beside the shop and it wasn't long before they decided it would make a perfect rocket ship and you'd see them playing in it for hours, equipping the firebox with old car seats, air hoses, pressure gauges, etc. Like all boilers, it had a firebox at one end and then a water tank laced with numerous hollow tubes so the flames from the fire could rise up through them and heat the water faster. The outlet end of the boiler where the tubes used to exhaust all the smoke still had a bit of soot caked around it and made a fairly realistic-looking rocket nozzle, which the kids made more realistic by loading the empty tube holes with dynamite. We kept dynamite for blowing stumps and the kids were warned never to go near the magazine where it was stored up the road well away from camp, so the dynamite they used consisted of wooden sticks roughly the size and colour of a stick of dynamite.

The men were endlessly fascinated by the kids and their games and somebody got around to asking them why they had the boiler tubes all plugged with sticks and got the story that it was loaded with dynamite ready to blast into outer space. This caused much hilarity and led to one of the guys claiming he had actually caught Howie, who was younger and a more plausible dupe than Marilyn, loading the boiler with real dynamite. Howie hotly denied this and I believed him, but it was such a good story it couldn't be stopped and it soon spread beyond camp and began travelling up and down the coast. Decades later, long after we had left Green Bay, men who worked there would come up to me and say, "D'ya remember the time Howie loaded up his rocket ship with stumping powder?" We got tired of denying it and took to accepting its place among the legends of Green Bay.

I tried to make up for the educational deficiencies of the situation by explaining things the way a teacher might. If there was a sudden hailstorm, well, I'd explain about transpiration and droplet formation, the freezing effect of updrafts and so on—it was hard to keep it simple enough and often I'd encounter stifled yawns and wandering eyes and realize I'd gone too far. But I was remembering my high school science teacher and how important it had been for me to get that logical explanation of how things worked as a child, and I thought the earlier I could give my own kids that logical outlook the better.

I never missed a chance to explain how plants and animals we came upon displayed acquired characteristics that gave them evolutionary advantage. I picked up a copy of Frazer's *The Golden Bough*, probably through one of Kay's messy go-rounds with the Book of the Month Club and found it answered a lot of my own questions about religion—where it comes from in all the different forms it takes. A book like this that

The gyppo family at ease, 1951. Me, Howie, Kay and Cindy on the camp wharf with the too-steep road and the too-high log dump behind. Marilyn is taking the photo.

made logical sense of the big mysteries I found very exciting and I'd do my best to pass it on to the kids. During my lifetime, I had seen scientific enquiry throw light on so many of life's dark spaces I couldn't help but feel mankind was passing through a time of great enlightenment, and this enlightenment would eventually eliminate superstition and prejudice and deliver us from poverty and hunger and pestilence and war and produce an era of unprecedented peace and happiness on earth.

Things were not looking so good right then with overpopulation, the bomb, the Cold War and famines in many parts of the world, but if you listened to humanist thinkers like Bertrand Russell and George Bernard Shaw and looked at all the people getting college educations you had to believe the advancement of knowledge would conquer all these problems. I wasn't troubled when I heard ignorant bastards like Joe McCarthy or Westbrook Pegler spouting backward ideas because they were uneducated slobs and their children would go to college and realize how wrong the old ideas and prejudices were.

What did upset me was when I heard a man like the rocket scientist Wernher von Braun spouting reactionary, warmongering ideas because he was highly educated and should know better. With the way I thought about education and intelligence, I just couldn't understand how what I thought of as primitive and ignorant ideas could exist side by side with high intelligence and great learning. It just didn't make sense to me. I had to believe people like von Braun were hypocrites who knew better but sold out for money and power. I contented myself to think the vast majority were benefiting from education and progress on things like birth control and UN peacekeeping and abolition of capital punishment. It gave me lots of reason to believe we were making overall progress toward a better world despite local setbacks. It would be a great place for our children and I wanted to make sure they were thoroughly aware of it.

I kept beating this drum as long as the kids were living at home and no doubt came to be avoided for giving boring lectures. I realized I was often trying to put a grown-up's head on a child's body and despaired at the seeming futility of it. If you'd asked me, there was a long period when I would have said parents' influence on the thinking of their kids is just about nil, but over the years I've come to realize this is wrong. At

Howie and Marilyn hoist a big catch while Cindy vies for notice with a little shiner. She never got over feeling left behind by the big kids.

the time, it seems like nothing sinks in and they even go so far as to reject what you tell them, but then you read their school essays and see your own ideas popping up in their words and you realize they were listening after all. All my kids grew up to be independent thinkers with strong social awareness and left-wing sympathies. It even gets a little scary at times and you think, my god, I should have gone a little easier on some of those opinions.

I'm sure there were a few people around who viewed me as a demagogue who polluted my children's minds with godless socialism but the kids themselves never complained. They think of all their opinions and values as their own and don't like to hear it suggested you had anything to do with it. That's the thing about kids, they soak up what's around them and that becomes who they are. Kay and I worried that Green Bay was a poor environment for kids, especially as we came to have our own misgivings about the place, but to hear the kids in later years, it was paradise on earth. They never miss a chance to go back up there and revisit all the places they used to play in their rowboat, trying to remember the funny names they had for every little cove and point.

The one who didn't benefit as much from our self-directed system of child-rearing in Green Bay was Cindy. At six and nine Howie and Marilyn were old enough to understand novels and make up sophisticated games but Cindy was just that much younger at three or four that she couldn't keep up, much as she tried. The two older kids were good in that they took her along and looked after her, but they couldn't help speaking over her head most of the time and leaving her out of their big-kid schemes.

This irked Cindy to no end, and she frequently came to Kay or me in tears because the big kids wouldn't include her in their games. I remember trying to referee a dispute following the *Giant* episode when Marilyn and Howie's pretend characters, Marilyn-of-the-Stores and Sevward Billington, were all driving Rolls-Royces and hundred-foot Chris-Craft yachts after having discovered a gusher up behind the camp's machine shop (in actuality, our used-motor-oil sump). Cindy's character, whom she called Bad Keeky, wanted to have a twice as fancy car and a hundred-hundred-foot yacht but the older kids were pooh-poohing such claims.

"How did old Keeky get all this stuff?" Howie demanded.

"She just got it," Cindy said.

"You gotta have a way!" Howie insisted.

"Well . . . well, she just looked under all the sofa cushions, and there was lotsa money there, so there!" Cindy fumed.

It was tough for her, but there wasn't much you could do because the older kids really did do a pretty fair job of looking after her, and you couldn't really ask them to pretend she understood more than she did. Another time I remember, Marilyn and Howie started a newspaper. It was all hand-lettered with columns and headlines announcing the cat had had kittens and Daddy was mad because the men all got drunk on Lil Poschner's homebrew, etc. It

When the seagoing missionary Canon Alan Greene came to camp shooting film for his fundraising tour, he couldn't take the camera off Cindy. He said later she filled donation plates from Edmonton to Edinburgh.

made for sensational reading around the cookhouse table and brought its publishers considerable acclaim—but Cindy was not to be outdone. She got out her crayons and quickly produced a sheet of scribbles which she then demanded I read. "See, Daddy? See? Me make newpapie too!" she clamoured, tugging at my sleeve.

Your heart just went out to the poor little thing. She was just as cute as could be, with cherubic features framed by dark curly hair like her Aunt Ruth, and yet she always had this aggrieved attitude. And do you know? She never got over it. To her dying day she had a great big chip on her shoulder, even with her master's degree and her Business Woman of the Year award, she never got over this feeling that she was being left behind, short-changed, cheated out of her rightful consideration and had to screech to be heard. Having watched her life unfold, I have to be a big believer in the theory that birth order has a great big influence on how people turn out.

My mother was just appalled at the way we were raising the kids. She was appalled at their uncut hair, their raggedy clothes, their unsupervised and dangerous play, the lack of milk in their diet, the lax approach to schooling, late bedtimes, the lack of Bible teaching, their exposure to grown-up talk and on and on. When we didn't immediately act on her complaints, she started giving Kay a hard time, inferring that this terrible breakdown in child-rearing discipline was a reflection of Kay's lack of qualification to be a wife and mother. Never mind Kay was doing the work of cook, flunky, bullcook, timekeeper in addition to wife and mother and making a good stab at most of it. But Mother wouldn't leave her alone, and took to calling Kay "that woman" even with the kids, and putting them up to saying hurtful things like "Nanny says proper mothers give their kids clean underwear every day." Kay didn't need this, and after she started coming to me in tears I told the old lady (Old! She was a mere sixty-five!) she would have to go. Damn her, it could have worked out so well if she'd only used some sense. But that had always been the problem with her.

7

In-Laws and Outlaws

Kay's sisters came up and stayed with us every chance they got. I think the old folks had moved off the farm and rented it out once their captive labour pool dried up. Ruthie had somehow managed to do what Kay had been unable to do and stayed in school long enough to become a nurse. She came up to visit and got on at the little hospital in Pender Harbour, where she married one of her patients, a tall, dark, handsome local named Les Kearley. At one point he came to work for me and the newlyweds lived in what we called the "Little Bunkhouse," the smallest of the three buildings perched on poles at the bay's edge. Les was a good man, big and strong with a lot of natural charm but like the kids he was enthralled with the store business and he soon left to become a store clerk, then a manager, then owner of Pender Harbour's leading store, Lloyd's. Later he started a marine supply store in Victoria and branched into boatbuilding with the well-known Pelagic line of fibreglass fishing hulls. They raised a girl and three boys and eventually retired to a fine estate on the Saanich Peninsula.

Jean, the next oldest Boley sister to Kay, had a more lasting impact on Jervis Logging. She came up to visit and hung around for a spell, helping Kay with the bunkhouse work a bit and amusing the kids. She was always a great yarn spinner and had a good way with kids, even though she never had any of her own. She was also pretty handy, having grown up on the

Kay's younger sister Jean made waves in Green Bay.

farm and done a lot of the rougher outside work. She just happened to be hanging around one day when the Workmen's Compensation Board inspector dropped by and noticed we were operating without a whistlepunk.

Whistlepunks are long vanished now, but their job was to relay signals from the rigging crew who were out at the far end of the yarding operation hooking chokers or cables onto the logs so the yarder could pull them into the spar tree with its mainline. The rigging crew consisted of two or three chokermen and a rigging slinger. Normally there would be an older, more experienced logger called the hooktender who bossed the entire yarding operation including the yarder operator or donkey puncher and the landing crew consisting of the chaser and head loader, but in our show this position was supposedly filled by Charley Trebett, who was punching the donkey.

The rigging crew was often out of sight and out of voice contact with the donkey puncher so in order to signal when a group or "turn" of logs was hooked up and ready to be pulled in, we strung a long electric wire out to where they were working and used it to activate a loud horn on the yarder. A system of long and short toots was used to signal "go ahead on the mainline," "slack off on the mainline" "go ahead on the haulback," etc. (The haulback was a lighter line used to pull the mainline back out into the woods after a turn was pulled into the storage space around the spar tree or "landing.") On small gyppo shows like ours where the job descriptions overlapped, the signalling was often done by one of the rigging crew, usually the rigging slinger, who had a few years' experience and maybe a few IQ points on the chokermen, who were recruited for brawn, not brains.

According to the rules, there was supposed to be a separate person whose only responsibility was to relay hollered signals from the rigging crew to the donkey puncher via the electric whistle. This was mostly a hangover from the days of steam, when the steam whistle had to be physically activated by a long pull-cable stretching out into the woods. Since the old cable was up to a quarter of a mile long and had to be laboriously strung through notches in tree limbs, the position of steam whistlepunk was more of a job. Once we went electric, the job of whistlepunk was really rather superfluous and soon after we were in Green Bay the position was eliminated altogether. But it was still on the books in 1952 and the WCB man told me I had to put a man punking whistles before we could operate another day.

Well, we didn't have a man to spare. I would have liked to put Howie doing it but the WCB probably frowned on child labour, too. There were no women in the woods in those days either, if you didn't count cooks or a few lady boss loggers like Sis Harris who co-managed a small show alongside her husband. But there was no law against it, and I asked Jean if she would like to fill in as whistlepunk until we could get somebody else. You'd have to know Jean to know just how eager she was to accept, and how determined she was to keep the job once she had it.

Having a woman on a crew of men changes everything. Suddenly the conversation is entirely transformed. The main topic, female anatomy, is no longer possible. Swearing is subdued. But nobody complains when the woman is young, single and good-looking. Suddenly every man is scheming to get next to her, the married no less than the single. Jean was not flirtatious but she knew what she had and when I realized which one of the crew she was interested in, I couldn't believe it: Charley Trebett.

I guess Charley was only about ten years older than her but it seemed more than that. He seemed crusty and musty even to me, although he was only about five years older than me. I couldn't imagine them together, but the first thing we know, off to town they go and come back married. This changes the dynamic of the camp considerably.

After his initial flurry of resistance to having me come in and take over, Charley had taken a back seat, mainly because he didn't want to put out the effort to do anything else. He had been content to let me do all the talking along with all the extra work of running the camp and welding up broken truck frames through the night. Now suddenly he was back asking questions and making beefs. He demanded that I pay board for the kids. He said it wasn't right that they got to live in camp and eat company groceries for free. I told him if he really wanted to get picky, Kay and I would start billing for all the overtime we worked and we could take the kids' board out of that ten times over.

He didn't have any answer to that, and I could only conclude it was because it wasn't his idea in the first place. Why was this suddenly an issue when there hadn't been a word of it before? But it was just the start. He began carping every chance he got about one pisant thing or another. Jean began speaking up whenever she got the chance as well. Her main theme was what a terrific asset to the camp Charley was and what a raw deal he was getting, with me keeping him in the dark on everything. She praised him up and down and put out quite a story about how strong he was and what a deadly fighter he was. I don't know if he was encouraging her in this, but he did nothing to disown it and he did become increasingly belligerent. Every time I gave an order he either contradicted it flat out or found some way to undermine it. It was really starting to eat me up, which made me doubly mad because I suspected that's just what they wanted.

The old *Suez* had been getting steadily more decrepit and instead of going looking for a replacement, I decided to build one. I'd spent a lot of time thinking just what qualities a good camp boat would need and I was eager to put them all together in one design. I started with a plan for a twenty-five-foot cabin cruiser called the *Flash* that I found in *Boatbuilding in Your Own Backyard* by S.S. Rabl. I liked it because it was beamy and roomy inside, had a planing hull for speed and was built out of plywood, which was the new-wave boatbuilding material just coming into use then. But I made a lot of changes.

I always hated boats you felt you were going to fall off when you were on the narrow catwalk around the cabin, so I doubled the width of that. I hated the fact that on most small powerboats the motor took up the best part of the cabin. Today stern drives get around this but there weren't any then so I put the *Flash*'s motor under the back cockpit and hooked it up to the shaft with a V-drive out of a truck. I'd never seen this in a boat, but Rabl suggested it as an option and I couldn't see why it wouldn't work. The *Flash* was designed with no keel or shoe, the prop and rudder just hung down where a chunk of driftwood could knock it off, so I gave my version a good skookum keel with a shoe strong enough to ride over a log. Rabl's plan had a kind of blunt bow with a light bow stem I didn't like the look of, so I skipped having a bow stem altogether and made a rounded nose that I carved out of a big piece of cedar. It gave it a real fifties look, like a 1950 Ford.

Then I decided to fibreglass it. This was not called for in the plans and I had never seen fibreglass on a boat up to that stage—I'm not sure there was one to be seen in BC in 1952 but I'd read about this new miracle material in *Popular Science* and I decided it would be just the thing to provide a permanent finish you would never have to worry about teredoes or shipworms boring into. I had to send away to the eastern States for the ingredients and I'm afraid I made kind of a lumpy job of applying it because the cello-finishing technique had not been perfected yet, but it gave our boat a tough shell we would never have to paint.

I had the whole family working on this dream boat every night until late. The kids seemed to enjoy the work and were very handy for tightening bolts and dabbing Cuprinol preservative in confined spaces. Some time not long after I came, I got the company to buy a good little Onan light plant and I strung wires through trees along the walking paths that laced the camp together and put electric lights in all the buildings. Normally we would start the light plant at dusk and run it until 10:00 p.m. We didn't usually have it on during daylight hours but I was eager to get this boat finished so I had taken to running the plant on Sundays to power my electric tools.

One Sunday I was drilling merrily away when the power went off. I thought, "That's funny, I'm sure I put enough gas in it," and walked over to the light plant, which was about five hundred feet away down a trail and around a

The *Flash*, aka *Marilyn Kay*, our family boatbuilding project, finally hits the water in 1955. The sad thing is, we never spent as many hours running it as we did building it.

bend, checked the plant over and restarted it. It didn't have an ignition key, just a red button for start and a black one for stop. I couldn't figure out why it had stopped, but shrugged and went back to my drilling. Ten minutes later, it stops again. I go back over, check everything and again, there's no reason it should have stopped. I'm suspicious so I look around. There's a big cedar tree about twenty feet away and I see the toe of a boot sticking out from behind it. I walk over and here's Charley standing there.

"What in hell are you up to?" I say.

"I've had enough of you burning up company gas for that damn boat of yours," he says.

"Charley, I don't think you really mean that. Somebody put you up to this. You don't have the guts to pull this on your own."

So he takes a swing at me. I dodge it and unload a real haymaker and he just stands there and catches it full in the face. I know then the big build-up about his fighting skill is just BS. He goes over but scrambles up and comes at me, arm cocked like something in a comic strip so I pop him again. The silly bugger keeps getting up so I keep knocking him down. Finally I knock him right through the salmonberries and down onto the beach. He doesn't get up from that so I start the light plant and go back to work.

I tell Kay and she's upset but not surprised. She knew something had to give. After an hour or so I get worried maybe I hit the chump too hard with that last shot and go over to take a peek through the salmonberries but he's cleared out. The next morning Charley and Jean walk down the path all dressed up in town clothes, get in a boat and leave camp.

That's it. The partnership is over. They move up Jervis Inlet where Charley gets a small claim of some kind but they don't stay together. Jean becomes an itinerant logging camp cook, travelling up and down the coast and Charley ends up a kind of hermit back in Port Alberni where he came from. He died years ago although Jean is still steaming along at ninety-six. We meet at family dinners during Christmas sometimes and we're friendly on the surface but there is a tension not very far below because of our past history. There may be forgiveness in families but not necessarily forgetting.

With Charley out of my hair, things smoothed out at Green Bay. I've never thought of it this way before, but Jean did me a favour by bringing things to a head. If she hadn't come on the scene, god knows how long I would have struggled along with Charley sticking to me like a wood tic. The main drawback was that he took the yarder with him, although we found out later he didn't even own it, he was just borrowing it from a logger up Jervis named Sampson who might have been just as happy to go on leasing it to me. It didn't matter. I had a new D8 cat by this time which I fitted with a logging arch and yarded into the tree with that, which worked better. We had a small loading donkey to load the truck. Without the yarder I was able to get rid of the rigging crew and cut back to a core of good solid men like Mike Poschner and Jack Spence, who moved his wife into the house at the top of the hill vacated by Charley and Jean, certainly the best accommodation in camp. We were getting out just as many logs with a lot fewer guys, so we started to make a little money. It was a lot less stressful not having all the unruly chokermen coming and going from the Harbour and not having Charley trying to trip me up at every turn. I was feeling pretty good about the future.

I was having a hard time getting enough time to finish off the *Flash* and I was kind of wishing I had chosen one of the smaller, easier models designed by S.S. Rabl. There was one in particular I really liked the look of called the *Porpoise*. It was an open runabout only fifteen feet long but it had high sides that gave it the seaworthiness of a much bigger boat. Like all of Rabl's plans, it made use of the new easy-to-build plywood construction method, but it incorporated another new innovation that captured my interest: it was designed to be powered by an outboard. Outboards had been around for years but they were unreliable and low-powered. Then in 1951 Johnson came out with a twenty-five-horsepower model that was reliable and affordable at $390. I bought some spruce 1 x 4's and sixteen-foot sheets of marine-grade plywood but with all the hassles of running the camp I couldn't get at it so I talked one of the crewmen, Mike Poschner, into taking over and by god if he didn't get busy and bang a pretty little boat together in jig time. The *Porpoise* had a V-to-flat bottom and with the 25 Johnson it got up and planed at twenty knots or better.

Well, this really changed the dynamics of living in Green Bay. Suddenly we were only twenty minutes away from the store and the

Cindy hoping to hitch a ride on Jim Spilsbury's float plane. We used planes a little—mostly Seabees flown by BC Airlines, but they were too expensive to make a habit of.

hospital and—most significantly—Gordie Lyons' beer parlour. Going to Pender Harbour was no longer a full day's occupation, it was something you could do after supper and get home before dark. The *Porpoise* got a lot of attention when it came zipping down to Gordie Lyons' for a quick one after work. There were other speedboats around—a local logger named Olli Sladey won the boat race every year at the Pender Harbour Regatta with his crew boat, a twenty-four-foot Sangstercraft with some kind of a big V8 inboard in it, but a boat like that was not something every Tom, Dick and Harry could afford. A light runabout with a 25 Johnson was something anybody could get, and it wasn't long before they were crisscrossing Agamemnon Channel and ducking in and out of every camp.

I always say the 25 Johnson liberated the BC coast. Overnight you saw them at docks from Prince Rupert to Sooke and everybody felt a lot closer to everybody else. They had their downside of course. These light speedboats went so far in a day people were tempted to take them places they didn't belong. My brother-in-law Les Kearley built a copy of the *Porpoise* but added a bit of length and width so he could put two outboards on it. If I'm not mistaken, by that time Johnson was making a 40-horse and he put two of those on it, which made it go like a rocket. It went fast enough to get up Jervis Inlet and back in one day so he decided to take a run up the inlet with my sister-in-law Jean Trebett as passenger.

Halfway up they hit chop and one of the plywood bottom panels pounded loose. The boat sank in a split second. Jean can swim but Les can't and of course he didn't have a lifejacket on. No grown man would be caught dead in a lifejacket in those days. He managed to find something to hang on to and they floated around hollering for help until just about dark before the camp watchman at Brittain River heard them and came out for them. They were goddamn lucky.

As mentioned we added a fourth child on July 4,1953, and named him Donald Wesley after Kay's brother and mine. It kind of gave us a new lease on life to have a baby on the claim again. Jack and Eve Spence had a couple of little boys named Johnny and Trevor and the Poschners added a baby and the camp took on a bit of a family feeling. We even got some neighbours. A small logger named Bill Hodgson had set up in another part of Green Bay and one day when I was over visiting I saw a familiar figure, tall and stooped with craggy features and a cackling laugh.

It was my old friend Sam Hately, who'd saved my bacon by loaning me his horse in the North Bend blizzard of 1950. He'd left canyon country not long after us and was now living in Pender Harbour renting himself out as a contract faller. Typically, he was doing it the hard way. Instead of sharing his earnings with a second man to help run the big two-man McCulloch, he had knocked the head end off and was operating it all by himself. This was when chainsaws had six-foot bars and weighed 120 lb and here he was

Kay holding baby Donnie at the Yates house, Green Bay, not too long after July 4, 1953.

packing that up and down side hills all day long. All I could do was shake my head. What a man.

We were getting to the end of the claim we were logging but there was a patch of really nice timber next to it and I couldn't wait to move into that. I would have to get rights to it first but that was pretty much a given. The way you got timber in those days was you did a map survey then applied to the forest ministry to make it available in the form of a public timber sale. You had to go to Vancouver and go through a public bidding process but you could usually count on outbidding any other gyppo because you were already established in the area whereas they would have to set up camp, build roads, build dumps and all the rest. There were a few other small operators who might have been able to take a run at it, the Kleins, the Duboises, Olli Sladey, Bill Hodgson or maybe Milligan over in Vanguard Bay, but we generally kept out of each other's kitchens. So when the time came I phoned the log broker I dealt with in Vancouver and told him to go to this auction and handle our bidding.

"How high do you want me to go?" he said. I was paying the government a royalty or "stumpage" of $8 per thousand board feet on the claim we had been logging up to that point. That's what you bid, the stumpage you're willing to pay the forest ministry on each log as you log it. I knew log prices were rising a bit so I told him he could go up to $12 or even $14 if he had to, but I didn't think he would.

The next day I get him on the phone and it turns out we didn't get the timber.

"How the hell could that be?" I said, stunned.

"I stopped bidding at $18 but it just kept on going up," he said. "It finally went for $40 a thousand."

It turned out there were things happening behind the scenes I wasn't aware of. In the late forties the BC government began parcelling huge tracts of BC's remaining unlogged forest in the form of Forest Management Licences, which became the exclusive preserve of big companies like H.R. MacMillan and BC Forest Products. The excuse was that small operators like me couldn't be trusted to manage the forest properly, whereas large corporations could hire foresters and log in a sustainable way.

I've seen this time and time again in the course of my life. It had been obvious that BC's tremendous forest resource was being logged at an unsustainable rate for decades and the big companies and their supporters in government had been denying it. But at a certain point it could no longer be denied. In 1945 Chief Justice Gordon Sloan chaired a Royal Commission on forest practices that proved beyond a doubt the forest resource was being liquidated faster than it could re-grow. At that point the big companies reversed their position and admitted that the forest resource was indeed at risk, and furthermore, they were the only ones with the expertise and means to save it.

You will see this every time. You see it now with global warming. Industry has doubled the level of carbon dioxide in the atmosphere and it's warming the oceans, melting the ice caps and altering weather patterns. Scientists are warning us that if we don't reverse the process immediately we will be facing huge natural disasters including global famine before the end of this century. But the big corporations fight it and deny it and billionaire reactionaries like the Koch brothers fund political movements like the Tea Party bent on denying industry's role in climate change.

This is the pattern. The first impulse of entrenched interests is to defend their turf and refuse to change their ways, because change threatens their bottom line. But eventually the problem becomes undeniable, so the business leaders and their political representatives switch horses and begin embracing the very thing they've been denying all along. This is just starting with the global warming problem. Some companies are seeing the opportunity to sell electric cars and windmills, but the bulk of the establishment is still pushing hydrocarbon energy. Eventually though, after enough floods and hurricanes and fires and droughts, you will see the likes of General Motors and the Republican Party wrapping themselves in the environmental flag and presenting themselves as the best people to bring in electric cars and solar power and emission controls and trying to make people forget they were ever against it. In 1952, this is the stage we were at in the BC forest industry.

The outcome of Sloan's commission was that the forest was placed more exclusively than ever under the control of the very people who had already done the most to destroy it, and they went on logging at an increasingly unsustainable rate until by the end of the twentieth century, many of those big companies like MacMillan Bloedel, BC Forest Products and Doman Industries had logged themselves right out of existence.

They and their supporters in government had only used a phony concern for the environment as a cover to go on pursuing corporate profit to the complete detriment of the forests, and the public didn't get wise until it was far too late. We saw the same tactic used in fisheries management and in a dozen other areas. I was vaguely aware of the changes going on in the background in the early 1950s and I was very skeptical but I was too busy trying to make payroll to get involved. Some of the smaller operators tried to put up a fight through the Truck Loggers Association but it was controlled by the bigger members who wanted to do business with the majors and they didn't get anywhere.

I kept my head down and hoped none of the changes would affect me, but they did. Smaller forest products companies who were being squeezed out by the Tree Farm Licences began scrambling to grab any small claims they could find as a matter of survival. Our timber sale had come to the attention of two of these independent mills and they had bid each other into the stratosphere, probably not even knowing where Nelson Island was. It was crazy. Nobody could log at a stumpage rate of $40 a thousand and make a go of it at that time. One contractor after another tried, but nobody lasted for long. By bidding the stumpage up so high, the stupid bastards had ruined what should have been one of the nicest timber claims around.

That quickly, the rosy future I had seen profitably filling Green Bay with fat peelers for the next decade or so vanished into thin air. If I had made my move a year earlier I probably would have had that timber sale all to myself, but I hadn't seen any need to rush. The Forest Service official line was that you couldn't ask for a new timber sale before you'd finished the one you were working, but I knew guys got away with it. The forest minister, Robert Sommers, went to jail for bribes he had taken around this time but it was generally accepted he was just the fall guy. The whole ministry was shot through with corruption and cronyism and once again I paid a price for not knowing how to play the backroom game.

I was left staring at a blank wall. I scrambled around looking for another claim somewhere in the neighbourhood, then further afield, but everywhere I went it was the same story. The good timber was already tied up and what was available was overpriced scrub. All I could find was a little patch of private timber over on West Lake that represented about two months' work for the cat and one chokerman. I let the last of the crew go and logged the West Lake patch with Howie and a green chokerman named Robert La Rue, an educated Parisian who was on a world tour. He turned out to be one of the smartest and hardest-working men I ever had, learning in two months what many men never mastered in a lifetime. He and I used to get into the goddamndest discussions about history and philosophy and science. Lunch breaks would go on for two hours and after-dinner arguments would last until midnight.

We had a problem in that the timber was on one side of West Lake, a large lake in the middle of Nelson Island, and we had to boom it in Vanguard Bay, on the other side. How were we to tow the logs across West Lake? We needed a powerboat. Well, I had a Palmer one-cylinder fishboat engine in camp so I mounted it on two cedar logs spiked together in an A-shape. I scrounged a shaft and prop in Pender Harbour and slung them under the logs. We steered with a big homemade oar. Putt-putting back and forth across West Lake in this makeshift tugboat was Howie's job. He was tickled to have his own command at the ripe old age of eight and couldn't have done a better job, making up tows by dogging together a dozen logs at a time, inching patiently across the lake and stowing them in a bullpen over at the Vanguard side, then returning for another tow, all day long.

When we had the logs all boomed on the other side I walked the cat through the brush around the lake, crossing much private property and knocking down a fair number of saplings. You'd pay a $50,000 fine for doing that today, but in 1954 it was just typical logger behaviour, you didn't give it a second thought. We spent a couple more weeks yarding the logs out across the narrow neck of land locals called "the portage" and booming them up in Vanguard Bay, the three of us camping in the old *Suez*, which we lined with cardboard and turned into a passable little bunkhouse. The portage was a nice grassy swale when we started but after

Howie got off to an early start running the cat. It served him well in later life.

the first day it turned to a sea of mud. It was bloody awful. The muck was so damn deep the D8 would get bogged down over the tracks and I'd have to pull myself out backward using the powerful winch that all logging tractors have on the back. Once I got so buried, the big cedar I was using for a tail holt pulled right over on top of Howie, who thought he was standing in the clear.

That was one of the worst moments in my life. I saw this huge tree go down over him, its branches snapping and popping and spreading out over half an acre, it seemed. I jumped off the cat into waist-deep mud and started wallowing toward him yelling, "Howie, Howie, Howie" at the top of my lungs. It was an eternity before I finally heard his little reedy voice, "I'm okay, Dad." God, what a relief! He'd seen the tree coming and dove behind a big boulder so the branches came down all around him and pinned him but didn't do any damage. If he'd given in to the urge to outrun the falling tree he likely would have been schmucked. I don't know why he took so long to answer my frantic calls. I think maybe he was trying to teach me a lesson.

There was an old man living in Vanguard Bay at that time, Walter Wray. Everybody called him Santa Claus Wray because he had a big white beard and a Santa Claus shape to go with it. He was a member of the Wray family that had been the first settlers on Nelson Island and had been in Vanguard Bay since the beginning of time, living in a mossy old homestead with a wizened-up crone we assumed was his wife but actually turned out to be his sister. Robert went over to visit them one evening and when they realized he was a cultivated Frenchman they proudly served him their homemade wine. Robert eagerly took a sip and discovered to his dismay that it was pure vinegar. He says the old lady took a sip and said, "I don't know why I thought this just now, Walter, but when you're in Egmont tomorrow you must get us some vinegar." She wasn't passing comment on the wine, except maybe unconsciously. They both insisted the wine was top quality. Robert thought this was very funny. He thought everything about Canada was very funny.

Old Santa Claus had been made a justice of the peace somewhere along the way and viewed Vanguard Bay as his private domain. He didn't like anybody disturbing his peaceable kingdom and when he heard we were going to yard logs through the portage he gave us a big lecture about replacing our divot and not disturbing anything. I was a bit worried about him because we were actually trespassing on Crown land and booming our logs in a prime shellfish area without any kind of a permit and who knew what kind of trouble he might dredge up for us? Still, we had to get the logs out of there somehow and the portage was the only place to do it. West Lake is quite large and scenic, it must be one of the biggest lakes on any Gulf island, and since the early days it had been taken up by summer cottagers from Vancouver who used this portage as kind of a public thoroughfare.

Well, as I said, we turned the bloody place into a sea of mud. We truly did make a hell of a mess and old Santa Claus Wray just went out of his skull. He came over and ordered us to cease and desist, ranting that we had "ruined Vanguard Bay" and he was going to get me put in jail. I figured he was bluffing and kept right on logging, I didn't have any choice at that point, and figured the sooner we got the hell out of there the better. I did what I could to grade the place down with the cat before we left but it's hard to do much with neck-deep mud and it still looked pretty bad. I guess today I might well be put in jail but in those days that was the way logging was done. Loggers had the run of the land and did what they had to do to get wood to the mills. It was the way of the coast and pretty much accepted by everyone concerned. I don't know if old Santa Claus ever did contact any higher authorities but if he did, they must have told him to go home and tend to his homebrew because we never heard from anybody.

Once we had the logs boomed up I got in touch with Gordie Cochrane, who as a younger man had run my best Mack logging truck over a cliff on Texada Island. He had done well enough for himself to buy a solid little tugboat with a 6-71 Jimmy in it called the *Hi-Tide* and I was happy to be able to give him some work towing our logs back around to Green Bay, Howie pushing from behind with his motorized raft. Howie, Robert and I finished making a two-section boom back in Green Bay and that was it. The Green Bay period was over.

I was forty and broke.

Part 2

ONE DAMN THING AFTER ANOTHER

8

Pender Harbour, Temporarily

The first five years after we left Green Bay are kind of a blur in my mind. I was knocked flat and didn't know what the hell to do. Kay was pretty deflated too but she had the kids to worry about and got busy setting up housekeeping in an old farmhouse we rented in Pender Harbour. It was on the waterfront like all the houses in Pender Harbour then, and had been the homestead of a family named Sharp, who had run a marine ways and boat works on the property until their shop burnt down some years earlier. Now it was owned by one of the teachers at the local K–12 school, a man named Bob Dick. The place had its own dock where I tied up the *Suez* and an old grid where I was able to beach the *Flash*, which was still not quite finished. We also brought down two bunkhouses that I had a local logger named Wilf Harper pull ashore at his gyppo logging camp, which was located right in downtown Madeira Park.

The only people to welcome us on our arrival were the Hatelys, who now had five children and were living in a rambling house Sam built only a few minutes' walk from the Sharp place. Sam greeted me like a long-lost brother and in the course of a long night drinking beer at the Madeira Park Legion, managed to convince me to buy the south half of his ten-acre property, which was bisected by Lagoon Road and Francis Peninsula Road. I didn't really want land in Pender Harbour at that point but Sam was being so neighbourly I agreed to take it for $500, nothing down and $25 a month, interest-free. I had no intention of ever living on it.

We were right out of money so as soon as I got Kay and the family settled I had to find work. I didn't want to run off and leave Kay with so much up in the air but there was no getting away from it. The cupboard was bare. I swallowed my pride and made the rounds of my old logging contacts. One sent me to another and finally I got to Blondie Swanson, who I'd hauled logs for on Vancouver Island during the war, and who had a twenty-five-man camp called Barzell Logging in Theodosia Inlet, which is an offshoot of Malaspina Inlet, the ten-mile-long inlet just north of Powell River. He had a full crew but took me on as handyman and I spent the better part of two years there, filling in on any job that needed doing, doing some monkey wrenching, hauling the odd load of logs and operating the cable shovel in the rock quarry, the first time I'd ever run a cable shovel. My head was still spinning from the abrupt turn my life had taken and it was hard to accept being reduced from camp owner to working stiff but it was good to be occupied and sending home a good fat paycheque.

I had never been around the Powell River area before and I kind of liked what I saw. I got a bone infection at one point and had to spend two weeks in the hospital, the old one down by their big pulp mill. I was completely healthy except for having to tow this IV stand around so I tried to make myself useful around the ward doing this or that, cleaning up the waiting room and giving the old people baths. I enjoyed it. There seemed to be something open and friendly about Powell River people you didn't always find in coast towns.

Blondie's camp was up the valley a ways from the ruins of a big railway logging camp operated in the 1930s by Merrill, Ring and Moore. It had been nicknamed Baloney Bay, partly because they kept a herd of pigs behind the cookhouse but mostly because it had the reputation of being one of the cheapest and most dangerous camps on the coast. During the Depression a lot of the big companies brought in what was called the "speed up" system, which mainly meant throwing safety rules out the window and driving the men like coolies. Men were paid by the log and those who didn't work flat out didn't last. Anybody who put his own safety ahead of production was instantly fired and an old-timer said the mail boat seldom left Baloney Bay without a couple of accident victims on it. Once they killed five men in one day.

This was typical of the way many big corporate camps operated during the Depression and of course it was all justified by economic conditions and condoned by the government, which ordered the safety inspectors to back off. And it wasn't just logging, it was everywhere during the Depression. The value of human life fell while money became more precious. It was a big eye-opener for a lot of guys including me and a big reason for the growth of unionism after the war, when the woods went solid for the IWA. Today the lessons of the 1930s have been largely forgotten, the loggers' union is just a shadow of itself and a lot of the bad old practices we thought were gone forever have crept back in. Logging once again has one of the highest fatality rates of any industry.

Apart from the men in camp there was nobody living in Theodosia Inlet then except an old widow named May Salo, who still lived on a ranch near where her father, Jim Palmer, had pre-empted back in 1900. This was the same Palmer family that gave its name to Palmer Bay, where I had gone contract hauling for Clare Smith in 1943. May's brothers had been famous pioneer loggers and I had seen one of them at Palmer Bay skipping across floating logs at age seventy carrying a 150-lb oxygen cylinder on his shoulder. May was a great old gal who loved company and was full of stories. One day I went down there and she was standing in the little creek that ran through her place pitchforking salmon carcasses onto the bank to use for fertilizer. This might have been considered slightly illegal under normal circumstances but as she told me, these salmon didn't officially exist. There hadn't been a salmon run in that creek until she had illegally planted eggs and built it up, and by this time she had such a vigorous run coming back in the fall they needed to be thinned out.

Just on the other side of the narrows that led into Theodosia there was another little homestead owned by a bachelor named Willy Bishop, who'd been raised in the inlet and was one of the most naïve and also most sweet-natured men I ever met. He had a shy stammer and couldn't say hello without blushing and looking at his feet. His father had pre-empted a homestead at Bliss Landing in 1911 and founded a settlement there, originally called Bishop's Landing, which he left in the mid-1920s after being burned out by an arsonist. Willy had a little schooling at a country school that had been operating in Malaspina Inlet for a few years, but he could barely write a letter. He had a nice piece of property on a small bay with a spare cabin so I rented it off him. When the weather warmed up Kay came up with Donnie, who was about four then, and we spent a very pleasant summer together. It sort of reminded me of the time in Nanoose Bay when we were first married and living in a cabin with a small child on the beach and had nothing to do after work but relax and read.

By this time I had the *Flash* running and I brought it up so I could commute back and forth to camp. One day when I was bringing the boat home from work I saw an eagle dive-bombing something in the water. I steered over and here was a mother otter with four little pups swimming along. The eagle had separated one pup from the group and was diving on it every time it poked its head up. The little fellow was going down for the third time when I got to him and I scooped him up and took him home. There is nothing cuter or more fun than an otter pup and he became our main source of entertainment. Some animals just seem to have an inborn sense of fun, and otters are at the top of the list. He was as agile and clever as a monkey and before long he was as tame as a kitten. He was a handful though. Nothing was safe from his prying little hands and he ate more than Donnie. As he grew he ate more than two Donnies. He wasn't great on training but we noticed he always pooped in more or less the same place so we put paper down there and caught most of it. Still, his entertainment value was worth it and when he chewed through the wall and disappeared one day we were heartbroken.

I saw a young otter when I was out in the boat the next day and chased it ashore and got hold of it—only to discover it was pretty well full grown and completely wild. It made hamburger of my hands and arms. Wild otters may look cute but they are absolutely vicious when cornered. I was still thinking maybe we could tame it like we tamed the other one and managed to get it into the back of the van I was driving and slammed the door. My god, you could see the roof and walls bulging out where he was flinging himself around in there. The whole van was rocking. I was afraid to open the door. Eventually it calmed down and I carefully opened the door and peeked in but the poor thing had blown a gasket. I skinned it and dried the pelt, and that's all the otter we had for the rest of our stay in

Theodosia. We had that skin for years, the fur was silky and beautiful, but I felt bad every time I saw it.

There was this young truck driver in camp, Howie Smith. He was a highballer and ran me off the road one time, not because he meant to but because he was just going too damn fast to avoid me. I was going to clean his clock, but then I thought, no he's just young and doesn't know any better. So I took him aside and gave him a fatherly talking-to. I told him being fast was one thing but being reckless was another and if he didn't learn the difference he was going to bust somebody up, most likely himself. He took it well and slowed down—a bit. I undertook to show him a few tricks about driving fast without driving dangerously and we became good friends. Well, he had a brand-new Cadillac, a lovely emerald-green

Donnie on the steps of our cabin, Theodosia Inlet, 1957. I'd like to say that's the pet otter he's holding, but the white booties give it away.

two-door and he said to me one day, "I want you to take that car and take your family on a holiday." I had been in camp a long time without taking any time off, so I said okay, I think I'll take you up on that.

This was in 1957 and this was the first official holiday we had taken since our honeymoon in 1939, so we decided to retrace the same route down through eastern Washington and up through the Okanagan to the Cariboo and back. It was a great trip and the kids were amazed at the change in landscape as we got out of the coast rainforest into sagebrush country just as I had been when I first saw it with my father and just as Kay had been in 1939. I stopped at the first sage bush and put a sprig over the heat vent so the scent of sage filled the car, just like my father had done when I took him on that last trip to the Interior just before he died back in 1929. I was happy to notice Donnie still doing the same thing when we went on what will probably be our last drive to the Interior a short while ago. It's become a family tradition, one of the few.

Everywhere we went on that 1957 trip the seas just kind of parted for us because of this swanky car. Customs agents, gas station attendants,

In 1957 we splurged and went on an actual vacation, retracing our 1939 honeymoon route past the Grand Coulee.

motel clerks, cops, all went out of their way to accommodate. Howie told me once it was the one time in his life he felt rich. My sister Gladys' family in 100 Mile House even rolled out the red carpet, and I didn't have the heart to tell them the car was a loaner. It was an eye-opener for a guy used to driving beaters. We burned through the nice paycheque I'd got before we set out but it was a wonderful time and I made a vow not to wait so long before the next family holiday. But I don't think we ever took another two-week trip while the kids were living at home. I meant to, but the years flew by, the kids got tied up in their own affairs and now here I am, grounded in my lift chair. A caution to all you young parents out there—don't put it off. Those calendar pages flip over faster than you can possibly imagine.

> Come, fill the Cup, and in the fire of Spring
> Your Winter-garment of Repentance fling:
> The Bird of Time has but a little way
> To flutter—and the Bird is on the Wing.

I had to hustle back to camp as soon as I dropped Kay and the kids off at the Sharp place and didn't find out until later what had happened. This Bob Dick who owned the Sharp place had been trying to get me to buy it off him. He was asking $2,500, then $1,500 then he just said, "Make me an offer." He'd had a bust-up or something and really wanted to unload. It was quite a property—a two-acre peninsula jutting out into Gerrans Bay with waterfront on three sides.

I guess I could have scrounged up a down payment somehow but we already had the property I'd bought off Sam Hately and to tell the truth I didn't want to stay in Pender Harbour. Part of Pender Harbour—the best-off part actually—was nicknamed "Hardscratch" and that was how I saw the whole town, a place where people scratched out a living doing a bit of fishing in the summer and getting a lot of pogey in the winter. The only people who had a steady paycheque were the teachers at the school, the postmaster and the foreman of the government highways crew.

And it wasn't just the economic prospects. It was a weird little place. There was no centre to it. Pender Harbour is just that, a harbour, a small

I think that's the Jermains' *Medusa* at the Irvines Landing gas dock in the right foreground. Ray Phillips would know. The long white boat on the left is Bill Cochrane's *Miss Victoria*, a sister ship to our *Suez*. This must be boat day to judge by the crowd.

inlet with many bays and coves just right for throwing up a shack on the beach and anchoring a small boat dock out front. So you had Lee Bay where the Lees lived and Joe Bay where Joe Gonsalves lived and Duncan Cove where George Duncan lived and Sinclair Bay where Bill Sinclair lived and Kleindale where the Kleins lived and Whiskey Slough where the Scotchmen lived, and Jermain's Island where Capt. and Mrs. Jermain lived and so on. Each family was kind of tucked away in its own private little compound. Jermain's Island perched right in the middle of the Harbour like a fortress. In fact it had a flag flying from it and not the Canadian flag either, but the British Union Jack. There was a rumour that Capt. Jermain raised it every morning as Mrs. Jermain stood at attention singing "God Save the Queen," which was no doubt as groundless as most of the rumours that swirled around Pender Harbour.

Capt. Jermain was said to be an actual British sea captain from the Royal Navy and the joke was that if Capt. Jermain was truly a captain, Mrs. Jermain must have been the admiral of the fleet. He was a stooped-over little shrimp of a guy who never spoke a word whereas she was tall and imperious and loud. They lived alone there in a stately home built out of vertical logs and nobody knew much about them, except to nod hello at the store on Saturday morning, a nod that was seldom returned. The only person they deigned to engage in conversation was Al Lloyd, the owner of Lloyd's General Store in Garden Bay, who had an imperious manner to match Mrs. Jermain's. They were cut from the same cloth, those two. Lloyd was the Harbour's leading businessman and he and his wife Queenie did their best to lord it over the town with a stately home of their own on a promontory looking across the harbour to the Jermains.

Not everybody in Pender Harbour dwelt in such splendid isolation as the Jermains, but it was definitely more of an each-to-his-own place than an all-for-one place. There was no main street tying it together and not even many good trails. There were three or four distinct centres—Irvines Landing, Garden Bay, Kleindale, Madeira Park—and they all pulled against each other as much as they possibly could. You had to go to Irvines Landing to get the mail or meet the steamer, you had to go to Pope Landing or Donley Landing to sell a fish, you had to go to Garden Bay to see a doctor, etc. The schools were at Donley Landing and Irvines, then at Madeira Park and Kleindale.

Cindy, Donnie, Howie and Marilyn in the pram I built for them. The kids struggled to adapt to life in the big city of Pender Harbour, but nobody had to tell them how to get around by boat.

They called it the Venice of the North because if you wanted to do anything—shop, visit, get the mail, go to church, grab a beer—you had to get in a boat and go to one of the other places. Even the kids went to school in a school boat instead of a bus. For everyday business Harbourites had kickers—open skiffs powered by air-cooled inboard engines. Every home had a dock in front and every dock had one or two of these kickers tied up at it. I'm not sure why they were called kickers—maybe because the little Briggs & Stratton motors would give you a kick if you didn't pull hard enough on the starting rope. It was a common term for any small boat in those days, although in Pender Harbour it only meant these ten- or twelve-foot skiffs with inboard motors. The classic Pender Harbour kicker

In the 1950s, shoppers flocked to Al Lloyd's revolutionary "self-serve" grocery store in small inboard boats called kickers. This family appears to be still getting used to their newfangled outboard.

was clinker-built and painted white on the outside and green on the inside. There was usually a little wooden box over the motor and for steering they had sash cord running around the gunwales that you'd just wrap your hand around and yank. Only the pretentious used steering wheels, and those were usually mounted along the side.

On Saturday morning you'd see as many as two dozen of these kickers clustered around the store dock like a flock of seagulls. Women used them to shop, kids used them to go to school, old people used them to go to the doctor—they were everywhere. But getting in your boat and putting over to a neighbour's wharf was not like chatting over a back fence or meeting people on the sidewalk. It took more of a conscious effort and also, you couldn't do it with any amount of privacy. Everybody in the Harbour could look out their window and watch you leave your wharf, wondering where you were going. It was hard to have an affair in the place without everybody knowing about it. When old Al Lloyd started slipping out on Queenie and spending quality time with Zoe Earle while her husband Tom was away fishing, we all knew because Al's boat was spending so much time at the Earles' dock "delivering groceries." The gossip mills were running overtime with that one.

So we weren't sold on Pender Harbour. Today jetsetters pay millions for a tiny scrap of its craggy headlands and gnarly trees but in those days nobody would give you a nickel for scenery. We were sick of looking at rock and Christmas trees and would have been happy to trade all of it for a bit of flat land with some soil where you could grow a decent crop of spuds. Pender Harbour seemed to us a backward, ingrown little place where everybody was suspicious of everybody else and newcomers weren't accepted until they'd been there two generations and preferably married into one of the seven big families that dominated the place. It didn't have home phones or hydro or cars and seemed to us to be mired in a past of gumboot yokelism we didn't want our kids to become part of.

The kids that grew up there generally dropped out of school by grade nine or ten and went fishing, logging or got pregnant. A lot of them grew up without ever having seen the outside world, or knowing there was one. Vancouver and Victoria might as well have been on another planet.

During the 1950s the event of the year in Pender Harbour was the mid-summer regatta, here being staged in Garden Bay with a three-man log birling contest in progress. Note all the boats, large and small—that's how people got around in the "Venice of the North."

The first settlers had been world travellers and people of vision but with each succeeding generation the vision narrowed until you had a bunch of hicks who couldn't see beyond the next drunk-up at Egmont or the next salmon season crewing on one of the Warnocks' seine boats, like a lot of the gumboot gang we had at Green Bay.

I remember sending one of those boys to Pender Harbour to phone a parts order in to Vancouver. This kid had his own boat which he had no trouble skippering through a howling winter gale but when it came to operating the old crank-type phone at the grocery store he was as spooked as a Kalahari bushman. He had to get one of the store clerks to make the call. This kid's grandfather had been a man of the world but here he was after two generations in the Harbour so bushed he was flummoxed by a common telephone. We desperately wanted to avoid having our kids grow up like that. In later years I came to be more than a bit sentimental about those innocent and long-gone days, but at the time we wanted them to go to college and have the lives we dreamed of for ourselves but got cheated out of by the Depression.

Kay and I were set on relocating as soon as possible to some go-ahead place like Powell River or Campbell River or Nanaimo where there was a healthy payroll circulating around and a guy stood a chance of making a decent living. My old foreman from Green Bay, Jack Spence, had started up an excavating business in North Vancouver and we liked the looks of North Vancouver too. We even got as far as making an offer on a place there and were ready to up stakes if it came through.

When Kay and I talked about the future, staying in Pender Harbour for the long term was never mentioned. We told Bob Dick we weren't interested in buying his patch of rock and Christmas trees for any price. Too bad. That property has a twenty-room mansion on it now and the land alone must be worth more than all the money I have earned in all the years since.

Anyway, when Dick realized we weren't going to buy, he told Kay to get out. I was in the middle of a three-month work stint at Barzell Logging and out of phone contact. She wrote me, but I think she took her time about it because she didn't want me to miss any paycheques. She couldn't find another place to rent so she did something I can't imagine any other woman I know doing. She went over to that bunkhouse I'd parked on the beach at Wilf Harper's logging camp and hired Harper to drag it over to the lot I'd bought off Sam Hately. Like all bunkhouses in those days, it was built on log skids so you could tow it around with a cat.

The only clear spot on the Hately property was a big rock dome so she had Wilf drag the old bunkhouse—actually it was the one we had used for our cookhouse—up on top of this bald rock, where he left it tilting at a decided angle. Anybody else would have taken the time to level a little pad and set it up properly, but not Haywire Harper. I had fixed Kay up with a fourteen-foot kicker before I left—a modern one with a five-horsepower Johnson outboard—and she and the kids transferred all our stuff down the length of Salt Lagoon skiff load by skiff load. When I came down on my next time off two months later, here was my family living in a cockeyed shack with no plumbing or power, using a makeshift privy and packing water from the neighbours. And quite proud of themselves. This was the woman I'd married. You could slow her down but you couldn't stop her.

And somehow, we were still living in that house, a levelled and expanded version of it, fifty years later. We still like to gather there with all the wives and husbands and aunts and uncles and cousins and grandchildren and great-grandchildren for weddings and funerals and Christmas dinners. They all have better places of their own but they like the atmosphere of what they consider the old family homestead and what I long ago came to consider my true home. Every board in that house, every salvaged window and hand-planed window frame, every mismatched fixture has a story for me and it's the story of this next part of my life.

I was getting tired of working at Blondie's. There was something funny about that camp I could never figure out. It seemed there was an in-group I could just never break in on past a certain point. There was this old bastard, a big fat guy who was just kind of a bullcook as far as I could see but he seemed to drag a lot more water with Blondie than I could rightly explain, and he really had it in for me. He was just kind of bitchy like a hostile mother-in-law. It wasn't until many years later I began to wonder if the thing I couldn't break in on was that the core group there were all gay. The guy who got me thinking about it was Blondie's brother Robert Swanson, the famous inventor and writer. I ran into him somewhere, it might have been at the Truck Loggers' Convention, and told him I'd worked for Blondie up at Theodosia and he gave me kind of a funny look.

"Oh, you were in *that* camp, were you?" he said. "How did you like it?"

I couldn't quite get what he was driving at.

"It was okay. I was damn glad to get the work," I said.

Donnie in front of our old Green Bay cookhouse, which Kay dragged onto a lot in Madeira Park when I wasn't looking.

"I'm willing to bet you didn't stay long."

"It was okay for a while but I had to get out in the end."

"That's right," he said. "It was no place for a family guy."

It was a strange conversation. At the time, I just put it down to bad blood between brothers but later I wondered if he was trying to tell me something. You heard about camps where everybody was gay but I was shocked to think I might have been in one and not known it. There was no doubt a lot more homo-sexuality in the woods than I ever knew, just like there is everywhere as it turns out. I lived my life pretty much as an innocent about things like that, I guess I could hardly be otherwise with the Bible-belt upbringing I'd had. It was one of the biggest shocks of my life when a man I'd known as a tugboat operator and land developer, a real mover and shaker, appeared at my door a while back in a skirt and lipstick and told me at age seventy he'd had a sex change. Not that it's the same, he's emphatic that it has nothing to do with homosexuality, it's just that all those years when he was moving and shaking he felt he was really a woman.

This wasn't only news to me; it was news to his wife of fifty years and his grandchildren. The point I'm making is that you might think you know someone but you don't know what's really going on inside them. This is one of the things that keeps life interesting—you think you know things to the point of being bored with them and it turns you didn't have a clue what was really going on.

9

Parenthood, the Terrors and the Triumphs

Each time I'd get a few weeks off work, I'd work on the house. I set it up on a proper foundation, wired it and dug a well. Then I began tacking on bedrooms and eventually I twinned the old cookhouse with a whole new wing and put a truss roof over it with three rooms upstairs. But I kept running short of money and having to go away to work. I met a guy on the Gibsons ferry who told me they were building a new hydro dam on Clowhom Lake behind Sechelt so I applied and got on there.

That was a crazy job. The contractor was some guy from Salt Spring Island, Tommy something. He had connections to the Social Credit government and they got the job of clearing the reservoir on a cost-plus basis. I'd heard of cost-plus jobs during the war but I'd never been on one. Everything was backward. The more time you could waste, the more bills you could run up, the better the boss liked it. The more cost the more plus. They were just hiring every guy who came by and getting him on the payroll without having any clear job for him so I went for one of the grapples. They had three cable shovels rigged up with crane booms and grapple buckets for lifting floating debris out of the reservoir as it flooded behind the dam. I'd learned the basics of shovel-running at Blondie's and liked it so I jumped on one of these shovels.

They had a big 2½-yard Northwest 80D there, a 1½-yard Model 6

Northwest and a 1½-yard Bucyrus. I tried the 80D but I couldn't get the damn clutch to engage. It was stiff as hell and I yarded on it until I was afraid I was going to break it off. Then some pushy kid who didn't know any better got in it and threw all his weight into it and got it free. So the operator who knew the least got the biggest machine. He was a menace. Meanwhile I grabbed the Bucyrus, and I spent the next six months or so on that, bailing wood into a huge burn pile. It was one of the softest touches I ever had. Just sat in one spot for six months, spinning round and round. You could pile up all the hours you wanted. It was fabulous money for the time.

One peril of that job was the drive home because it went right past the old Wakefield Inn outside Sechelt and all the guys stopped there to cash their cheques and drink up as much of it as they could. I think every able-bodied man on the Sunshine Coast was working up at Clowhom and it was quite a party at the old inn on shift-change nights. I got on some awful drunks and ended up in a few messy scrapes that didn't stand me in too well with the wife, but she was used to it, poor woman. I didn't drink a lot but when I did I tended to go all the way. That was the 1950s style. We looked down on people who just sipped all the time. Drinking was something you saved up for, then you did it up good. Luckily as I got older I was able to make the spaces between my binges wider and wider until I pretty much stopped altogether. Now if I have one beer that's pretty much it. My poor brain is so muddled up at the best of times there's nothing much beer can do for me anyway.

I came out of Clowhom in 1959 with a pretty good stake. I spent a few months working on the house and got it pretty much up to scratch—although I never completely finished everything I set out to do on it.

I was tired of being away all the time and began to look around for something I could do and not leave home. Driving back and forth through Sechelt I had noticed a little hydraulic backhoe on the side of the road with a "for sale" sign on it and it gave me an idea. I had bought an ancient RD6 cable dozer off Willy Bishop when I was in Theodosia Inlet and I had tried doing a bit of contract work with it but the old cat was really too big and too beat up. It threw a track every time you turned. Hydraulic backhoes were a new thing then and I'd never run one, but it struck me as a machine that would be just right for the kind of light-duty residential work there was getting to be a bit of around Pender Harbour.

This was a very early Case backhoe mounted on a Case farm tractor with a Lull front-end loader. The story was this guy brought it into Sechelt and his competitor sabotaged it, dumped carborundum powder into the hydraulic tank so the hydraulic pump ground itself up and all the hydraulic rams ate up their packing. He had flushed it all out and got a new pump and claimed it was just fine but nobody around Sechelt wanted to touch it. So it was going at a fire-sale price, $1,500. I checked it all over and could see there was no lasting damage so I went to the credit union and took out a loan and bought this thing.

It was just a toy by today's standards but it was considered quite a marvel then. I saw a picture of it the other day and it looked like something out of a museum. Hoses and rams sticking out everywhere, it looked like something hacked together by engineering students for an experiment. And so tiny. You could pick the whole thing up in the bucket of the big 4WD backhoe my son Don runs now. What I could have done with a machine like that! But the little Case was the latest and greatest at the time, and by god, I built half the town of Pender Harbour with it once I got it.

I went to Vancouver and found a 1949 Ford dump truck for $500 and started looking for work. When I needed to move to a job, I would just drive the backhoe up behind the truck, hang the bucket of the front-end loader over the tailgate, and lift the backhoe's front wheels clear of the ground. The machine was too big to fit in the little five-yard gravel box and I couldn't afford to hire a low-bed, but it wasn't the most secure way of moving you ever saw. I shudder to think of it now, but it worked as long as you didn't try to turn too tight or stop too hard, which would cause the hoe to crash against the truck like a loosely coupled coal train.

Once I was pulling the backhoe up a steep hill on Egmont Road and missed a shift and stalled the truck. The whole affair started rolling backward, causing the backhoe to jackknife sideways so it was teetering over a steep bank. I dynamited the brakes and reefed on the emergency brake as hard as I could. That stopped it but I was locked in position and couldn't get a hand or foot free to start the motor.

Howie and I loading our HD5 track loader into the eight-yard Dodge tandem we had in the 1960s. The White family has been gouging the side hills around Pender Harbour for over fifty years now.

I must have stayed there for half an hour, stomping on the brake pedal and reefing on that emergency lever with all my might. The strain drained me of every ounce of strength, but whenever I began to ease up the truck would creak and inch backward and the hoe would jackknife harder over the bank so I would bear down again. It was torture. When I hear athletes talk about coming up against the wall of pain, I know exactly what they mean. I began to shake uncontrollably and was just about to let go and meet whatever disaster fate had in store for me when I heard another truck coming.

It was one of my least favourite people, a gyppo sawmill operator named Reg Spicer, who seemed to feel he was placed on this world to lecture me about my faults, but I was never gladder to see him. He pulled up right tight behind me so I would wreck both of our trucks if I let go and shambled over.

"Frank!" he said. "What in the hell do you think you're doing?"

"Block wheel," I gasped.

"What? You're blocking the road. Nobody can get by."

"Reg! Block my wheel before I roll back and wreck your truck," I spat between gritted teeth, letting it slip back a little to demonstrate.

"Oh, all right," he says and shuffles back. I can hear him rooting around and cursing for an eternity. I don't know if he's got me blocked or not, but finally I can't hold any longer so I begin easing off. The truck lurches backward, then hangs up. He yells to keep holding, he's not done, but I am done. Anyway, he has piled up half the boulders in the country, blocking every wheel, even those that didn't need it, and he's still piling. I couldn't have rolled back any more if there'd been an earthquake. I couldn't see this but I should have known it. Reg was one of the most slow-moving, slow-thinking, overcautious men I ever met. Still standing on the brake, I free a hand to hit the starter, get into low gear, burn up about two years' worth of clutch, and crawl up to the top of the hill. Reg pulls up alongside and I wave a thanks to him.

"You can't keep carrying on this way, Frank," he says. "You've gotta use your head more. And you better go move those rocks off the road. I piled them up but I don't think I should have to clear them off."

"Thanks, Reg," I say.

Reg Spicer was a tall, thin, sandy-haired man with a patch over one eye. He had a funny habit of twitching his lips before he said anything, like he was chewing over his words. I guess he wasn't a bad guy and did his part, serving on the school board and helping organize the kids' ball team, but I just found him painful to deal with. He was never satisfied just to take your money and give you your lumber—he always had to express his reservations about what you were doing with it, at least in my case. And the pissoff was, when I looked at whatever I was doing through his eyes, it always did seem haywire. It's hard to like a guy who makes you feel that way. He'd been raised in Pender Harbour but didn't seem to be all that chummy with the old Pender gang. He held himself aloof in his private little bay in Bargain Harbour where his sawmill perched at the water's edge and he tied the little black-hulled tug he used for scrounging drift logs. His place actually backed up against mine, or more precisely, against Oyster Lagoon, the little saltwater lagoon that separated our two properties. Sawmills of course produce a lot of waste in the form of slabs and sawdust, and disposal of this waste is always one of the challenges facing mill owners. Some used beehive burners while others sold it for home heating or used it for fill but it makes very poor fill. Reg dealt with his by dumping it into our pretty little lagoon, transforming it into a fetid, stinking cesspool. He's been gone now for forty years but the lagoon is still a foul-smelling mess. Worse, people today blame me for the pollution. I don't know how they think I caused it, I guess they just think it's the kind of thing I would do.

It's true, things like this weren't so uncommon in the era I come from. Wilf Harper also had a mill down on his land in the centre of Madeira Park village and he also dumped his sawdust and slabs into a small salt lagoon there. He filled in about half of it and built the building that now houses the Madeira Park post office on top of it. I keep wondering when the old sawdust pile is going to rot out and tip Her Majesty's Service into a devil's brew of sulphurous muck. A few years ago some locals got the idea to pretty up what remained of Harper's lagoon and turn it into a nature park. They pulled out the old oil drums and built walkways across it and put up little signs pointing out the natural wonders. But it wasn't long before the toxic ooze from Wilf's old sawdust dump began reasserting itself and covered the pond with an iridescent scum, which kind of spoiled the effect. I don't know if they ever figured out what the problem was.

Thinking of Reg Spicer puts me in mind of another incident he came into. When we first moved onto the former Hately property at Kent Road and Francis Peninsula Road there was a big cedar leaning out over Francis Peninsula Road. It was about five feet on the butt and had a schoolmarm about halfway up that squealed like a banshee whenever it blew. It wasn't particularly in the way and it was leaning hard right over the power lines so I left it standing. I guess I could have put a line on it and pulled it back against the lean with the cat, but then it might have hit the house. I figured it didn't pose any real threat to anything except the power lines, so I left it for the hydro crew to worry about. The worst thing about it was that damn schoolmarm, which made such a racket some windy nights a guy couldn't sleep.

During this one storm in about 1959 I was lying in bed listening to it sway and kind of holding my breath every time it reached the end of its squawking swing, thinking for sure this time it was going to go, then telling myself I was a damn fool, since it had stood for two hundred years and would fall harmlessly away from the house if it ever did go. I was just convincing myself of this for the umpteenth time when—snap, crack—kerwhump! The house seemed to jump sideways ten feet. I was out of bed in a flash and ran around to the stairs. The way up to the kids' bedrooms was completely blocked by cedar limbs and splintered rafters. I was hollering, "Howie! Donnie! Cindy! Oh, my god!"

I had to go outside and climb up the fallen tree trunk to get upstairs. The front room where Cindy slept was unscathed but the old cedar had scored a direct hit on the back bedroom where the boys were and you wouldn't have believed anyone could live through it. The roof was completely flattened. There was broken lumber and tree limbs and branches everywhere. The first thing I saw was a splintered beam jabbing right through the middle of little Donnie's cot, but it turned out he'd been scared by the storm and climbed in with Howie. Howie's bed was nowhere to be seen. The main trunk of the tree was right across it, pressing down on the tangle of rubble. I was out of my skull, pulling madly at wreckage and calling out, "Howie! Donnie!"

Finally I heard Howie's muffled voice, "We're okay, Dad!"

It was a miracle, really. I'd had a bunch of surplus five-eighths fir plywood salvaged from a sunken barge and I had used this for the upstairs ceilings even though it was way too thick. The tree had smashed into this heavy plywood but it was so strong it just came down on the bed and pressed the two boys flat against the mattress, collapsing the bed but not harming them. I had to get the power saw to free them, but they didn't have a scratch. I spent a lot of time shaking my head and thinking what a damn fool I'd been to leave that old tree standing, but at the same time it was such a freak occurrence I could hardly blame myself.

The only saving thing was that the tree was completely sound so I sawed it into log lengths and loaded it into my trusty Ford gravel truck and hauled it next door to Reg Spicer's mill. After giving me a lecture about the dangers of danger trees, Reg cut enough lumber out of it to rebuild the house. There was even a chunk left over that we were able to split into shakes to patch the roof.

The excavating business was slow coming, but I found enough to keep at it and gradually added a bit more equipment—a tiny John Deere dozer, then an old TD9 track loader. In the late fifties things started to open up a little and I teamed up with a developer named Syd Heal to do some of the early subdivisions around town—Bowsprit Drive, Narrows Road, Mt. Hallowell Road, Lee Road. It was a living, but hard scratching all the way. Whenever it started to look a bit promising, somebody else would start up. Wilf Harper, the local logger who filled his lagoon with sawdust and who Kay got to tow the cookhouse through Madeira Park to Sam Hately's lot, was my first competitor. When he saw I was making a dollar or two he horned on the business with some of his haywire old logging equipment.

The cash flow was small beer compared to logging and neither of us really believed in it enough to get good equipment so we both spent most of our time fighting breakdowns. I called him Haywire Harper and he called me Haywire White and we fought over every driveway job from Egmont to Middlepoint. I got the best of it, but he had amazing staying power. Just when I thought I'd finally run him out of the business he'd show up with another lopsided truck or slightly obsolete rubber-tired loader and start in all over again, bidding jobs at half what I was charging, which was already hardly enough to pay for fuel. People said his mother financed him but she was just a teacher and I could never see that she could have saved all that much. But he seemed to have a small but endless trickle of money coming in from somewhere.

Then a young Finn named Larry Spara (everybody called him "Sparrow," which suited him) came in with a brand-new backhoe and big sixteen-yard diesel truck paid for by his stepfather Oscar and took all the good business away from both of us even though he was charging double what we were. He hadn't a clue about drainage or grading but people went for the shiny new machine. It was a lesson I never learned as I kept fighting with old, obsolete equipment that ate up the profits in downtime and lost work, but it seems all wasn't lost. My sons both learned to become heavy equipment operators and Don carries on as Pender Harbour's main excavating contractor today with a fleet of shiny new excavators and trucks I could only have dreamed of.

Don was too young to do anything but watch when I first started up but I used Howie like a hired hand and had him coming out to my jobs after school and working until dark. Sometimes I let him skip school to do a second job on his own when I got in a jam and of course skipping school to run equipment had been his favourite pastime since Green Bay. People were sometimes a bit taken aback when a thirteen-year-old kid showed up to install their drain field but inevitably they would be marvelling and singing his praises once they saw he could handle the backhoe and set the tile as good as any grown man.

I sometimes wondered if I was doing the right thing by him, and always made a point of letting him off work if he said he had home-work to do or a baseball practice. The girls had adapted to school and started getting top marks right away but he really struggled. Marilyn had pretty much kept up with her correspondence lessons in Green Bay and was able to step right into her proper grade at Pender Harbour and never look back. Cindy was young enough to start in a grade only a year behind for her age and did well from the start but Howie should rightly have been in grade four when we first came down and he was way behind. Kay had secretly finished his first-year correspondence lessons for him, doing the printing exercises left-handed, so he had grade one on paper but hadn't really done it.

The Pender Harbour teachers decided to try him out in grade three, which only had a couple months left to run when we first arrived. He did poorly but he had a very sympathetic teacher, Mary Caesar, and she passed him into grade four. The next year he had the infamous Bob Dick and it was a disaster. He ended up with an average on his final exams of something like 25 percent. He was already so far behind they didn't want to fail him, so after many meetings and solemn promises of homework help by Kay they let him into grade five. He still had Dick and he still did very poorly. I stayed awake nights worrying that my "throw 'em in the deep end" method of kid-raising was as bad as my mother and old Jim Ross had tried to tell me back in Green Bay and I had bone-headedly gone and crippled this young life before it had a chance. I just felt sick about it.

I can remember the day I stopped worrying about Howie.

I think it must have been a weekend because I had him out with me hauling fill from the pit up Silver Sands hill. There wasn't a good gravel pit in Pender Harbour then and everybody used this free-for-all pit on government land up an old logging road near where the McNeill Lake water reservoir is now. It was lousy material—just fine sand—but it was all we had and we used it for everything from road base to fill to cement gravel. It didn't have enough coarse material in it to make good concrete and it's the reason a lot of older houses in Pender Harbour have crumbling foundations today.

It was never hard to get Howie to come with me to the Silver Sands pit because the road wasn't public and he could drive the truck, the one machine he never got to run because he was too young to have a licence. Normally I just let him drive it up the hill empty and I would take over to bring it down loaded but this time I figured he was ready to get the feel of driving with a load, which is a whole different experience. The road was a couple miles long and gently sloping for most of the way but just before it came out on the highway, it dropped off into a very steep, very long hill.

We had agreed he would stop at the top of this hill to let me take the wheel, and just as we came to the crest I saw him stand on the brake pedal to slow the truck down. Then suddenly we leapt forward and headed over the brink. "No, Howie," I yelled, but he paid no attention to me. Instead, to my horror I saw him grab the gearshift and take it out of gear. I just about had a heart attack. It had been in third, which had been enough to hold it back on the gentle part of the slope but I normally stopped and put it in low for the big hill. On that steep of a hill, you want to stop and get in your lowest gear before you start heading down, because it's almost impossible to make a downshift on the fly, especially loaded. You have to do a really extreme double-clutch. It's hard enough that only an experienced driver can do it, and an experienced driver wouldn't try because if you miss, that's it, you can't hold the truck back with brakes alone and you have a runaway.

Now here I was with a novice driver trying to make this impossible shift. I could see the hill falling away before us and cars going by on the highway below, with a steep bank and big trees on the other side. It looked like the Grand Canyon right then. I thought, I've lost him. I should never have put such a heavy load on. I should never have let him get this close to the brink. I should never have let him drive it loaded at all, he wasn't ready. I should never have sent him through the bush that time at North

Bend when he was four. I should have let Mother raise him and send him to Sunday school. Then I heard the engine revving. Really revving. Just about exploding. Then I saw him slam the shift lever into low. There was a crunch and a thunk and the truck slowed with a lurch. He made the impossible shift! But why—

Only then did he say, "Dad, the brakes are gone!"

I couldn't believe what I'd just seen but there was no time to ask questions. I reefed on the emergency brake, which was the old driveshaft type, and the truck flew down the hill bouncing over the humpy road like a mogul skier with the engine screaming, smoke pouring out of the emergency brake and sand flying everywhere. The wheel was kicking like a mule but Howie had himself braced and was hanging on to it for dear life. As we came charging into the highway I saw him get himself ready then reef on the wheel for all he was worth. The truck heeled over so hard half the load flew out onto Highway 101 and it felt like the truck was going to flip over but somehow he made the turn. Once we were on the flat he pulled over onto the shoulder, got it into low gear and coasted to a stop.

I was speechless.

It wasn't just that we'd lost our brakes, which is unexpected enough, but we'd lost them on the steepest hill around with a beginner driver at the wheel. It was a million-to-one set of circumstances—all bad. But the kid had responded like an old pro. He had saved the truck and likely some broken heads. I asked him how he had figured out what to do so fast and he told me he had been visualizing what could go wrong and planning his moves just in case, the way I'd taught him. It was true enough, I was always telling the kids to think ahead, you just never expected them to actually do it. For a happy moment I figured my efforts to raise the kids to think on their feet hadn't been such a waste of time. And I figured Howie would be all right, bad grades or no bad grades. Later I asked him what his next plan was, if he'd missed the shift.

"I was going to hit the ditch," he said.

"High side or low side?"

"High."

"Right."

Right now I can't remember exactly which truck that was. I started with a 1949 Ford three-ton, then moved up to a slightly newer one and I think this may have been the second one because it had a two-speed axle and the first one didn't have that. Both of them were great little trucks and we used them for everything, shopping, taking the kids to school, taking Howie down for his driver's test on his sixteenth birthday, going to town to visit the folks.

One time in about 1959 we were coming back from one such foray to the Valley loaded up with our winter's supply of spuds, a side of beef, machine parts and late back-to-school clothes. We caught an afternoon ferry out of Horseshoe Bay. We were late as usual and they just managed to squeeze us aboard. We had Cindy with us, she must have been about ten then, but she'd fallen asleep and we didn't want to wake her up so we left her to get some rest while Kay and I went upstairs for a coffee.

Those old ferries only went in one direction, they had to back out from the slip and turn around, and when the skipper threw it into forward the old boat would shudder and shake so you'd have to hang on to your coffee cup and it had just finished doing this when a crewman came up to me with a funny look on his face and said, "Did you have a truck on this sailing?" I said I did and that it was the one parked right out on the apron.

"That's what I thought," the guy said.

"Why do you ask, what's wrong?" I could tell by his look something was.

"I-I . . . I don't think it's there anymore," he stammered. Naturally our first thoughts were for Cindy. I tore down the stairway and by god, the truck was gone. Immediately the cry went up, child overboard! The ferry stopped, lifeboats were launched, the coast guard was called and everybody lined the rails searching as we began slowly retracing our route. Kay and I were having seventeen heart attacks when Cindy walked up rubbing her eyes wanting to know what the fuss was all about. She had woken up and gone upstairs to the bathroom.

That solved the main problem, but the truck was still unmistakably missing. They found some of our stuff floating right around the place where the boat made its turn and it was clear they hadn't blocked the wheels and when the boat started shaking it shook the truck right over the edge. What I figured out had happened was, I had parked it in gear but with the two-speed axle in high range. You weren't supposed to do this because it was vacuum-operated and when the vacuum leaked down, it could slip out of gear. Naturally I kept this to myself, insisting I had both parked in gear and applied the emergency brake.

It was a pretty major disaster, but it had come so close to being so much worse we actually felt lucky. The ferry company was terribly worried and willing to do everything for us, including raise the truck, which was in four hundred feet of water. I chose to have them do this rather than take an insurance payout because I had taken the tilt ram from the backhoe in to get straightened and nobody seemed to know where I could get another one. Dumb thinking, I should have got one made from scratch at a machine shop and let the ferry company pay for that and a new truck. The old Ford was never any good again after its swim and I had to buy a new one with my own money.

To this day though, all I can think of is how lucky we were that Cindy woke up needing to pee and got out of that truck minutes before it went over. It puts things into perspective. We had our share of grief with equipment and business, but we never had anything bad happen to the kids. Not that it was exactly a bed of roses, especially once the girls reached their teens.

Our girls had never been anything but angels but, as I learned, even angels can give their fathers fits when they hit their teen years. I guess boys are just as bad but you don't worry as much because they are less vulnerable. They can have scrapes with the law and bang up their cars but generally they come through it and get on with life. With girls, I don't know if it's because the hormones hit them harder or what, it's easier for them to lose their way, especially in the kind of place Pender Harbour was in the 1950s and early 1960s. You'd see them sailing along in school doing great, planning to be nurses or airline stewardesses and see the world, then pow! The hormones would hit, you'd see them glued to some young galoot like a Siamese twin and the first thing they'd drop out of school and have two kids by the time they were twenty.

No matter how responsible and well-behaved they've always been, now suddenly no trick is too low or sneaky to get off somewhere with their boyfriend. Every time you turn around they've snuck out and you have no idea where they are. Well, you do actually, and it's not a good one. The trouble is, they're so starry-eyed. They think they've discovered the first love in the world and it's all so heavenly and glorious and their boyfriend is such a knight in shining armour, while in the parents' eyes of course it's not quite so noble, they view the situation more like cats in heat. The girls think they are so virtuous and their boyfriends so gallant nothing bad could ever happen. They are wounded to the core that you don't trust them and there is just no way of getting them to see it your way.

All around them their friends are being rushed off to church but that's always an exception, that would never happen to them. Don't forget this is the fifties and early sixties, before the pill and before birth control was even legal. One of Sam's daughters, who was a real smart kid and looked to be headed for great things, got pregnant and left school. But it isn't just the risk of pregnancy that upsets parents of teenage girls, it's their heads become so completely turned. Here you've been encouraging them to want to be something when they grow up or at least go out and get a taste of the world and make a good marriage and they're all for that but when the hormones hit that goes out the window and all they can think about is being with their little peer group and their boyfriend twenty-four hours a day. They lose all interest in anything else.

I tried to lay down the law but that just led to the most godawful fights. It created problems in the community for me too. I remember one time, I was quite a good friend of one of the boyfriends' fathers and served on several committees with him. He was an upstanding local citizen but from an old Pender Harbour clan and he couldn't see anything wrong with girls getting married in high school, starting families in their teens and settling down to be good Pender Harbour fishwives. Maybe he was right, but at the time anyway, Kay and I, our whole thing was to get our girls through school and into college so they would have the chance we were both denied. Our whole lives had been built around that dream and we were both ready to fight for it.

The boy's father wouldn't have it but that I was being a snob and figured his son wasn't good enough for my daughter, but I tried to tell him it wasn't that, it was just that the kids needed a chance to get out of the Harbour and see what else the world had to offer. He didn't go for that at all. Pender Harbour in those days was still the closed little world it had been for fifty years, almost as closed as Abbotsford was in the 1920s. Most parents didn't see a reason in the world why their kids should want to look beyond the local scene and I got the reputation not only as a real badass dad but as a high-hat who thought he was too good for Pender Harbour. As I've said, we just kind of washed up on the beach at Pender Harbour without ever consciously choosing it as the place to make our stand. I have lived to be considered a community builder who was here before the dirt as somebody said, but the truth is we spent our first twenty or thirty years here planning to get out and find a more normal town.

People say it's hard to fit in now, but they should have tried it in the fifties. It was still dominated by these big families that were all intermarried. What's more, many of them were fishermen. I was viewed as a logger and loggers and fishermen were on the outs with each other, kind of like the cowmen and the farmers in the movie *Oklahoma!* So this trouble with the girls and their boyfriends didn't help our local standing a bit. Now I not only had the fathers giving me the fishy look, I had their kids doing it as well. Our house was right on a busy part of Francis Peninsula Road and they would squeal their tires outside late at night and yell stuff and keep us awake. Our house was like it was under siege with the fair princesses held hostage in their rooms and these heroes in loud cars trying to set them free.

The media was all full of this teen rebellion, *Rebel Without a Cause*, *Blackboard Jungle* stuff and our teens picked up a full load of it. They listened to rock and roll music, which was new and seemed all part of this frightening transformation that was seizing the children's minds and turning them against the values we had tried to instill in them. The boys were all wearing their hair in big greasy waves with ducktails and shuffling around with surly looks on their mugs that made you feel like taking a swat at them to smarten them up. I did take a poke at one punk who threw a beer bottle at my backhoe and that was added to my list of sins although some parents phoned me on the quiet and told me I'd done the right thing.

This was the first real emergence of teenagers as a special group with their own distinct culture and we parents didn't know what to make of it. We were spooked by it, although I didn't see it as anything but a local problem at the time. Other parents around Pender Harbour seemed more easy with the whole teen thing but I put that down to the fact that they lacked the vision to make something out of their kids. It might seem funny now but at the time it was absolute hell. I felt like it was taking ten years off our lives, but since I seem to have survived a way longer than my three score and ten, I guess I can't say that.

I was working at home by this time and I just bore down and eventually things got better. I think the years thirteen to sixteen are the toughest, or were then anyway. After grade eleven they seemed to come back down to earth and start taking school seriously again. Marilyn was the first one through and I couldn't believe it when she got accepted into UBC.

We drove her down to the campus and helped her move into the residence, which I can still remember was called Mary Bollert Hall. I don't suppose it's still standing. Oh man, what a day that was for me and Kay! It seemed like everything had been worth it, not just everything we'd gone through to get Marilyn into college, but everything we'd gone through, period. Both of us had grown up worshipping the ideal of education and when we'd been deprived ourselves we transferred our ambitions onto Marilyn. Finally getting her into college seemed like a vindication of all the years of struggle and frustration. It was the best day of our lives, maybe next to the day Kay first brought Marilyn back from the hospital. But we'd worked a lot harder for this one.

Marilyn wasn't at UBC long before we began hearing rumours of a new boyfriend and one day she brought him home. Well, what a difference from the local yokels she'd been dating in school! This fellow was a classic college type. He had an Austin-Healey sports car, wore a scarf, probably smoked a pipe, had been raised in the high-rent part of Victoria and didn't exactly say "bawth" but had that articulate English way of talking that came from being educated in private schools.

When she announced they were coming up to see us one weekend we were very nervous. Suddenly we were looking around at our comfortable digs noticing the messy heaps of old *Popular Science* magazines, the partially dismantled outboard motor in the front porch, Kay's little stacks of salvaged building materials everywhere—she never gave up on a chunk of 2 x 4 longer than twelve inches. It was like Ma and Pa Kettle getting ready for the tax collector—we were rushing around hiding stuff behind the shop, Kay was throwing quick coats of paint on doors that were beyond washing, it was pandemonium.

Howie got the idea that we should take the new guy on a picnic to some nice place, so as to send him back with an impression of our great scenery rather than the ramshackle joint we lived in. We ourselves never paid any attention to the alleged great scenery around Pender Harbour but knew it existed because city people constantly came up and yakked about it, so this seemed like a plan. The question was, where was this alleged scenery and what did you do with it? What did tourists do when they came up, go sport fishing? We didn't have a reliable boat at this point. The outboard off our skiff was in pieces all over the front porch and needed parts we couldn't get in a hurry. The *Flash*, aka *Marilyn Kay*, was at anchor in Salt Lagoon but not operational and anyway I'd never quite got around to finishing the interior.

In all the time we'd lived on the coast we'd only ever deliberately tried to do something recreational twice that I could recall, apart from our periodic car trips to the Interior. Once was in Green Bay when we went on a camp picnic. I forget the reason. I think probably Jack Spence's wife Eve was behind it. She was always griping about the work-work-work scene in Green Bay and angling for better things in life, though mostly she kept these battles under her own roof. Jack would come running down to the cookhouse all hours of the day trying to get some peace.

Anyway, it ended up that we took everybody left in camp at that time, which included our family, the Spences and somebody who was pregnant—maybe Lil Poschner—and all piled onto Parky Higgins' boat and went up to Egmont. Parky's boat was a horror show but it had a good three-cylinder Easthope motor that was more reliable than the rusting Chrysler Crown in the *Suez*, and he was eager to show us the high points of Egmont, so we reluctantly went along with him. There were heads sticking out of every porthole. I could smell raw gas—you could always smell raw gas on Parky's boat and I think it did eventually blow up—but I crossed my fingers and hoped for the best.

A logging friend, Teddy Bride, was renting an old estate in North Egmont that had landscaped grounds with a bit of open meadow, and that's where we planned to spread our picnic stuff but I seem to remember the adults getting waylaid in this draughty old house where quite a bit of beer was consumed, while the kids ran around outside. On the way back or to, I can't recall, Parky decided to provide a little entertainment by steering his overloaded, unseaworthy boat into the Skookumchuck rapids.

I remember looking over the side at a big whirlpool that was making ominous sucking noises only a boat length away, and looking back at all the babies and kids and pregnant mothers and thinking of the many boats and people that had met their end there, mostly skippered by overconfident locals like Parky. I remember yelling at Parky to get the hell out of there and seeing him laughing his head off and making ape noises and kind of jitterbugging around the way he liked to do and wondering what the hell kind of an idiot I must have been to agree to this.

A rare family picnic on Sakinaw Lake, probably 1952 since it looks to be pre-Donnie.

On balance, we didn't think this example of recreational activity held much promise for our present needs.

The second outdoor outing we went on was organized by Les Kearley, the husband of Kay's beautiful younger sister Ruth. I forget the occasion, but Les was full of bright ideas and good at organizing things, even as a young squirt, so there may not have been any special reason. He had grown up in Pender Harbour and knew about this nice little lodge on Sakinaw Lake run by a couple named Cotton, so this is where we went. Not to lodge in the lodge but to rent rowboats.

We spent a pleasant afternoon rowing around this large lake, the men trolling for trout while the women and kids swam and explored the pretty little islands, discovering a loon's nest complete with eggs. It was truly like a little wonderland and everything was going well until the cry went up that the game warden was sighted, which caused a stir due to the fact none of us had fishing licences. There was a rush to stash our brand-new fishing rods on one of the islands, which worked, except it was done in such a panic we couldn't find them later and we never did get those rods back.

Now, ten years later, it was determined the Cotton resort was still going and still renting out rowboats so this is where we decided to take Marilyn and her beau. The weather cooperated and it was a very nice outing, but this fellow was quite something to behold. I realize now he was probably as nervous as we were, but he had a different way of showing it. He had all this good breeding and manners he could call up when in doubt, and so he seemed very much in control of the situation, starting all the conversations and generally carrying the ball. His name was Charles, Chas for short and I'm sure he smoked a pipe. He had a bad effect on me. I had been surrounded by people with well-bred English manners all my life and it always made me feel awkward and uncomfortable.

Not that his performance was flawless. On the way to Sakinaw, which was down a rough logging road, he unwisely insisted on taking his Austin-Healey sports car with its three-inch clearance and drove like he was on a cross-country rally, knocking off his muffler on a big rock he should have had the sense to steer around. But I felt as though that was our fault, for having such big rocks. Then when Howie had started a little fire and got it just to the right stage for toasting wieners, Chas jumped up, strode down to the lake's edge, gathered up a handful of wet rocks and plopped them in the fire, putting it out. We all kind of shifted uneasily as Marilyn piped up, "That was brilliant, Chas, you've killed the fire!"

"The principle is that the surplus heat energy from the oxidization process is being transferred to the rocks," he said in his composed way. "Once that process is complete the rocks will radiate it back at an even rate, which will prevent overcooking." We all sat there with straight faces holding our wieners over these cold rocks, too tongue-tied to say anything. Kay tried to salvage the situation by announcing wieners were already well-cooked and fine to eat as they were but I noticed the kids slinking off to make their own little fire on the other side of the island.

It was very uncomfortable. It was as bad as the first time Kay took me to meet her folks. This guy was stiff as a poker and scared everybody into glum silence. Making conversation was like chipping granite. I was afraid we had disgraced the poor girl and ruined whatever chances she had with this highly presentable college chap.

No worries there. I didn't realize this until he told me over many glasses of wine years later, but our family was exactly what he was hoping it would be. He'd been brought up in one of these cold ex-pat English families in Victoria where his nanny would dress him up and lead him into the drawing room on Sunday morning so his father could quiz him on his times tables, then shoo him away for the rest of the week. He spent much of his childhood in boarding schools and only experienced real family warmth when he was allowed to go home with his nanny, who had a big family in a poorer part of town. It was their image of home life he aspired to, not his parents', and apparently what he saw of Marilyn's home on that visit did nothing to shake his conviction that she was the one for him.

On a later visit he formally requested a meeting with me and very stiffly asked for my permission to marry my daughter, vowing to be the most loyal and worthy husband, etc. I was a bit disappointed that this was happening so fast, before Marilyn had a chance to finish her degree, but they did seem very much in love and anyway it was out of our hands. Their backgrounds were so different a marriage counsellor probably wouldn't have given the match very good odds, but it's lasted fifty years now and produced two admirable sons, both of whom have an unbeatable blend of

Marilyn's warm heart and Chas's scientific mind, and four terrific grand-children, so you just never know.

We felt pretty good about Marilyn but we still had the three younger ones to worry about. Howie had turned into an egghead. After three abysmal years of getting such bad marks it seemed we were looking at another chokerman, in grade six he suddenly caught fire and shot to the top of the class and stayed there. He became so bookish the other kids took to calling him "professor" and I couldn't help noticing he was a bit of an outcast. He got bullied on the way to school and harassed on his paper route and I tried to coach him in some of my old brawling techniques but he was no fighter.

It was queer to see my son reliving the same experiences as an outsider I had gone through myself and I had no doubt I had infected him with my own inadequacies and condemned him to a miserable life. He had his own small group of fellow eggheads he chummed with but I don't think he had a girlfriend all the time he was in Pender Harbour. It didn't seem to bother him. He affected a towering disdain for the school in-crowd and busied himself writing for the local newspaper, putting on skits with his friend Raimo Savolainen, writing poetry, going off on ski holidays with his other friend Sean Daly. He spent all his energy gearing up for the day when he would ride his educational ambitions out of Pender Harbour and never look back. This is the true history of the guy who not only chose to return to Pender Harbour but to stay there and become the great champion of small-town life on the BC coast. Anyway, he did graduate from the local high school and did follow Marilyn's path down to UBC and so we had a second kid living our dream.

Cindy wasn't far behind. Poor little tagalong Cindy, as usual she worked twice as hard bringing up the rear and got better marks than either of the others. In fact she had such a stellar school record that in 1965 she was selected as one of a handful of students from around BC to be invited to go to shiny new Simon Fraser University straight out of grade eleven, skipping grade twelve. She was also the only one to actually carry through and treat Kay and I to a graduation ceremony—which she did twice, first for her bachelor's degree and ten years later for a master's. She was the one who fulfilled the family's educational ambitions most fully, and yet as I said before, she was never able to shake that conviction she had somehow failed.

The one who was literally bringing up the rear was Donnie. He was eleven years younger than Marilyn. It was almost like he was in a different family. Certainly he inherited an older and more worn-out set of parents than the other kids had enjoyed. I was thirty-nine by the time he was born and for his first five years I was away working in Theodosia, then up at Clowhom so I didn't have the chance to form that early bond I'd had with the others. Then soon after he started school we started running a gas station business and that kept us tied down morning, noon and night. I didn't spend as much time discussing comparative religion and evolution with him as I had with the others, not that he ever complained.

Funny the way you get all knotted up and blaming yourself about your kids. As a young boy Donnie was shy almost to the point of a handicap. He got bullied at school and I figured, boy this time we had really fouled up our duties as parents. Ha! Today Don is the most sociable, most confident member of our family who organizes all the big dinners and is ten times as successful in business as I ever was. And the thing I like best about him, he does it his way. He speaks his mind and doesn't kiss ass.

10

Pender Harbour Chevron

oday there is a lumberyard, a small mall and a health clinic at the junction of Francis Peninsula Road and Highway 101, but in 1965 it was all just bush. I drove past it several times a day, and every time I did the idea grew on me that this was a very strategic location for future business development. Pender Harbour is a sprawling community with miles of prime waterfront but it has a shortage of space when it comes to any kind of town centre.

For a long time the centre was at Irvines Landing, at the mouth of the harbour where the steamer dock was. That's where the action was when I first came in 1950. There was an old general store there that had been built by the town's first magnate, Portuguese Joe Gonsalves, who also had a hotel and a gas dock. He was long gone but the store was then being operated by a man named Bill Pieper. His main competition was Royal Murdoch, who had a store, fish dock and gas barge across the Harbour on the south side. We started buying our camp supplies at Pieper's then went across the Harbour to Murdoch's, who had a little more to offer. We never did deal at the third store, Hassan's, which served mostly fishermen in the Whiskey Slough area.

Then a clerk who had been working at Pieper's, a transplanted Englishman named Aleth Alexander Lloyd, borrowed $5,000 from Cedric Reid and a few others and started a new store in Garden Bay that was a bit more up to date and we took our business there. He installed my brother-in-law Les Kearley as manager and Les took all the goods down from the high shelves behind the counters and laid them out on tables where customers could touch them—self serve! That was quite the big deal in the 1950s and took all the business away from the old leave-your-list stores.

These stores were all close to the water and were patronized mainly by people who came around in boats. When the roads came through from Sechelt and then connected up to the Powell River ferry in 1954, cars began slowly replacing boats and the waterfront stores lost their advantage. Irvines Landing and Murdoch's were in the right spot when traffic was coming by sea because they were right there when you first came into the Harbour but once traffic started coming up the highway from Sechelt they were at the wrong end of town. Garden Bay was closer to the highway but after the old mission hospital was moved down the new highway to Sechelt in 1964 it lost much of its reason for being.

All of these old store sites had their backs to rock bluffs that left no room for expanded commercial development around them. The new hot spot was Madeira Park, which was inland, more accessible to cars and had at least a bit of room for development. Two clerks from Al Lloyd's store, Clint Anderson and Frank Harding, copied his example and started a more modern store in Madeira Park that planted the seed of what became the

Murdoch's, aka Pope Landing, one of Pender's busier commercial centres in the 1950s with a store, fuel dock, water taxi and fish buyer.

For years Pender Harbour's main claim to fame was St. Mary's Hospital, built with volunteer labour in 1930 and the only hospital on the Sunshine Coast until being closed in 1964. Now an inn, it is still the most impressive structure in town.

main business centre there. There was a school, a community hall, a post office, a credit union, a small convenience store, a Forest Service station and a government dock. In the 1970s, two newcomers named McQuitty and Alexander built a strip mall with an IGA supermarket. The trouble was, even Madeira Park didn't have much space to expand and I felt the town could use another centre at the busy Francis Peninsula Road intersection.

The land surrounding the intersection was owned by an old logger named Charlie Heid, who lived in a small yellow house hidden by bushes on the east side of the highway. The obvious thing was to put a gas station on the corner opposite Charlie's place so I hit him up about it and we made a deal to buy a chunk suitable for a gas station for $1,500. I worked away clearing it and levelling it over the next few years and started looking around at the different oil companies a guy might partner up with. The one that showed the most interest was Chevron, which had a bulk station down at Davis Bay and had stations in Gibsons and Sechelt but none further north.

In those days the big oil companies felt there couldn't be too many places to sell gas; there were already two in Pender Harbour and must have been thirty on the entire Sunshine Coast. Since then they've swung the other way and started thinking there can't be too few filling stations to please them; now there's only one left in Pender and less than ten on the whole Sunshine Coast including Sechelt and Gibsons. Anyway, Chevron was all for it and put up a bit of money in exchange for what they called a product contract. They would put in the tanks and pumps and signs and keep us supplied with gas and oil and we would have to solemnly promise to only sell Chevron-approved products and participate in their promotions. We were all too happy to agree, it was like yeah, twist my arm, but in the end that contract was to cause us a lot of grief.

Kay was all for the gas station. The excavating business had never got any better. Just when you'd almost get all the bills paid off, there would be another big breakdown or a lull in business and you'd get behind again. As the town grew, more guys started up. At one point Gordie Cochrane, who as an underage kid had wrecked my logging truck on Texada Island, even got into the act. His old man Bill had a girlfriend, Eunice Fincham, and he set her up with a beer parlour in Madeira Park—the one that burnt down in 2013. They called it the Pender Harbour Hotel although the pub part was nicknamed the Rigger's Roost because when it just started they were putting a power line through and it spent its first few years filled up with rigging crews. At the time it burned it had been rebranded The Grasshopper, though nobody could figure out why. You don't see many grasshoppers in Pender Harbour—I think they all drown in the rain.

I guess Bill saw me going back and forth pulling my wonky old backhoe along behind my little five-yard gravel truck and figured I shouldn't have all that lucrative enterprise to myself so he bought Gordie a better backhoe and truck than I had. Gordie hadn't improved over the years. He had a bad drinking problem and had done a stretch in jail for robbing the Irvines Landing post office with a local baddie named Ronnie Wray, a real bonehead move if there ever was one. The story was they only got $60 cash, which is about all you'd expect to find in a little pissant joint like that. If he'd robbed the grocery store he might have got more and probably would have got away with it. But you touch the royal mail, they bring in the cavalry and make you do time.

Gordie didn't make much of a go of the gravel business even with his father's help and gave up in short order but managed to take away any cream there might have been for me during those few years. There was always somebody jumping in and making a noise for a few years then drifting off to greener fields. This continues today. My son Don must have a dozen competitors, most of them starving. They will dry up and blow away, most of them, and leave Don to carry on. If you date it back to when I started in 1959, there's been a White digging ditches and hauling gravel around Pender Harbour for over fifty years as I write this. It's a credit to inborn cussedness if nothing else.

One thing having a deal with Chevron did for us was it kicked things into high gear. I'd been fooling around talking and daydreaming about building a station for years, but once the gas company came on board, they wanted results. There was a very attractive gas station beside the Upper Levels highway in West Vancouver that Kay always admired, it looked more like a classy house than a garage, so we had got the plans for that and hit the bank up for a $20,000 mortgage.

I had been figuring to do the building myself and I did a lot of it but it was coming slow so I went to a local builder named Wilf Harrison and, wow, did things ever happen fast after that. Wilf had built houses all over the place before semi-retiring to the Harbour, and that guy was like a crew of ten men in one body. He took one look at the plans and that was it. He did all the rest off the top of his head, and made no end of improvements to the original. I had a stack of logs I'd cleared off the place so he got them cut into timbers and framed the main shop area out of heavy fir timbers. It was truly a beautiful job. Chevron sent a crew up to install the tanks and pumps and we were in business.

It was the classiest-looking building in Pender Harbour, sitting in the most prominent location and I remember Kay and I just driving up on summer evenings to admire our handiwork. We both felt a glow of pride unlike quite anything we'd ever felt before. I'd been proud of my fleet of Mack trucks at first, but I hadn't built them. We had been proud of our house in Abbotsford, but it had been undercut by the fact that by the time it was ready to live in we'd already decided there was no future for us in Abbotsford. This time it looked like the right thing in the right place, something that was going to provide us with a nice clean living for the rest of our working lives and give us an asset to sell off at the end of it.

How we could have been so wrong it's hard to imagine. It's true we had built ourselves a fine facility, but that didn't get away from the fact it was still located in Pender Harbour, which in 1968 was still the little fishing town with seasonal income and hardscratch economics we had come to know too well in the sand and gravel business. People bought $2 worth of gas at a time. (Of course, in those days that got you five gallons.) And they expected to be able to charge the $2. And since $2 was such a small charge, there was no use paying it, at least not until it built up to something worth writing a cheque for, like $50. But $50 was a lot of dough, so how about $10 till the next pogey cheque and since I've just made a payment, how about filling my tank?

Pender Harbour Chevron, the gas station Kay and I built at the corner of Francis Peninsula Road and Highway 101. People said it looked good enough to be a private home and in the end it became one.

We were glad to see credit cards come in because that got us away from carrying credit ourselves to a degree, but we lost a lot of money there, too. Chevron put out a list of cards that had been revoked each week and you were supposed to check every card you took in to see if it was on this list. Well, the list was about six feet long and in type so small you needed a magnifying glass to read it and when you got busy there was just no way you could do it. As a result, we began to get a steady stream of charges that had been rejected at head office, and that went against our account.

We still couldn't stop giving our own credit because most of our customers didn't have good enough credit to get credit cards. Cutting anybody's credit off was a drastic measure that courted a feud with their whole extended family, and many of the big interconnected families we had first run afoul of in the logging camp were still going strong. Besides, we had competition, and they gave credit.

My old nemesis, Haywire Harper had built a B/A gas station next to the school in downtown Madeira Park and put his daughter Bev and son-in-law Johnny Divall in to run it. I am sure they had exactly the same trouble with credit we did, with the same people, but that didn't stop the culprits from playing us off against each other. If we'd ever sat down over a beer and agreed to both stop giving credit our lives would have been a lot easier, but we were not on speaking terms. When you go into business in a small town, the degree of animosity you build up for your competition puts the Orangemen and the Catholics to shame. You start dividing the town up into those that buy the other guy's gas (infidels, unwashed) and those that buy yours (the saved, the chosen people). You have to laugh looking back, but at the time it was deadly serious stuff.

The real problem with the gas station was the gas company. They allowed you just enough profit to barely survive on. At that time we were selling gas for about forty cents a gallon. Litres hadn't been invented then, but if they had it would have been something like ten cents a litre. For selling the gas we got about three cents out of the forty. So every time some SOB skipped town and left us on the hook for ten gallons, we would have to sell 120 gallons to make it up.

The gas company controlled prices absolutely. The office in Vancouver would order a hike but we wouldn't know about it until the local bulk agent, Dicky MacDougal, delivered his next load and sprung it on us. We were always struggling to get enough cash in the till to pay for the next load so we would phone Dicky and try to find out what the price of the day was but he wouldn't tell us because he was afraid we might put our price up and make two cents a gallon extra for a few hours. If we had a hundred gallons of the old cheaper gas left, he would even try to tell us we couldn't change our price until we'd sold the old stock. He was always reporting us to the head office for this and other transgressions and they would send some young twerp in a suit up to give us a lecture.

One of the sore points was Supreme. We had two grades of gas, Regular and Supreme. The Supreme had an octane rating of 91 compared to 87 for Regular and cost a nickel or so more a gallon. They had it worked out that you should be selling one gallon of Supreme for every four gallons of Regular whereas in fact nobody ever wanted Supreme in Pender Harbour at all. Nobody owned a car that required high-octane gas. This was beater country. Even those who did fall heir to some ex-luxury car that was specified for Supreme never bought it. The only time we sold any Supreme was when we ran out of Regular, and then we had to sell it at Regular price and lose five cents a gallon.

Dicky never quit chiding us for failing to sell the prescribed quota of high octane and reporting us to the company for failing to meet it. They would then send up one of their emissaries who would drill us in sales pitches about valve damage and reduced performance that we were supposed to deliver to local cod fishermen and salal pickers in their rusted-out Cadillacs. Dicky knew damn well there was no market for Supreme in a poor country town like the Harbour, but he was one of those guys who just lived to quote stupid rules. He always wore a company uniform with a peaked cap and was always trying to get me to wear one too. He'd strut around the shop shaking his head if he saw an oil spot I hadn't got around to wiping up yet and giving Kay a bad time about the state of the washrooms.

The company was always launching phony promotions, like the one where you were supposed to put plastic palm trees around the pump island and don grass skirts to tie into their "Come to Chevron Island" jingle on television. They'd send up crates of sales paraphernalia which we wouldn't open and Dicky would report us for non-compliance. It was none of his goddamned business, he was just the bulk agent and had nothing to say about how we ran our business but he was such a company man he took squealing on us as his solemn duty.

I would have liked to have knocked some sense into him but he was a skinny little git and always half-crocked. I could have fixed his wagon any time if I'd wanted to because you seldom saw him any time of day without whisky breath, even first thing in the morning. I doubt the Chevron public image people would have been too pleased to know their trusted emissary was three sheets to the wind while wheeling up and down that twisty goddamn road packing enough raw gas to blow up the whole town of Sechelt. How he managed to do it all those years without getting in trouble I'll never know.

I sat down and worked it out once and figured that we would have been further ahead if we'd never sold a single gallon of gas. If you added up all the money we'd lost in bad debts and rejected credit cards and times we had to sell Supreme for the price of Regular, and then you added in all the hours when there was no traffic but you still had to pay someone to sit there manning the pumps, that more than ate up the paper-thin profit margin you made on a gallon of gas.

The only money we ever made in that place was in the shop, doing brakes and mufflers and the odd bigger thing, like a transmission or occasionally an engine. I'd never thought of myself as a mechanic as such but I'd been around machines so long I figured I could handle anything that came in. I picked up a scope at the auction and started boning up on automotive mechanics and built up a pretty good clientele. At first Chevron tried to get us selling their approved line of batteries, tires, fan belts, etc., but I soon learned I could make my own deals and double the profit.

For a while I had a great thing going selling retreaded tires for $13 each. The beater crowd went for that big time but they'd get going down Halfmoon Bay hill full tilt and the goddamn things would fly apart and they'd come in mad as hell, wanting their money back. It did no good to say, "What did you expect for $13?" so we had to get out of the retread business. We got our new tires from Firestone and we still made a good dollar on them. Those were still the days of the old-style bias-ply tires and a car would go through a set every year on the gravel sideroads we had then. But then Michelin and Bridgestone came along with their steel-belted radials that lasted forever and kind of knocked the tire business on the head.

The trouble with the shop was this: the people who had decent cars didn't need much work done. A regular oil change, sometimes a $20 tune-up maybe, but I never got into the practice you run into in most places today, where you go in for a $40 oil change and they won't let you go until you've bought $300 worth of hoses, wipers and belts. If all a guy needed was twenty bucks worth of brake pads, that's all I'd sell him. I wouldn't stick him for $900 worth of brake lines, master cylinder kits, rotors, drums.

I only fixed what needed fixing. It wasn't a good business model. They wouldn't thank me because they had no way of knowing what I hadn't stuck them for. Then often as not, they'd go down to some clip joint in Vancouver with ads on television and pay the $900 and come back and tell me how much better they'd been treated. I only ever had one person thank me—an old retired salesman named Jack Edmonds. He came in to shake my hand when I sold the place and said, "Now people are going to find out just how lucky they've been all these years."

The good customers paid up promptly but their bills were insignificant. Meanwhile the beater crowd would come in needing a $500 exhaust system and ask me what I could do for $25. You'd weld them up a homemade tailpipe and get them back on the road, but three months later their rotten old muffler would blow apart and they'd be back in mad as hell, demanding you fix it for free because you hadn't done it right the first time. If you were smart you'd tell them to come back when they had $500. If you were me you would explain this was a different thing than you'd fixed the first time, and offer to stick in a cheapo replacement for $50. By the time you'd drilled out all the rusty bolts and faked up more homemade parts, you'd have spent your morning working for two bits an hour.

There were some good things about our years at Pender Harbour Chevron. I never felt so much a part of the community. Whenever somebody smacked up a car, we would be the first to know the gory details. If somebody got a visit from the cops we would know, either because they asked us for directions or the next five customers gave us reports. People told us things because they wanted us to tell them things. If anybody new came to town, we would be the first to meet them. You would often get a heads-up on which well-known citizens were having affairs, because cars need gas at the most inconvenient times.

Every summer people from Sakinaw Lake would make us their first stop on July first to load up on propane and kerosene and outboard gas. They came in with their kids and dogs and in-laws in overloaded station wagons and needed to hose down the car where the dogs had puked and were always going through such hell I felt lucky not to have any vacation. For those years at the corner of Fran Pen Road and Highway 101 I knew more of my neighbours and more of their doings than at any time before or since. And it worked in reverse—we were known by everybody. It was kind of like being a celebrity without the money or goodwill that normally goes with it. I wouldn't have given you ten cents for all of it but after it stopped and I drifted back into obscurity I kind of missed it.

It was funny, I got reacquainted with quite a few of the guys who'd worked for us in Green Bay fifteen years earlier. It gave me a bit of a turn to see those fuzzy-cheeked punks as potty middle-agers showing the effects of beer and bad living. Some had graduated from pogey to welfare and weren't good risks for a tank of gas but others like Gerry Bilcik, who had crews working all over BC, were obviously doing well for themselves. Davey Pollock succeeded his father as foreman of the local Department of Highways yard, and Barrie Farrell, who used to amaze us with his natural drawing ability, became famous as a designer and builder of fishboats. Young Pete Dubois, who had graduated to just plain Pete after his father Old Pete died, built up a fleet of rubber-tired skidders and got killed when one flipped over in the hills just above Green Bay where I had got him started in the logging game.

A lot of guys were killed on skidders, not because they were so unstable, but because they were so versatile guys would try to drive them straight up cliffs. They were an innovation that has kind of come and gone now, a cross between a cat and a logging truck that eliminated the need for both. They allowed small-scale loggers to mop up even smaller remnants of timber than the 1940s gyppo with his 10-10 Lawrence gas yarder and truck. Those of us who'd been watching the progress of logging since the days of the railroad shows could see the end coming in logging decades before Greenpeace started making noise about it. I remember guys shaking their heads back in the twenties and saying the industry was logging itself out of existence back then, and the Green Timbers controversy of the 1920s worked through every argument for and against controls on cutting that we've heard since. It's always been clear what needed to be done, and it's always been clear nobody in authority was going to do it.

This was causing big changes in Pender Harbour. They always called it a fishing town but when I first saw the place in 1950 more families were supported by logging than fishing and the two accounted for probably 90 percent of the community income. By the mid-1960s the logging jobs had probably been cut to a third and the fishing fleet was just starting to shrink. I remember when we first started the Ratepayers Association we did a study and figured there were eighty boats going out every summer. All on salmon. I doubt there's ten working a full season anymore, and not one surviving on salmon alone.

For a long time the Chamber of Commerce was pushing tourism as the thing that was going to rescue the local economy, mostly because it was dominated by Len Larsen and John Dunlop, two owners of tourist businesses, but you could see from the start that wasn't going to work. Tourism only generates jobs for the summer months and even then doesn't pay half the wages logging or fishing did. For a time marinas and motels were going in like gangbusters, but that bubble burst sometime back in the eighties. Today there are only a handful left.

11

The Tic and I

While we had the garage, that was our life. You'd get up at six in the morning, climb into your greasy clothes, grab a bite and hustle up to open before the traffic from the 8:30 ferry went by. I'd have half a dozen repair jobs waiting so Kay would have to look after the pumps while I worked. We'd spell each other off for lunch and again for supper. Often I'd work late into the night trying to finish some job I'd promised for the next morning.

Seven days a week, 365 days a year. You can't close Christmas day because your customers are burning more gas than any other day of the year. It was like the dairy business I had started in back in the 1930s. You can't take a day off. The cows always have to be milked. The gas pumps always have to be on. This was the thing that finally drove us around the bend. It was like being in jail. Your life was not your own. You couldn't get a grip on your problems because you couldn't get away from them far enough to see what they were. Kay and I both started to go batty.

One positive development concerned the property across the road. There was a flat, two-and-a-half-acre piece on the southwest side of our inter-section and when it came on the market for $12,000 we'd taken out a mortgage and bought it, partly because we were afraid someone would start another gas station on it and partly because I still believed this was going to be the commercial centre of Pender Harbour. On dark days when we couldn't find much to be hopeful about we'd sit in the office looking out across the road at that fine piece of property and daydream about what we would do with it if we ever got free of the garage. We had plans to build a little shopping mall with office space overhead, much like the one that the Gerick brothers later built on the east side of the highway. We figured we would retire on the rents. It was the only retirement plan we ever had.

Jim Tyner had plans for it too. Tyner was the kind of character you'd only meet in a place like Pender Harbour. He was an accountant who'd once held a high position in the Ottawa civil service, but he and his wife Violet longed for the simple life so they'd moved into a little shack with no electricity or indoor plumbing down on Lily's Lake a few minutes away from the service station. They could easily have had water and electricity brought in but didn't want it. This was the more noteworthy in that Jim was a paraplegic who got about with crutches and leg braces and wasn't exactly suited for roughing it in the bush.

Jim was a strange man, quite twisted and paranoid in some ways, but highly skilled at backroom politics. He and I had formed a local Ratepayers Association when the provincial government had unilaterally placed Pender Harbour and Egmont under the jurisdiction of a new layer of government called the Regional District in 1965 and we basically set about lobbying to keep the area from becoming too citified. We were very successful and Jim got elected to represent the area on the new body and got re-elected for about ten years, eventually serving as chairman of the entire Sunshine Coast district from Port Mellon to the head of Jervis Inlet—all the while roughing it in his un-electrified cabin.

Our first order of business on the Ratepayers was to torpedo the too-restrictive zoning regulations the first board had drawn up, then we moved on to a long-standing Pender grievance, which was lack of good medical facilities. After the old mission hospital at Garden Bay was relocated to Sechelt in 1964, the area had gone from having the best health facilities on the coast to the worst and we formulated a plan to build a community clinic that would have a full-time doctor and nurse and provide a good range of services. This was a long, complicated struggle that was opposed by the medical establishment and that we finally succeeded in 1976 is completely a credit to the skill and determination of Jim Tyner.

Now, I knew Jim had his eye on our property across from the service station as the site for the clinic should we ever succeed in getting it, but to tell the truth I wasn't crazy about the idea. Kay and I were hoping to keep it and build it into a valuable holding worth maybe in the hundreds of thousands or even millions in time, whereas if we gave it for the medical clinic we would lose that opportunity and would probably be obliged to accept a low price, since the whole project was being funded by donations. This was especially unappealing since the value of the property had come up nicely since we'd bought it and was now in the $50,000 range.

As if things weren't tough enough at the garage, I began to have some serious health problems. I had back trouble almost steady and the doctors didn't give me much hope. They showed me X-rays of my spine that looked like an elongated ink blot, it was so spiky with arthritis. They told me I wouldn't be able to work at all in a few years and should start planning for life as a disabled man. I couldn't afford to pay any attention to them, and just as well since I was still working twenty-five years later. I don't know what happened to all that arthritis. It seemed to go away. I've got some now, but nothing unusual for a man of my age.

My real problem was a bit harder to get a fix on. I mentioned earlier that I had been getting a pain in the face. It had started as a tickling sensation, like worms wriggling under the skin. Sometimes shaving or washing would set it off, sometimes it started by itself. For many years I ignored it but it became more regular and more intense as I got into my fifties so finally I started to go to doctors about it. I heard all the usual brush-offs and got all the usual pills, but it just kept getting worse. During my first couple years in the garage it went from an attack once a week to several times a day and the feeling grew from being pricked by a needle to having a red-hot nail digging into my face and being twisted around. I have always had a high threshold for pain but these bouts were so intense I would just drop my wrench and close my eyes and hold on to something while it lasted, which might be several minutes. You never knew when it was going to strike, so even your pain-free times were stressful.

I kept going back to the doctors and finally they sent me to a neurologist and I was diagnosed with trigeminal neuralgia, also known as tic douloureux or "the suicide disease." It's fairly well known for a disease as uncommon as it is because its effects are so dramatic. To this day they have never figured out what causes it but its symptoms have been known for several hundred years. The pain it causes is said to be the most intense pain known to mankind. I haven't tried them all, but I have sampled a good selection and I'd have to agree with the statement as far as my experience goes. The reason it used to be called the suicide disease was because that was the only effective cure.

There are supposed to be better treatments nowadays but they can't be perfect because a doctor at our clinic had it a few years ago and despite all the resources available to her as a member of the medical profession, she ended up committing suicide. In the early days, sufferers usually ended up in insane asylums. In my day they had a handful of treatments, each of which I went through. First there were the medications, mainly the same medication they gave to epileptics. They kept raising the dose until I was so blitzed I was walking into walls but it still didn't stop the attacks. Then they tried shoving a big needle into my face and injecting alcohol. That had no effect, maybe because I had already put so much alcohol into my face it was immune.

Finally they sent me to Vancouver's grand old man of neurosurgery, Dr. Frank Turnbull. I was a bit spooked by Turnbull because he seemed kind of like the Tin Man, no heart. I assumed this was simply because I was not on his level and could never know him like his peers did, but later through pure coincidence Howie ended up publishing a book of his life story and reading it I realized, no, actually, the man really was a kind of robot. A very intelligent, very competent robot maybe, but I defy anyone to read that book and come away thinking this is a huggable guy. Not that there's anything wrong with that. When you have somebody cutting a hole in your skull and digging around in your grey matter you don't want him to be too emotional.

One thing I found out from that book that I'm glad I didn't know when he was working on me was that he pioneered the practice of giving BC mental patients lobotomies. He rather casually mentions that he did three hundred or so, noting that they usually cured the aggressive behaviour although there was some loss of vitality. He was the first brain surgeon in

BC and though I found him cold I will say he was a straight shooter. He told me I had exhausted all the treatments known at the time except surgery inside the skull, which he was willing to perform if I wanted, but he had to warn me it had a mixed success rate combined with substantial risk. This was not encouraging and I went home to mull it over but after a few weeks of worsening attacks I phoned him up and made the appointment.

Did I say Dr. Turnbull was a straight shooter? Most of the time, maybe. Something went terribly wrong on that operation and I never did get a clear explanation from him. What I think happened was that he accidentally broke a blood vessel and caused a man-made brain haemorrhage. I came out of it barely able to speak my own name. It was like I imagine a stroke to be, except if I'd had a stroke I might have known what I was up against. I was staggering around bumping into things not knowing which way was up for six months and not knowing why this was happening. I had lost the hearing in my right ear, and worst of all, the goddamned tic was just as bad as ever.

I tried to go back to work, but most days I just stared at my tools and couldn't figure out what I was doing there. I had a big bandage around my head like a turban and I kept banging it on everything, especially when I had a car up on the hoist, and whenever I banged the sore spot I'd let out a string of curses fit to peel paint, which scared the hell out of our few remaining customers. I felt miserable and was miserable to be around. Kay tried to make excuses and I guess turned work away, and I've no doubt the word went out that poor old Frank White had gone off his rocker.

This didn't mean that Dicky MacDougal eased up on his harassment or the oil company cut us any slack. Quite the opposite. Our creditors became nervous and decided this was the time to start playing hardball. Kay would try to get Dicky to bring half a load because that was all we could afford, but he wouldn't do it and we would frequently be out of gas. So with nothing getting done in the shop and no gas being sold, we were in danger of being foreclosed by the bank. How I came through that without shooting myself, I don't know. I thought about it enough.

I'll tell you something about suicide though, it gets harder the closer you get to it. When it's just a distant possibility, it seems easy as pie. Oh, yeah, think I'll kill myself, that would be a nice easy way out. But if your options have all been removed and you're sitting there thinking, is this the morning I do it? How should I do it? You only get one crack at it and I don't want of be one of these chumps that only blows his head half off. When it gets down to practical matters, suddenly it doesn't seem so easy.

Should I wait until I finish this muffler job? Or maybe I shouldn't leave Kay with an empty Regular tank. I should wait till it's been filled. And really, how can I leave her with this goddamn place to run all by herself? I should burn the place down, then do it. But that would be too obvious and she wouldn't get the insurance, she'd be stuck with the mortgage. Maybe I should just tough it out until we can sell, then do it.

It becomes another big problem, the kind you have no ability to handle when you're in that end-of-the-road state. It becomes easier to just keep on keeping on. But when a big long spasm of face pain hit, I would be back thinking, "I've got to put a stop to this, this can't go on."

The kids pitched in as much as they could. Donnie had been working in the garage since it opened and by age twelve could do most of the routine jobs including fixing tires and installing exhaust systems, but we didn't think it looked right to leave him running it by himself, although he was happy enough to do it. He had become best friends with Sam Hately's youngest son Stewart and they would spend whole days there racing each other out to the pump and making the most of free access to the pop machine. Howie was away at UBC in the winter and off working for Bob Hallgren's construction company during the summer so we didn't see much of him but he sent Cindy tuition money so she could afford to spend the summer helping out.

The business was going down the drain and although my brain was starting to get back to normal, the pain attacks were worse than ever, so I went back to Turnbull and asked him if there were any options left. He checked me out and studied the files and said, "Well, we could try again." He explained that he had intended to sever the middle branch of my trigeminal nerve, which was the one most commonly associated with tic douloureux, but nerves grow like the roots of a tree and you never knew exactly which branch led where, so he wasn't sure he'd got the right one. I have to hand it to old Turnbull. Most guys would have thrown up their hands and said, sorry, buddy, we did our best. He had got in trouble on the first operation and nobody would have blamed him for not wanting to go back for more. But we both knew my life wasn't worth a plug nickel the way it was, so he made the offer and I took it.

The second operation was a complete success. I woke up free of face pain for the first time in years, and with no side effects at all, at least no more than you'd expect from having a one-inch plug cut out of your skull for the second time in a year. It was like a death-row reprieve. I have had the odd mild jolt since then, but effectively I've been cured for forty-five years. I never did get the hearing back in my right ear, though. Later on guys told me I could have sued old Turnbull for a few hundred grand over that but Christ, how could you do that to a guy that saved your life? Lots try, I know, but I knew all too well he didn't have to go back that second time and most doctors wouldn't have. I owe a lot to that guy. I'd phone him up and tell him so but he died young. He only made it to ninety-seven.

Looking back I try to remember if I felt a new lease on life or anything, but really I can't say I did. We were still in a pretty bad fix, and I still didn't feel that great. When they cut your head open and stir things around in there, it's a while before you can see straight again, and I was tired of being everybody's damned whipping boy.

When you become a garage mechanic, especially in a place where everybody drives broken-down wrecks, you become the keeper of trouble—this lady burns out her clutch every three months, this fellow stores gas in a dirty barrel and has chronic carburetor problems, this other one parks at the pulp mill and has a rotted frame—and all their stupid problems become your problems. You sometimes perform amazing feats of haywire genius but there is nobody to witness it but yourself, and nobody thanks you. You're just doing what you're expected to do, and taking too long to do it. But then the carburetor gets clogged again, and the patched frame buckles in a different place, and it's "Goddammit, Frank, I paid you fifty dollars to fix that only last year!"

We talked it over and decided to put the shop up for sale. This would be about 1970. I think we first opened up in 1966 or '67. I hated to do it because there were still some mornings when I drove up and saw the place sitting bright and fresh in the early sun and felt a twinge of that pride I felt when we first built it. It was still the best-looking gas station in BC and the finest thing I'd ever owned. But most of the time I couldn't stand the sight of it. Kay and I both came to hate it the way a lifer must hate the sight of his prison cell.

Well, it took a year before we got a serious bite and we began to think we would be stuck there for the rest of our lives. I know Kay thought seriously about sneaking up at night and putting a match to it. She laughingly mentioned it enough times I felt I had to warn her off it. Christ, the fire marshal would have seen through anything like that quick enough. The thing to do would have been to stage some kind of accident in the middle of the day. God knows, I almost set the place on fire without meaning to often enough when a welding spark hit a greasy rag in the corner. No way they'd ever be able to hang something like that on a guy. I knew what my old Abbotsford mentor Les McGarva would have done, or his father-in-law Milton Nelles, who torched his barn with all his livestock in it. They would have jacked the insurance up and torched it without a thought, then brazened it out with the officials and the neighbours but I just wasn't built that way.

12

Goodbye to Gas

Along about 1969 or '70 Howie spelled me off so I could go take a busman's holiday working in a logging camp up Bute Inlet for a few months. It was good for me to get away from my usual troubles and try on some different ones for a change and I did feel a little better for showing I could still drive a truck, but it wasn't long before I was mired in the same old sense of futility as before. I couldn't put my heart into it anymore and hated to wake up in the morning knowing it meant another day up there battling the list of overdue jobs that probably wouldn't pay anyway. We still had it for sale but had almost given up hope anyone would ever come along.

Then one day, a summer resident named Clary Rowls told me he had a prospect for me. It was funny, we'd helped him find his place, a five-acre property on Bargain Harbour that was going for $5,000 sometime in the early 1960s (it recently resold for $2.5 million), but he was a persnickety character and we had never had much more to do with him. I would have placed him in the enemy rather than the friend category but it turned out he'd been paying attention to our struggle and he stuck his nose in at this point and gave us a real lead. His furnace oil delivery man in North Vancouver had just sold out and was looking for something else. Clary thought our gas station would be just the thing. A number of well-meaning people, seeing how badly we wanted to sell, came up with suggestions from time to time and we had learned to take them with a grain of salt, but

Clary's contact called, then came up to take a look. This was more interest than we'd had from anyone and we got pretty excited.

The prospect was a Dutchman named Frank Roosen who had become a minor celebrity doing a stage routine called "Jake the Peg" about a man born with three legs. I heard it a few times but between my 50 percent hearing and Roosen's Dutch accent, I couldn't make out a damn thing he said. The way he danced with the fake leg was pretty slick, though. You had a hard time keeping track which one it was. At one point the Australian comedian Rolf Harris had bought rights to the routine and incorporated it into his touring stage act. I saw it on TV once but with Harris's Aussie twang, I still couldn't get the words. You might have thought Roosen would follow up his success by coming up with something else, but Jake the Peg was his one stroke of inspiration and he went on repeating it at Lions Club dinners for the rest of his life.

We didn't find Frank the slightest bit amusing when we dealt with him. He was hard as nails. He had obviously been well primed about our situation and set out to take full advantage of us. He screwed the price down to where we couldn't even clear our own debts. Worse, he demanded we throw in our treasured piece of land across the road, which Jim Tyner still wanted for the proposed Pender Harbour Health Clinic and which Kay and I wanted to keep for our retirement nest egg. But Roosen insisted he had to have it or he wouldn't buy the gas station, and not only that, he would only pay $18,000 for it, not the $50,000 we valued it at. There was no good reason for this. He just saw that we were beat and he wanted to take full advantage by stripping us of this valuable asset at less than half of what it was worth. We were devastated by this turn of events but we were just so damn desperate to get out of the gas station we agreed to his offer. I immediately wished I hadn't. When Tyner found out, he was furious. He told me I was being robbed and counselled me to get out of the deal if I got a chance.

The offer was good for a month and we didn't hear another word from Roosen. We didn't know if the deal was still on or not. All we had was a $1,000 security deposit. The month came and went so I had my lawyer call his lawyer and give notice that since his client had not completed the purchase within the prescribed time we considered the deal off and we were withdrawing the vacant lot from the market, although the gas station was still for sale. Roosen screamed like a scalded witch but he had let the offer expire and legally didn't have a leg to stand on, even a wooden one. If he had, he would have sued in a minute. To our vast relief he did go ahead and buy the gas station, but he spent the next thirty years meowing about the raw deal he'd got, claiming *we* had taken advantage of *him*.

Once again a chapter in our lives closed on a less than victorious note. I still felt we'd accomplished something in building that business, which sowed the seeds of a new commercial district in that part of town, but we had put in five hard years between 1967 and 1971 (it seemed like twenty years) and came away with nothing to show for it. Roosen kept the station another four or five years then sold it to start a truck farm up on the salt flats at the head of Pender Harbour. After that it passed to the Hunsche brothers, who passed it along to one of their sons and his partner, but they really ran into bad luck. Before approving their mortgage, the bank did an environmental survey and found that Chevron's buried gas tanks had been leaking and polluted the soil.

The new buyers were stuck. They had sunk their savings into the place and now it wasn't worth a plug nickel. In fact it had negative value because it was an environmental hazard that would take untold thousands to clean up. Meanwhile the land had to be taken out of service and be stripped down to mineral soil so that was the end of Pender Harbour Chevron. The one happy note is that the actual garage building, which people often said was pretty enough to be a house, was moved to Egmont and actually converted into a house.

As anybody who lives in Pender today can tell you, Jim Tyner eventually succeeded in convincing us to sell him the vacant lot and had the Pender Harbour and District Health Centre built on it in 1976. He wanted that location so bad and Kay and I had worked so hard on the campaign to get the clinic, we didn't really feel we could deny him. There were other sites he could have found, in fact the owners of the little strip mall in Madeira Park, McQuitty and Alexander, made a strong play to add it to their complex, but Tyner's vision was of a facility that would expand over

The Pender Harbour Health Centre as it looks today.

the years—as it has done—and he wanted a big property where it would have room to grow.

Besides, McQuitty and Alexander had been on the wrong side of the campaign and he hated them. He would have built the clinic on top of Mount Daniel to keep it out of their clutches. Under his banking and accounting exterior Tyner was a socialist and supported the NDP, while McQuitty and Alexander were raw-meat right-wingers with good connections to the Social Credit government of the day. Just when it seemed Tyner had finally got all the medical clinic ducks in a row, Art Alexander would use his pipeline to the health minister, Ralph Loffmark, and screw everything all up again.

The clinic would never have got off the ground if it hadn't been for the NDP government of Dave Barrett getting elected in 1972. The new health minister, Dennis Cocke, was a proponent of community-run health clinics and with the help of the local NDP MLA, Don Lockstead, the clinic preparations went into high gear. It came close to being cancelled again when the NDP got turfed in 1975, but Tyner made one final, desperate, skilful thrust and pushed it through.

He knew there would be talk about buying the land from someone who had been so prominently involved in the campaign so he brought in certified appraisers and did everything by the book. The appraisal process set the value at $55,000 and that is what we got. I still would have liked to have held on to the property and put commercial buildings on it, which would have been worth a million today and been a legacy for my great-grandchildren, but it did turn out to be a good location for the clinic, which has been the community's greatest source of pride. They did a big expansion a few years ago and I was asked to say a few words:

> *I only wish some of the old-timers who campaigned for this clinic back in the 1970s could be here to see their dream come into full bloom . . . We never could have succeeded but for the extraordinary efforts of one man, a very special person, the late Jim Tyner. Jim was an accountant and former civil servant. He was also a polio victim who walked with the aid of crutches and leg braces. He was a man of great ability and even greater determination. The rest of us would have given up in the face of all the red tape and political tricks we encountered along the way, but Jim refused to quit, and in the end his doggedness paid off . . .*

It felt good to be able to say a few words for old Jim, a truly remarkable man who is almost forgotten today despite the many decades he spent working his heart out for the community of Pender Harbour.

13

North to Alaska

A short time after we sold the garage Donnie and I went on a six-week driving holiday to Alaska. He had been away working for a contractor named Digby Porter and wanted to see the country and I hadn't started with the water board yet so he hit me up and away we went. He had a Ford pickup he'd bought in Chase, a pretty decent truck with seventeen-inch rims which came in handy on some of the rough roads we ended up on, and we bought a little tent trailer. We wore the wheels off that little trailer. We towed it down into Bella Coola and up the Stewart-Cassiar, over to Atlin and on up the Alaska Highway to Whitehorse and Dawson then over the Top of the World Road to Fairbanks, down to Anchorage and around through the lower loop through Valdez and back up over the mountains to rejoin the Alaska Highway and back home. We started out with Cindy and Marilyn's older son Doug, who was about ten then.

They were with us going down the big hill into Bella Coola. This was the famous road the government wouldn't build so the citizens built it themselves. It's a big point of pride in Bella Coola history, the little town that could, people taking things into their own hands, etc., but my old logging pal Blondie Swanson had a different version. He was logging up at the top end of the Bella Coola Valley and had a lot of timber he couldn't get to, so he got on the Chamber of Commerce and fanned these local ambitions to have a road connection to the BC Interior.

Donnie's Ford pickup with the tent trailer we towed to Alaska and back.

Up to that time Bella Coola had to depend completely on steamships and it was holding them back. So once he got these townspeople all fired up about taking vigilante action he supplied them with cats and drivers and road crews and incited them to put in this illegal road through the wilderness. If he had tried to do it himself, the Forest Service would have had him in court but the government had been promising the people of Bella Coola a road for ages and couldn't really blame them for taking things into their own hands. So Bella Coola got its road and Blondie got his timber. At least that was his story.

There is a big escarpment dividing the Chilcotin plateau from the floor of the Bella Coola valley and the section of the road that goes over the escarpment is built just like a lot of the logging roads I hauled on, where the cat driver laid in switchbacks just as steep and tight as he could get away with and pullouts for passing since they couldn't get enough width for two lanes. We pulled out in one of the pullouts to take in the view and the edge of the road just dropped out of sight. The boys started rolling rocks down and boy, they just took off like runaway freight trains. Cindy and I joined in the fun and before long we had a mini landslide going, although there was something telling me this wasn't a good idea. A few minutes further down it came to me why: here on the next switchback were all our rocks piled up blocking our way. We had to spend half an hour rolling them aside, with the help of several other cars that came along.

"Must have been a landslide."

"Happens all the time."

We took every backroad we could find. After dropping Cindy off in Prince George where she had to get back to her job at Caledonia College, we turned left and took the less travelled road to Alaska through BC's great northwestern wilderness with stops at Dease Lake, Telegraph Creek, Cassiar and Stewart. Doug had to get back home so we put him on a southbound float plane at Stewart. It was a bit worrisome because Doug was so young and hadn't been out much on his own but the plane company said no worries, they would make sure he made his connection in Prince Rupert. We didn't know then that the seaplane base at Seal Cove is miles from the airport out on Digby Island or we might have been a lot more worried than we were.

As it was we were worried enough because no sooner had the plane taxied away from the dock than we heard sirens and every police cruiser in the area came screaming up to the dock. They wouldn't tell us what was going on but when we went up to the bank to get some cash we found out they had been robbed that morning and the robber had made his getaway on the float plane with Doug! We didn't know what to do. We didn't want to phone Marilyn because we didn't know for sure anything would go amiss, and we didn't want to admit we had sent her boy off in company of a bank robber if we didn't have to.

Apparently the authorities decided to let the plane carry on to Rupert, which seemed a bit risky but that's what they decided. We didn't want to lose a day waiting around fretting so we headed north and it was several days before we

My first grandchild, Doug Plant, around the time we sent him off in the company of a bank robber.

had the relief of knowing Doug got home safe and sound. He hadn't known a thing was amiss until they landed at Seal Cove and were met by another fleet of police cruisers, who cuffed the robber and spirited him away. Not the smartest getaway plan on his part.

Apart from the cars using it, the famous "Hill" at Bella Coola hadn't been that different from a lot of logging roads I'd spent my life yo-yoing up and down with logging trucks—a little longer, but not steeper—but the road into Telegraph Creek, now there was a real dilly. It goes through kind of rolling hill country that is cut through every so often by tributaries of the Stikine that have sawed their way down through the volcanic rock over the millennia forming deep, steep-walled canyons. The first one we came to the road just seemed to end in mid-air. There was road, then there was no road. Just open space.

We stopped and got out of the truck, thinking maybe there'd been a bridge washout or something. When we got to the edge, my guts took a spin. The road didn't end, it just dropped away so steep you couldn't see it. And it was so narrow and had so many tight hairpins I just didn't think we could get around it with our truck let alone with our trailer. It didn't even look stable. It was made out of loose glacial till crumbling away at the edges. I couldn't see any way in the world we could manoeuvre down there but obviously others had done it, so Don wanted to give it a try. The trouble was, there was no turning back. Once you stuck your nose over that edge you were committed.

I will admit I was scared on that hill. But we were reading that book *Notes from the Century Before* and he had made such a big thing of Telegraph Creek we felt we just had to see it. Don headed over the edge and handled it like a champ. At the bottom of this canyon was a foaming little river with a rickety Bailey bridge over it. Some tourists had pulled their car up beside it and a woman was leaning over the rail fishing. It looked like the first time she'd ever had a rod in her hands from the way she handled it, but she had two nice steelhead. "I can catch them but I can't get them up," she complained. She would get a strike almost as soon as the line hit the water, but she wouldn't play the fish at all, she'd immediately start cranking it in and the fish would be so lively it would flip off before she could reel it the ten or fifteen feet up to the bridge rail.

Telegraph Creek was disappointing. It looked authentic all right, but it wasn't swarming with amazing characters and stories of the area's Wild West past the way the book had made out. In fact, it looked practically deserted. It had an air of history about it that made you think it had a story if only you had the time to seek it out but we had miles to go, so we kept moving. On the way out it started to rain and the switchbacks turned to grease. There were places where Don had all four wheels locked and skidding. I had my foot up on the dash to keep from pitching forward, and one hand on the door handle. I was sure we were going to join the rusty hulks of old cars at the bottoms of the gorges and it was a huge relief when we finally got back on the main road.

In Dawson City we got into a bit of a rhubarb. We hit the beer parlour and ran into two old-timers who invited us back to their place. This was a kind of old folks' home for people who could still make it on their own a bit and it was full of old miners. They were a grand bunch and I'd bought a bottle of whisky and got drinking and talking and I guess it was a bit slow for Donnie so he went back to the pub. He got drinking with some younger guys there, Indians, and buggered if they didn't spike his drink. He was just about out of it but had enough sense left to realize they were going to roll him so he pretended to go to the can and took off. They chased him, but he found a gas station and locked himself in the washroom. He passed out right on the floor and didn't come to for a couple of hours. By that time his pursuers had gone away to find somebody else to roll.

Don came and rousted me out of the old guys' home but I took a wrong turn on the step and went right over on my head. Lucky I was drunk or I might have broke my neck. Actually, I did. Back home I found I had two fractured vertebrae but by then they were half healed and there was nothing to do for it. I managed to get my skull split pretty good in the fall and probably could have used a few stitches but Don was anxious to get moving before we ran into any more hostile Indians so we got across the Yukon River and started up what they call the Top of the World Road toward Fairbanks.

At the Alaska border there are just two little guardhouses, one on each side. It was early in the morning and neither was open yet so we pulled up in front of the US one and had a much-needed snooze. We woke to the sound of a very tinny rendition of "The Star-Spangled Banner" being played. The door of the American guardhouse opened and out marched a customs agent dressed in a smart uniform with a flag under his arm. He pivoted on his heels, ran the flag up the little bitty flagpole, saluted it, about-faced and goose-stepped back to the guardhouse. Then up went the shutter and he was ready for business. About fifteen minutes later the Canadian officer comes boiling up the road from Dawson in an old junker of a car and jumps out holding a coffee mug in one hand and tucking his shirt in with the other. He gives a big friendly wave and the US agent gives a stiff nod.

We hadn't expected anything like this. We didn't even know if there would be an official border crossing, it was so far out in the middle of nowhere, and we hadn't prepared for close scrutiny. To begin with, we were both about as hungover as you can get and still be alive, and just to emphasize the point, my face and shirt front were covered in dried blood. I must have looked like I'd encountered a Kodiak bear on the way up.

This martinet of a US customs officer was not amused. He grilled us and went through our stuff for an hour. He asked us over and over again what we were there for, and we kept saying we were tourists but I guess we didn't look like tourists. Don had brought a pretty good bunch of tools and he must have figured we planned to stay and work on the Trans-Alaska pipeline, which was being built then. He kept repeating how illegal it would be for foreigners to take any kind of work and how many months in jail we would get, but finally he ran out of reasons to deny us entry. Then he asked, "Do you have any firearms?" Damn! Donnie had brought his .22, and we had been too wasted to even think about hiding it. We had no choice but to admit, yes, we did have a gun with us.

"Good," he says, and stamps our passports.

As we headed down the road to Fairbanks we began to get glimpses of Mount McKinley, which must be one of the most impressive mountains in the world. It's over 20,000 feet, but unlike most big mountains, which are merely peaks rising a little above the other peaks in a high range, Mount McKinley is a free-standing mountain. Kilimanjaro is the same way, and it's supposed to be the highest free-standing mountain. I've seen both of them now and wouldn't want to choose between them. They're very different. Kilimanjaro is a huge brown rockpile jutting out of the African plain with only a cap of snow on top, whereas McKinley is more the classic pyramid shape blanketed in snow from top to bottom. Measured base-to-peak, McKinley is the tallest mountain on land, according to Wikipedia. It is truly breathtaking. At first sight you don't realize just how bloody big it is, but you drive and drive and it keeps getting bigger and bigger until it's completely blocking out the horizon.

Fairbanks was a crazy place. It was just swarming with construction workers working on the Trans-Alaska pipeline from Prudhoe Bay to Valdez, a massive project being built at breakneck speed. It was everything you'd ever heard a Wild West boomtown should be. The pipeline workers must have outnumbered the residents three to one and during changes of shift every road would be bumper to bumper pickup trucks. Drunks would be plugging the streets all night long, yelling and brawling. You could see why the customs agent was suspicious—it would have been easy to get work and make some real good money if we'd wanted to.

We kept on rolling down to Anchorage, which was completely different, a very clean, city-like little city swarming with bush planes of every kind and very well behaved in comparison to Fairbanks. We stayed there a few days and got cleaned up and rested up, then started back up over the mountains to Valdez and on around the southern loop to rejoin the Alaska Highway. We put over 5,000 miles on the truck before we were done. I think we must have changed the tires on that little trailer twenty times. We had two extra wheels but we should have had ten. It began to seem like an ordeal at times but it's all good to look back on, like a lot of trips.

14

Herding Water

I was fifty-seven when we left the gas station and the days when I could work double shifts for weeks on end were long behind me. To return to the idea of a man being like a drum of gas, now when I looked down the bung hole the level was so far down I couldn't even see it. I had become so used to being unsound physically I couldn't even remember when it was I had had that wonderful confidence in being able to move mountains. I used to think there was no job I couldn't do if I put my shoulder to it. Drive thirty hours straight? Unload five tons of milk to change a flat, then reload it? Chop back a whole load of fir butts jammed against the bulkhead of the logging truck? Build a bridge out of hundred-foot logs? Throw up a house in a week? I used to just roll up my sleeves and get to it. Now I looked for another option.

We had more money in the bank than at any time in our lives, thanks to the sale of the gas station and the clinic property, but it was far from being enough to retire on and I had to do something. Howie was back in the Harbour by this time and hit me up one day about applying for the position as maintenance man for the local water district. I'd helped start that district back in the early sixties when we were all on wells that dried up in summer and it had been operated for most of the years it was in existence by a slow-talking, slow-moving, careful man named Gene Spicher. It was the kind of old man's job I would have scorned at any other time and I was inclined to scorn it now but Howie convinced me it would at least pay the grocery bill while I decided what I wanted to do with my life, and he did a little politicking to make sure my application got its due. He was running his little newspaper, *The Peninsula Voice*, and he had become quite the political operator.

I got the job and stayed at the water board for the rest of my working life, which didn't end until I was seventy-six. It was the longest I'd worked at any one job in my whole life, over fifteen years. It wasn't a bad job. It was only about half-time really, although I worked at it pretty steady. The hardest part wasn't the work, it was the politics. They had a volunteer board of six guys and a part-time secretary who seemed to take it as their duty to make the job of the poor guy who actually ran the thing as hard as possible. It was a bugger never being able to just go and do what you wanted without going through a wrangling session with those fussbudgets but as time went by I pretty much did what I wanted anyway, and let them try to catch up if they could.

One good thing about having had only two long-term maintenance men in thirty years but a constantly changing board is that you were the only guy that knew anything. The board didn't even know which roads the mains were on, let alone where all the hundreds of feeder lines and services were. That had all been in Gene Spicher's head and now it was all in mine. The board was always after me to write it down on maps but they didn't want to pay me to do it so I never got around to it.

It might seem to be a pretty static job, watching over a system of buried water pipes but actually it kept you on your toes. If there was a big fall storm, leaves would plug the intake and if you didn't hustle up there and clear it, everybody in town would run dry and hot water tanks would be burning up. We had a primitive chlorinator to kill off the bugs that flourished in our swampy reservoir and you had to set the level manually. In hot weather the swamp water stewed like tea and you had to increase the chlorine to disinfect it, but it took careful judgment. If you guessed too low the phone in the office would be burning up with complaints about how bad the water smelled and tasted and looked. If you turned it up too high, all the goldfish in town would die and the phone would be burning up about giving people bleach to drink.

It was something you had to be thinking about but I got so if it started raining heavily in the night I'd wake up and think, "I gotta get up there and increase the chlorine setting two clicks." You always had complaints when you increased it to the point people at the start of the system could taste it—the chlorine got neutralized by organics as it passed down the line so it was the first people who got the heavy dose—but after I got the feel of it I never had any real problems. Later they put in an automated gas system and it didn't work half so well. A bunch of people got sick, oh, there were lawsuit threats and everything else.

The water system itself had only been built for about half as many homes as were now hooked up to it and it was unstable. Some areas were constantly losing pressure or running dry and the politest and mildest housewife can turn into an absolute terror if her water stops, as I came to know. I could have fixed the damn thing if I ever had a board that would just give me a few bucks and let me do what needed to be done, which was to increase water supply. When we built the system back in the sixties, we stuck the intake in a little puddle up on the mountain because we didn't have much demand at that time and it was high enough to give us natural pressure, eliminating the cost of pumps. But its day had long passed and the system desperately needed an increased source of supply.

Really, the ultimate solution to this was to drop an intake into the enormous Sakinaw-Ruby lake watershed, but in the meantime you could resupply the system much more simply by poking down a few wells. There are some first-class aquifers right under the ground our mains run through, and all you would have to do would be to tap into them and use them to recharge the storage tanks during the night the way they do in Gibsons. This would be the purest underground water, it wouldn't be subject to drought and it would be dirt cheap. But that was too simple for any board I ever had to deal with. Once in a while I got a chairman I could talk sense to but most of the time they insisted on spending all their money on engineering studies by clueless pencil necks who only made problems worse. Twenty years later they still hadn't done anything and people were so exasperated with the bad water they voted to turn the system over to the Regional District and my old board went out of existence.

I'd like to be able to say that solved the problem, but all it proved was that bigger governments can make bigger blunders. Instead of developing one of the readily available sources of better and more abundant water, the Regional District doubled down on the inadequate source we already had. As I write they are putting the finishing touches on an elaborate filtration plant designed to purify the bog tea coming out of that little swamp and the budget is up in the multi-millions. Our water rates are going through the roof and they still haven't increased the water supply by one cupful. Millions more will have to be spent if we are to avoid the kind of disaster they had a few years ago in Tofino, where the taps suddenly went dry one hot summer day.

It was a real education working in that job, not so much in digging ditches which I already knew enough about but in watching the democratic process at work. First you have all the wrong people running for public office, and for the wrong reasons. We had chairmen who put family in the paying jobs, others who got on the board just to eliminate the controls we had put in to conserve water—one chairman put meters on all the houses, the next one took them all off. Now they're putting them back on again. Meanwhile the public refuses to pay any attention until their tax bill gets doubled or their tap water runs brown. Then they're mad as hell but it's too late. As a diehard left-winger it hurt me to see up close how badly government runs things, and I'm glad I've had enough experience with big corporations to know they're just as bad. I guess I'm forced to agree with that old Tory Winston Churchill when he said our system is the worst one there is, except for all the others. Still, I think we can do better. We have to do better.

It's been forty years since we sold the gas station and I have a hard time remembering what happened in that time. It seems to have gone by in a blur. It's not like the earlier years where every day stands out, and yet plenty did happen. In some ways more happened than at any previous time in my life, but whole years, whole decades are missing and I have to get out the photo album to try to piece it together. One difference is that the stuff that happened was happening to me instead of being done by me. And as I keep saying, your ability to respond dries up. Things don't make as big an impression after you pass middle age. You tend to shrug and move on. And forget. When I reached my middle age I thought my biggest challenge would be boredom. I knew there wouldn't be any big new projects for me, though occasionally I thought of getting back into the excavating business. I bought another old backhoe off Marshall Rae mainly to use on the water board job and occasionally I took on a bit of landscaping or a septic system on the side but I just didn't have the steam in the boiler to do anything more.

It seemed like life was winding down and nothing would happen that hadn't already happened. Kay and I had been through it all and didn't hold any surprises for each other anymore. It's funny how a couple weigh each other down after a while. You get locked into your routines. If you think of doing something different, you immediately give it up because you know the other person would find it strange and you don't have the nerve to introduce a shift, to break step. For instance, I never cooked a meal the whole time I was married to Kay. I never did anything around the house. I never did any gardening or worked in the yard except when she needed something big done involving a machine. It was just the way it was. I didn't mind cooking and enjoyed it the odd time when I was away batching in a camp or out on the boat. I would have liked to, and I would have liked to have friends over. But in the system we had developed, Kay did all the cooking and we never had people over.

Later, after I was alone, I did all my own cooking and housekeeping and often had big groups in for dinner. I also took an interest in the yard and made a bit of a showplace of the old homestead. But while Kay was around I wouldn't have dared do any of this. It would have been too much of a departure from the habits we had fallen into. So you stick to tried and true. It's a hell of a thing, a straightjacket. You don't even realize it, unless something happens and you find yourself alone with the world full of possibilities again, then you think, what the hell was wrong with us? We could have done all sorts of things and our lives could have been so much better. I've since read this is where a lot of marriages come apart, right when you think you've finally got it made with nothing but clear sailing ahead, and having been there I can completely understand how this happens.

Without the old terrors of survival, life becomes predictable and monotonous. I tried to get back to reading the odd book about the Civil War or electronics but when your life is dull and uninspiring everything else seems the same way. I went on the odd drunk with Blind Bill Milligan or old Sam Hately but the old feeling wasn't there and I paid a hell of a price, not just the next morning but for two or three days after. It was just another reminder of how much time had passed and how much things had changed. The kids were all gone and getting on with their lives. Marilyn was well established with her two boys and her home in Vancouver where Chas worked as a high school science teacher. Howie had moved back to the Harbour and was getting started in his publishing activities, doing a little excavating on the side to pay the bills. Cindy married a guy she'd met at SFU and moved to the Interior.

The last one to leave the nest was Donnie but he'd been away living with Marilyn in Vancouver since high school so his going off to vocational school didn't give us the jolt the older kids did. He came home and worked in the gas station a bit and I could see he'd really made the most of his mechanical courses. He had an old muscle car and took the motor out and rebuilt it right on the porch of the house. He stripped that motor down in a matter of hours and had all the parts laid out like a surgeon in an operating room, then had the block re-bored and buttoned it all back together and painted it up. My god, I had overhauled a few motors but

Me with one of my six Corvairs and Don with the Firebird he overhauled, early 1970s.

he did it with such confidence and competence I was in awe. Some guys go to school and don't learn anything, others go and learn twice as much as they're taught and you could see right away Don had really been transformed into a pro.

He went out working on big construction, got his apprenticeship hours and became a first-class diesel mechanic who could tackle any engine or any piece of equipment made. Right in his twenties, he achieved a level of expertise I'd never had. I'd never specialized; I'd always been the guy who could do a lot of different things and I took pride in that, but I'd always admired the guys like Don who mastered one particular field. I just didn't think that would hold my interest indefinitely, and as it turned out that was true for Don too in the end. But it was a great way to start his working life and gave him a lot of confidence. You could just see him grow as a man and I couldn't help but feel a lot of pride. He'd had to fend for himself more than any of our kids, but he had come through.

15

Hairy Times

Up to the seventies Kay and I had enjoyed a pretty good marriage, or at least I thought so. We'd been through some rough patches but she had never complained. She bought into every scheme and joined in fully, pulling up stakes and moving hither and yon, raising the kids, doing the books, running the cookhouse, passing wrenches when I couldn't afford a helper. She not only didn't mind being called out to run a boat or a truck while I attended a towline or worked the loader, she did it with a will. She preferred it to housework, which it must be said, was never her strong point. I came to take her willingness for granted. Then one day it came to an end.

Actually it didn't happen that suddenly, it just seemed like it because I hadn't been paying attention. I would hear her telling the kids: "They tell you to work hard and be honest and you'll get ahead, but that's not how it works. That's just what they tell you so they can take advantage of you." It wasn't that unusual to hear somebody saying this kind of thing and it wasn't too different from what I thought myself when I was feeling down, but it was disturbing to hear Kay saying it. She had always been so optimistic, it represented a 180-degree change in the way she always thought about things.

I guess I'd adjusted my thinking gradually over the years to knowing there was no pot of gold at the end of the rainbow and it didn't bother me too much. I had hoped our various enterprises—the contract log hauling, the logging camp, the gas station—would pay off, but the fact they weren't financially successful didn't make them total failures in my mind. A guy had to do something with his life and I would rather do what I did than just punch a clock for years on end. It bothered me that Kay seemed to think it was all just a big fraud that had been played on us by MacMillan Bloedel, Charlie Philp and Chevron gas, but that was how she saw it. Along with this idea that our life had been some kind of bad joke, she became quite rebellious in the way she thought about everything else.

About 1970 the hippies started showing up on the Sunshine Coast. It was quite a surprise to everybody. We'd read about all the trouble in the cities but most things that happened in the news never touched our lives way up at the end of the road here and we never expected it to. But after the San Francisco scene went sour, the young people began looking for a new start by going "back to the land." Opposition to the Vietnam War was a big part of the sixties youth movement, of course. The US Army was drafting young men so a lot of back-to-the-landers targeted land on the Canadian side of the border where they could dodge the draft.

Somehow the Sunshine Coast got identified in the underground press as one of the good places to go and by 1971 hippies from all over the continent were rolling into Roberts Creek, Pender Harbour, Egmont, Powell Lake, Lund and Texada Island. It was quite a scene. It had become quite common even that long ago to decry the fact that our own young people seemed to be abandoning the coast, leaving it to an aging core population and various schemes were discussed for attracting youth, but this was a real case of be careful what you wish for. All of a sudden the old-timers were being swamped with young people and they didn't like it one bit.

Most people were appalled by the hippies' long hair, bad smell, drug use and "world owes me a living" attitude but Kay thought they were all just wonderful. The whole idea of giving society a poke in the eye and saying to hell with the rat race jibed exactly with what she'd come to think herself. She would have filled every room in the house with these long-haired refugees if I'd let her. As it was she "rented" them a summer cabin she looked after for a woman we knew as Miss Dodman. Why we always called her that I don't know. Her name was Bernice, but for some reason we always referred to her as Miss Dodman. She was what I think they call statuesque. She had some kind of business in town, maybe a travel agency. My old drinking buddy Lloyd Wiley and I had built that cabin in a week back in the early sixties, using an axe and a chainsaw. It is still giving good service as far as I know.

We were still in the garage when the hippies started appearing and it was bad for business to have them lounging around all the time using the phone and toilet and scaring good customers away so I blew up and told Kay to get them the hell out of there or I would clear them out myself. She wasn't with me on it but she must have told them I was being difficult and got them to back off. Always in our earlier years if I laid down the law on something like this, there would never be any trouble getting her to see it my way. Now I could see there was something different in her attitude. She went along with what I said and stopped encouraging the hippies to use our place as a hangout, but she didn't stop fraternizing with them and assisting them on her own. It was a quiet defiance I hadn't run into much before with her, but which I would come to know better.

Actually, I agreed with the youth revolt of the sixties—in principle. I wasn't much of a war guy at the best of times, and the Vietnam War had less to recommend it than most. It was the same old story, a bunch of miserable old bastards who couldn't be happy until they'd sent all the young men off to war to get killed. Tell every lie, break every law, make every excuse and feel perfectly justified in doing it. Gotta stop the infidels. Gotta stop the commies. Terrible threat, those commies. Then the dreaded commies collapse under their own weight. Well, okay, back to the infidels. They were our friends yesterday but today they're a threat to our way of life. The military-industrial complex has to have somebody to use up bullets on. But whoever the enemy of the day is, you young fellows must go out and get killed fighting them because us old bastards say you should. Yours is not to reason why.

Well, these young fellows had gone off to school and learned how to reason why. They were telling the flag-wavers to stuff it and heading for Canada. I was sympathetic to that. I was sympathetic to their idea of getting away from big corporations and taking their lives into their own hands, too.

The only trouble was these kids could barely tie their own shoelaces and didn't have it in them to do the kind of work it takes to live off the land, even though they had books on it and could talk all day about the theories behind it. I remember one character they called Bum Bank whose claim to fame apparently was that he had talked hundreds of guys into dropping their drawers so he could snap a picture of their bare butt. He then filed all these photos in his "Bum Bank" and that was supposed to be great art. This goof spent the winter over at the scout camp in a lean-to made out of clear poly stretched over a few wobbly poles. By spring the poly had got all covered with green slime. He pointed to the slime and said proudly, "It's getting more organic all the time."

They were in a dream world, that was what I couldn't accept. If you're going to drop out and live by the sweat of your brow, the first thing is you have to get practical and learn how to grow spuds and split wood. I saw one of the gardens these guys were making, they'd planted a crooked little row of beans right between the trees, right in the native soil without clearing away the salal or anything. You could see at a glance that not one plant was going to survive. One of them complained the stove in Miss Dodman's cabin wouldn't work and when I looked in he'd been trying to start it with chewed-off lengths of green hemlock sapling, wood you couldn't have got to burn with a blowtorch.

I thought, "This is utterly hopeless. These guys will be running back to their parents in Ohio before winter's half done." And that was true for a lot of them, but not for all. Some couldn't go back because of the draft, so they adapted. That guy who couldn't build a fire in a stove is today a hand-logger who has his own camp up north and everybody thinks he's an old coastal pioneer. Another equally lost character became a commercial fisherman and even became some sort of a wheel in the fishermen's union if I'm not mistaken. A lot of them blended into the scene so well in a few years nobody knew them from the locals, but you never would have bet on that in the beginning.

At first, though, the town was really up in arms about this alien invasion. People assumed they were all dangerous drug addicts who might infect their own young people and undermine community values. Up until this time I don't think the people of Pender Harbour were aware we

In the early 1970s the Sunshine Coast was overrun with dropouts and draft dodgers who didn't look like much but sometimes had well-hidden talents. This group comprises a printer, a photographer and two artists who helped start *Raincoast Chronicles*.

actually had any community values and I'm sure most people would have had a hard time saying what they were beyond we didn't believe in getting stoned (except if it was on homebrew) and we believed in supporting ourselves by the sweat of our own brow (although not until your pogey ran out) and none of this free love stuff although the hippie girls would tell you they couldn't venture out into the light of day without being hassled by local guys who wanted to try some just to be sure.

Cleanliness became a big issue, too. That would be the first thing most guys would complain about, that the hippies didn't believe in personal hygiene. You'd hear guys sounding off on this who themselves subscribed to the practice of taking a bath once a year whether they needed it or not.

A lot of the friction was over the girls. In a town where there never seemed to be enough single females to go around here was a whole army of good-looking young babes not wearing bras but they made no secret of their preference for their own long-haired mutts who didn't have any money, didn't have decent cars and looked too wasted to give a woman what she needed. But when any of the Harbour's stout red-blooded buckaroos offered to give them something better, they just got the cold shoulder. Ohhh, that made them mad.

Hostility against the longhairs built up to the flashpoint and although drug use was the official reason, sex was behind a lot of it. Free love. We'd heard rumours about it and the newspaper write-ups all hinted at it. The Pender Harbour men all showed a keen scientific interest in this, and of course that was enough to fill their women with moral outrage about it. Nobody ever saw this free love actually taking place and most of the hippies seemed paired off into couples by the time they reached Pender Harbour but that did little to stop the talk. It got pretty hot for them. The boys were routinely attacked and beat up outside the Rigger's Roost and the local RCMP took a free hand in harassing them. The corporal in Gibsons seemed to take a personal interest in making their lives miserable and sent a lot to jail for marijuana possession and got in the news for taking attack dogs after a group that was squatting in an abandoned logging camp up Howe Sound. A couple of kids got chewed up bad enough to be put in the hospital, but most people figured that was no more than they deserved.

We had a prize specimen up here, a local cop who really took it as his mission to singlehandedly turn back this mass migration of young people. He would stop and search anybody he saw hitchhiking or carrying a backpack and give them a hard time. Most were smart enough not to be carrying drugs but if he found anything that looked like it had once been in contact with drugs, like a pipe, he would seize that and have it analyzed and if there was a molecule of cannabis to be found it was off to jail with you. "Traces," it was called and it got you thirty days. Later this was found to be unconstitutional but these kids had no money to defend themselves and the local judiciary wasn't discerning.

A college friend of Howie's named Hank Cohen came up to visit during the summer and went out for a row in a skiff. This young fellow wasn't a hippie and didn't have long hair although he was a bit scruffy looking and was an obvious out-of-towner. The cop appeared in a fast outboard and charged him for not having a lifejacket, saying that if he left the Sunshine Coast before sundown the charge would be withdrawn.

This was phony to begin with because there was no law requiring you to have a lifejacket in a rowboat then, and since the heyday of Dodge City, cops haven't had any legal grounds to tell a law-abiding citizen to get out of town. Hank was quite a smart lad and researched the law and decided to stay and fight the charge. In those days we still had the old magistrate's courts where they got some local yokel who wanted a bit of pin money and made him into a magistrate. At that time the Pender Harbour magistrate was a retired RCMP officer named Charlie Mittlestead, popularly known as Muddlehead.

They held court in Muddlehead's living room with just him and the cop present and the kid started in to defend himself, quoting the law chapter and verse and pointing out what he was doing was perfectly legal. Charlie went red in the face and cut him off, shouting that his type was not welcome in Pender Harbour and giving him twenty-four hours to get off the Sunshine Coast or else be jailed for contempt of court. The poor kid was scared to death and nothing we could say would stop him from taking the next ferry back to Vancouver, never to return. That same cop came into the gas station one time and started giving Kay a bad time about renting to hippies. I was pissed off at him for meddling where he had no right, but I was madder at Kay for getting us into that spot.

Within a couple years of course, everything changed. The anti-war movement became mainstream and the US was forced to retreat from Vietnam with its tail between its legs. Hippie fashions and music became mainstream too and soon you couldn't tell the local kids from the outsiders. The very same guys who had been beating the hippies up were partying with them and not only smoking pot, they were growing it for a living. Sam Hately, whose twin sons had got mixed up in the drug trade and did time in prison for it, stopped into the garage one day and said, "You'll never believe what I just saw." He'd been driving by Bear Lake, a favourite hippie swimming hole, and had seen a bunch of people skinny-dipping including one that almost made him lose control and drive into the water. It was Al Lloyd, owner of Lloyd's Store, sometime president of the Chamber of Commerce, School Board Trustee and arguably the town's most respectable citizen, standing bollock naked beside the road with a bunch of stoned longhairs.

"I never thought I'd live to see the likes of that," Sam marvelled. "This isn't the world I know anymore."

It was truly amazing how much things switched around in those few short years. I had to change my thinking a lot too. My own kids got all caught up in it. Howie grew his hair long like a woman's and got a big bushy beard. I suppose he smoked pot like all the rest, I never asked. Cindy and her husband, they adopted the lifestyle and Dave grew a beard. Even Donnie grew a long pigtail. One Christmas there in the early seventies somebody brought a bag of pot to the family Christmas and damned if they didn't all get into it. Oh, it was an awful schmozzle. But for a while there that's how it was, it was all bets off. It made me more than a little uncomfortable.

I used to argue with Howie about it. He was all full of this revolution stuff, the hell with career, the hell with progress, the military-industrial complex is going to collapse and we're all going to have to survive by the work of our hands. I tried to talk some sense to him but it was fighting a whole generation that believed this kind of thing. It disappointed me because I had great hopes he would turn out to be something we could be proud of and here he seemed to have decided the highest calling he could aspire to would be to become the kind of country layabout we had spent our lives trying to steer him away from. Then one day he started up his own underground newspaper spouting all the radical attitudes of the time and I began to think, well at least he's doing something. Who knows—maybe it will develop into something worthwhile.

I built him a proper shop to print it in and helped him get set up, and pretty soon he was turning out a pretty respectable paper with all the local businesses advertising in it. Even Harold Clay advertised. He brought his girlfriend Mary up from town and bought Dennis Gamble's old pink house trailer, which he set up on the vacant lot across from the gas station. Mary had bright red hair and was hard to take your eyes off and I kind of wondered if Howie had been completely objective in appraising her assets, but whatever, he lucked out.

Mary was as smart as a whip and steady as a rock but also game for the rough-and-tumble course they set out on. She just rolled with the punches and made the best of it. She kind of reminded me of Kay in that way. But

I managed to find a tie for Mary and Howie's wedding although the groom didn't. They held it at our old Fran Pen Road homestead, as did Donnie and Crystal a few years later.

Kay had always been a bit disorganized where Mary was just the opposite and introduced an element of discipline that Howie of all people needed. She was the one who really shaped his fuzzy-headed ideas into a working business. She bought the town's first real computer, an Apple II Plus. They started publishing a history magazine called *Raincoast Chronicles* in 1972 then branched into books in 1974 and over the years built up a nationally known publishing house, Harbour Publishing. Their successes over the years have given me a lot of satisfaction.

Cindy continued to take her lumps, but she kept bouncing back like the little fighter she was. The guy she teamed up with, Dave Wilson, wasn't a bad guy but took a long time to get it all together, like a lot of people from that generation. They got married and seemed to have a strong relationship but he ran off and left her for one of their friends. It was a hell of a way for a young woman to start off in life, but Cindy pulled herself together and moved to Prince George and started over. She found another guy up there, an accountant with the provincial government named Ken Carling.

Ken was a right-winger and a playboy and I was dubious about him for a long time but he was very devoted to Cindy and treated her well.

They travelled a lot and enjoyed life and everything seemed to be going well for her. She worked her way up in the college and in her spare time started her own book publishing company, Caitlin Press. She published writers from Northern BC and made quite a name for herself as a promoter of the Northern Interior. One year she was chosen the Prince George Businesswoman of the Year. She often said she went up there to get away from the family and show she could make it on her own and that seemed to be just what she was doing.

16

The Perils of Peace

Like a lot of dumb bastards, I thought I had it made when the wife and I hit middle age. The kids were all launched on their lives, we'd escaped the tyranny of the Chevron gas company, I had my health back, we had our house paid for and we had money in the bank for the first time in our lives. It wasn't enough to live on but I had the water board job to keep the grocery money coming in. I thought I was lucky. Finally Kay and I would get a chance to do some of the good things we'd been putting off for the last thirty years. I could never remember exactly what these were but trusted we'd have no trouble figuring them out when the time came. It would be such a pleasure to sit down together and draw up our list, and we would agree on every item.

How wrong could a guy be? I guess one thing I could say I learned is that any time in your life you get thinking things are all set—look out! This is a sure sign life is getting ready to deliver you a big fat curveball. I wouldn't have believed it if you'd tried to tell me then that the middle years after you've fought all your big battles and got the kids away and you've come to terms with the kind of life you have, far from being calm waters, are exactly when a lot of marriages hit the rocks. God, there ought to be better instructions handed out when you get married.

I noticed that Kay was becoming more and more independent and you think I would have seen something in that, but no, I just dismissed it as some shift of female mood to do with the change of life. I knew the hippie girls had got her all hepped up on women's lib and gave her this book, *The Female Eunuch*, which she would often read passages from that would just about give me apoplexy. I came to think of that book as a kind of Satanic text and was even heard to accuse it of ruining our marriage, although I later realized I was blaming it for a lot of things that were just part of the atmosphere of those times.

She wanted to get back to painting, which was one of her old unfulfilled dreams from her school years, so she cleared out Cindy's old bedroom upstairs and set up an easel and paints. Then she moved in a padded chair and a bookshelf and started spending a big part of her day there. Then the next thing I know she's got a little cot in there, and I'm not seeing her much at night either.

If I asked her anything about what she was up to I would get put in my place with some quote about male chauvinism. It's painful for me to think about it now, not because I have any lingering resentment, but because I handled it so damn badly. But at the time it just seemed so silly. I mean here we were—we were partners. We'd been through the wars. We'd raised a wonderful family. We had a level of understanding that went beyond words. Now we had to communicate in slogans? I thought she was going off her rocker. I'd get mad and shout, which is what I'd always done. She had never fought back and didn't now, but whereas I'd always got my way before, I didn't now. She'd just go up to her room and close the door and leave me standing there with steam coming out of my ears.

When things got too much to handle I would just jump in the car and go up to the Roost. I could usually count on some old drinking buddies like Lloyd or Doug being there grousing about their own old ladies—as long as the wives themselves weren't present.

Doug's wife liked her beer just as much as he did and the two of them would sometimes close the pub down together. One night well past twelve there was a bunch of shouting and pounding on the door so I go to the door and it's Doug. He's falling down drunk and tells me he rolled his truck over the bank a little ways down the road. He and his wife were both in it but he'd managed to crawl out and find his way to our place. I pull on some pants and drive him down to where I can see it down the bank with the lights still on. I pull over and Doug says, "Ah, don't bother stopping, just take me home."

"What about your wife?" I say.

"Ah the hell with it," he says. "We'll get 'er in the morning!"

I always felt better about my own troubles after hanging around with Lloyd and Doug for a while.

It does funny things to you when you see your life partner suddenly going through changes you don't share. Whatever was going on with Kay, I was completely shut out. Looking back now, I think she was abnormally afraid of getting old. She was absolutely nuts about giving out her age. She wouldn't put her birthdate down anywhere and if it turned up on any kind of official paper, she'd grab it and burn it. Earlier on she'd never worried about time going by, a year here, five years there, we had lots of time to wait for things to work out and start a family, get a nice house in a nice town, she was very relaxed. But suddenly here we were, the sands were running down without a lot of what we'd set out to do getting done, and it seemed to put her into a panic. I sometimes wonder if she had a premonition of just how short her time would be.

Her main beef seemed to be that we had spent all our lives butting our heads against brick walls and not enjoying life. We spent all our time raising pigs, hauling logs and pumping gas instead of doing what the better class of people were doing, namely having elevated conversations, taking part in the arts, travelling, and generally enjoying the finer things in life. I wasn't as sold on the finer things in life. To me it was leisure and leisure was always of secondary importance. She seemed to want it to be primary, and that struck me as schoolgirl stuff. Still, I was worried about the gulf that had opened between us and I was ready to try and bridge it.

I thought maybe if we went on some trips and had some good times together, that would help to put things back together. Maybe go over to the Island and revisit some of the places where we'd lived as a deliriously happy young couple, but she wasn't interested. I asked her if she still wanted to have our ashes spread on Winchelsea Island according to the promise we'd made each other when we picnicked there as young lovers but she brushed it away as silly old nonsense.

At one point we even went to a marriage counsellor. I forget whose idea that was but I suppose it came out of my wanting to find out what the hell was going on—she thought everything was just fine and was in denial about any changes in her or grief they might be causing me. We only went a couple times. This counsellor, he was a pretty decent guy really, he just kept saying, "What are two nice down-to-earth people like you doing coming in to see me? How long have you been married? Thirty-five years? You should be giving me advice!" It wasn't terribly helpful.

While I was getting the cold shoulder, she was spending a lot of her time cultivating new friends on her own. She had a bunch of women she painted pictures with, especially a woman named Ada Priest who was kind of a spiritual guru type. I got to know Ada later and she was a great old gal but at the time I was suspicious and resented all the time Kay spent with her and people like her. She took night school lessons from a local real estate agent who fancied herself a painter and got so she could paint pretty good water and skies and mountains, but she couldn't put it all together with any assurance.

She did one oil painting she was pleased with enough to frame, it was a seascape with mountains and everything looked like it should except the picture was empty right in the middle. The trees and mountains and waves all seemed to point your eye toward the centre, but there was nothing there. It bugged me. It bugged her too, so she painted a little sailboat right smack in the middle. That made it worse. It hurt to look at it, it was so centred or something. I think if she'd been more confident she would have put it a little out of balance and painted things a little off what they really looked like, I don't know. I just noticed Ada's paintings were a lot more blurry and off-kilter than Kay's, but they had more spirit somehow. But then Ada had more spirit. She had been limbering up her spiritual muscles for years, she did astrological tables and tarot card readings and all this malarkey. Kay was just taking baby steps in her mid-fifties, with her bones all aching and stiff and her mind the same. It was sad to see her struggling away and spinning her wheels, I know she must have felt she'd missed her chance and I felt it too.

Looking back, I wonder if things could have been different. If I could have gone along with what she wanted instead of getting my back up. God knows, in my second marriage I learned how to take the back seat and keep my mouth shut.

Maybe if I had showed I was ready to let Kay go her own way and supported her more, bought her a ticket to one of these fancy art retreats at Yellow Point Lodge or something and taken more interest in what she was trying to do, I could have helped her. The trouble was I didn't know the first thing about art or good things in life then and neither did she. She was groping blindly for something that was lacking in her life, something she didn't have but idealized. I didn't sympathize as much as I could have because I thought it was all a pipe dream of hers that was bound to disappoint her in the end.

I think I may have been right about that, because the crazy damn truth is I lived to experience the reality she was dreaming about, and I know now it is nothing like she imagined, nothing she would have felt comfortable with. But the way I see it, her dream of art and books and elevated company wasn't foolish, it came out of a genuine desire to get back to that place we left behind so many years ago when you could feel alive, to live a little before it was too late.

Kay was still very attentive to the kids and got quite worked up over any family occasions like Christmas. She would spend days cleaning the house, which always really needed it, and would be rushing around shopping and making preparations for the big dinner and building up a lot of stress. She was like that. She was one of these people who always seemed calm and cheerful on the outside but would be tearing herself apart inside. She developed ulcers when she was in her forties and had to have several operations on them. She was so sunny and cheerful people always found this surprising, but I came to know better. She hurt just as bad as anybody, she just kept it bottled up.

This would have been a Christmas Eve in the early 1970s. Marilyn and her bunch were up and I guess probably Donnie, but Howie was away with his wife Mary at her folks' place in Mission. They had a dog, one of the black Lab–Doberman crosses we had been raising for years and Kay was supposed to be looking after it. It had got late and she was worried about this dog being shut in their trailer, so she took our dog Peppy and walked up to their trailer, which was about a half mile away. About an hour later we heard the dogs in the porch and opened the door and here was Kay looking like she'd been hit by a truck. She was bleeding from the forehead and was completely out of it. When we asked her what happened, she couldn't speak although it sounded like she was trying to say "dogs." We thought maybe the dogs had knocked her down and given her a concussion or something. They were full grown but still in the puppy stage and very rambunctious when they were together. She was white as a sheet and wasn't in full control of her limbs. I had never seen her look so weak and vulnerable and it panicked me. We got her into a car and rushed her down to the hospital in Sechelt. They put her into intensive care and the next day medevaced her into Vancouver.

She'd had a stroke. The dogs had nothing to do with it, except maybe they'd been the last thing she remembered before she went out. She was in St. Paul's for several weeks then went over to stay with Marilyn for a few more weeks. It had been a moderate stroke and knocked out one arm and left her without speech, which it took her a couple years to get back fully. But there was something else. While she was in hospital she lost a lot of

Kay and I with the dogs Jason and Peppy in front of our place on Francis Peninsula Road. We went through about four generations of black Lab–Doberman crosses and some neighbours thought it was all the same ageless black dog.

weight and got so thin one of the nurses noticed a tiny lump in her right breast. They did a biopsy and found it was malignant. So as soon as she recovered sufficiently from the stroke they took her back in and gave her a mastectomy. It was a radical one that took the lymph nodes under the arm as well as the whole breast.

She came home and healed and relearned speech but she couldn't get over what they'd done to her. She lamented the loss of her breast and hated the disfigurement. "I like my breasts," she said. She had a hell of a time accepting it and accepting that she had come so close to dying. She did get back pretty close to normal, although there was always a slight hesitation in her speech and one arm remained weak, not from the stroke but from the operation. In her characteristic way, she was secretive about it. She hated to be reminded that she'd been sick and wouldn't utter the word "cancer." She was supposed to go into Vancouver to have a checkup each year at the Cancer Clinic, and she always went but we sometimes wondered if she really had the checkup.

Things improved a little between us but never went back to normal. She became more and more private and I got used to it. She recovered her feisty nature and became more outspoken and iconoclastic than ever. I remember when Howie and Mary came to us in 1975 to say they were getting married, her response was, "Why?" She made no secret of the fact she thought marriage was a crock of "itshay." (She never did learn how to cuss properly.) Two years later when they told us they were having a baby, she was no more enthusiastic. "Having children makes you a hostage to fate," she said. Little Silas was about the most perfect little baby you ever saw, but she didn't show much interest. I babysat him lots but I don't think she ever did.

I was now working at my water board job and that kept me occupied. Howie was getting more established, doing his publishing with Mary on the one hand and financing the whole effort on the other hand by doing excavating. I'd kept the little Allis-Chalmers HD5 track loader I'd had before we built the garage and he had started up using it to do roads and clearing jobs. After a few years he took the contract for maintaining the local garbage dump and got a newer, larger, HD7 track loader and a

When Mary and Howie named their first child Silas in honour of my father, I couldn't help feeling a little biased toward him but he was such a thoughtful little guy he made it easy.

twelve-yard dump truck so he would work a few days a week on that and a few days in his print shop. Eventually both things built up to where it was too much to handle, so he turned the equipment over to Donnie and went full time on the publishing while Don built the excavating business up into a serious enterprise with half a dozen excavators, a couple of graders and about five trucks. He uses my old machine shop and the back half of the land I bought off Sam Hately all those years ago, which gives me the satisfaction of thinking some of those efforts of mine were not entirely wasted. This is getting a bit ahead of schedule however.

In about 1977 I began to think Kay wasn't looking too swift. She was losing weight and seemed listless. I asked her if she was feeling all right and of course she wouldn't discuss it. All she would say is that she had a sore back. I mentioned it to the kids and they were all concerned but her doctor said she had checked out okay. But she kept losing weight and getting weaker so we went back to the doctor and finally got him to agree she was looking bad. He sent her in for a thorough examination and they found cancer in her spine. She'd been complaining about her back for over a year but instead of connecting the dots between that and the weight loss he'd been sending her to a chiropractor. Exhibit 999 in don't leave it to your doctor. The way things unfolded it probably didn't make any difference. The spine is very tricky to treat and anyway her cancer was the aggressive kind. Within weeks it was in her lungs and then her brain and on March 15, 1978, at sixty-one years of age she was gone.

It's taken me decades to get my head straight about it. Losing your wife of thirty-nine years is enough of a shock to the system to rock you back on your heels for a good long spell but I had the added confusion of our strained relations toward the end. I didn't know what I felt except that I was good and properly messed up. Now with the distance of thirty years, I can see her more clearly without my own confused feelings getting in the road. And all I can see is this fine, good-hearted woman who gave her all and got cruelly cheated. Cheated by her mother, cheated by society, cheated by me and cheated by death. She had every right to be bitter. If only a man hadn't been so blind, things might have been different.

17

On My Own Again

fter Kay died I spent about two years being too depressed to do anything but eat, sleep and work. It's lucky I had the water board job to take my mind off myself or I might have put a boomchain around my neck and jumped off the dock. Even though toward the end she had left me feeling pretty down on myself, that made it no easier to lose her. A man learns a lot about the true meaning of love when he loses a wife of forty years. It's like those double stars that orbit around each other. One day he's chafing about the limitations of his paired-up situation. Then he loses his partner and finds himself tumbling through space not knowing which way is up and he'd give anything to be back in his old familiar orbit even with all its limitations.

I saw many of my old acquaintances go through this. Old Bill White there, while Ivy was alive he never paid much attention to her. But after she died he just went all mushy about what an angel she was and how life was no good without her. Every damn one of those guys who used to give their wives a hard time went like that. It was kind of pathetic and made you wish you could step in and give them a little glimpse of the future to smarten them up. But I had the same thing happen to me.

People make all sorts of helpful suggestions but you can't even consider them. You can't think about going travelling when you don't even know if you want to go on living. You can't look at another woman any more than a lovesick kid can look at any other girl than the one who has his heart. I had no self-esteem. Kay had done a good job of convincing me I was such a slob and a loser that it exhausted even her infinite patience, and I couldn't believe I would ever find another person who would want anything to do with me. I was about as low as a man can go and still be breathing and I was back to thinking I should just bail out. The kids were good, they had me over for dinner damn near every night and Cindy kept wanting to take me on trips with her and Ken, but you had to think they were doing it out of a sense of duty and that only goes so far, at least in the funk I was in. You have to feel you deserve it. You need to feel you actually make someone appreciate you by your own efforts.

Then one day I woke up and decided to get on with the rest of my life. But I didn't start by going around the world. When you rebuild your life you start with sweeping the floor and watering the plants. You start from the bottom up. I started puttering around with Kay's old garden, which had overgrown to brambles, and I got the camellia and lilacs and rhododendrons blooming again. I took satisfaction from this, and started spending a lot of time on the yard, more time than I had ever spent while Kay was living. I built a trellis and got a nice clematis going up the garage, covering up the pile of plate glass salvaged ten years earlier from Beaver Lumber I still couldn't part with and soon I had the old place perking up a bit.

I had four acres there at one of the town's busier intersections and over the years I'd made use of it to store a lot of valuable stuff I didn't have immediate use for. I still had my good old loading donkey from Green Bay rusting away in the salal, as well as my old car collection. The main piece was my good 1956 Cadillac which Howie had rolled over the bank on his way home from Dick Gooldrup's stag party in 1970, and which I intended to get running again one of those days.

Then there was my Corvair collection. I bought my first Corvair sometime in the early seventies, mainly because it was so cheap. GM had pulled them off the market in 1969 after Ralph Nader killed demand by claiming they were unsafe and you could get a fairly new one for a couple hundred bucks. I found it a good little car, and started picking up any I saw around going cheap for backup and spare parts. I ended up with seven altogether

I think, all of which were now parked around the property waiting for me to have time to fix them up.

I also had a couple of good non-working trucks stashed around the place including the cab off the old Clark logging truck from Green Bay and my great old water board truck, a former BC Tel boom truck that I had bought for $600 after the boom had been removed. It looked a bit funny, especially as the previous owner had painted it bright yellow, but it was a lot of truck for $600. The back was all fitted out with tool cabinets and parts bins which were handy for packing waterworks fittings and I used it as my daily driver until the motor went.

Then there was the *Flash* aka *Marilyn Kay*, the dream boat I had built with my own hands back in Green Bay. It truly was a great boat with only one fatal flaw, namely its owner could never bring himself to take time off to make use of it. I had long cherished dreams of cruising up and down the coast with Kay and the kids but now Kay was gone, the kids had boats of their own and the poor old *Flash* aka *Marilyn Kay* had sat on blocks so many years the topsides had all gone rotten.

There was also a fair selection of salvaged building materials piled around the place, waiting for me to get time to build more buildings on the various bits of property I had accumulated over the years.

All this stuff represented a lot of potential to my way of thinking but I was disappointed to learn a lot of the passersby, which there were more of each year, viewed it as an unsightly junkyard. At one time there were a lot of guys like me with fine collections of old logging and fishing gear in their yards but as Pender Harbour progressed into the modern age and city people began moving in and planting lawns, the rusty equipment began disappearing. I was one of the last holdouts and I started to get a lot of flak from uninformed types who didn't understand local history.

Now that I was getting the beautification bug myself I began relinquishing a few of the less promising candidates for revival like the old donkey and the boom truck. A collector came along and made me an offer I couldn't refuse for the Cadillac and Donnie hauled all the Corvairs away when I wasn't looking, which I'm still mad about. The toughest one was the old boat. It was the number one eyesore and it was too far gone to ever be fixed, but it just about killed me to drop the backhoe bucket on it. It wasn't smashing up the boat that hurt as much as giving up the dream. But it was also liberating to get out from under all the unfinished business and all those old stillborn schemes that junk pile represented, and I had to agree—the place did look a lot better. People driving by would yell encouragement and give me the thumbs-up and it really began to feel as if I was starting a new life.

I'd been watching with fascination the coming of the personal computer and clipped a coupon from *Popular Electronics* to get one of the very first kits, known as the Sinclair ZX80. It was too basic to be of much practical use, but you could see this idea was going to go somewhere and I kept up on developments through *Popular Mechanics* and *Popular Electronics*. Marilyn's two sons Douglas and David were both very technically inclined and we played around with computer stuff together. David was a bit over-active and unmanageable, but a whiz at anything technical. When the first IBM PC came out he and I put our heads together and built our own souped-up version using mail-order components. It worked well enough that Howie bought it for his publishing business, so we built a couple more. Everybody was terribly impressed by this, the sixty-five-year-old grandfather and the twelve-year-old kid building computers, and we took full credit, but of course we were just following simple plans. We didn't understand how the thing worked. At least I didn't. David just might have.

We probably could have gone into production and got a jump on the no-name PC boom that followed in the next decade, but we weren't set up for it. Still, it was a bright spot in the gloom and great fun to get together with my two grandsons. I gave them one of the computers to take home and they were banging it around and modifying it for years. Both of them went on to careers in electronics, Doug as a computer scientist and David as an electrical engineer. I always felt good about both of those boys. We had a genuine friendship that buoyed me on dark days.

Then I did something I'd thought about a dozen times but never got beyond the thinking stage, and that is, I phoned up the kids and invited them over for dinner. I had been eating off them for months but never had them in for more than a coffee on their way by. Don had rented a place with a local girl he'd been going with for a long time, Crystal Cummings,

Bill Milligan, myself and Jason admiring some of my precious junk sometime in the 1980s. Milligan had only 2 percent vision but liked to do things like hire out as a danger tree faller.

and Howie and Mary had bought a little house out on the end of Francis Peninsula by this time. I think I also invited Bill Milligan and his wife Mary. Bill was 98 percent blind but refused to let it slow him down, working as a carpenter, a deep sea sailor, an upholsterer and danger-tree faller, just to begin a long list. He was a great character and good company, although he tended to break things when he got a few drinks in him. Once I got launched on the project, I really got into it and cooked up a big stew with cornbread and a clean tablecloth and all the trimmings. They were a bit leery at first just because this was such a new thing, I don't think I'd ever cooked a meal at home in all the time they'd been growing up. Milligan claimed he'd seen me stirring the stew pot with a crescent wrench, which was a damn lie. I can never find my crescent wrench when I need it. But we had a great time, the stew was a hit and they all congratulated me to beat hell. This was the beginning.

A few days later I really stuck my neck out and put a dinner on for one of the few single women I knew, Dawn McKim. She'd been a teacher at the high school and had always seemed friendly when I fixed her muffler, so I thought what the hell. We got on well and took to taking in the odd event. She was a bright, cheerful thing who always welcomed a chance to get out of the house but didn't have any great expectations beyond companionship, so we got along fine.

One day I heard that Mount St. Helen's was erupting so I phoned her and said, "How'd you like to go down and take a closer look at that?" "Let's just do that!" she said. Dawn was partially disabled due to childhood polio but she tried not to let it slow her down. I had an old 1969 Cadillac so we jumped in that and headed south. We crossed the border about two in the afternoon and the sky was dark with ash. You could see the huge mushroom cloud rising up 60,000 feet. Just a huge pillar of boiling muck going up, you couldn't even see the top of it.

What I didn't know is that the mountain had blown again that day, May 18, 1980. This was the main blast that tore the top off the mountain and they'd started evacuating the whole area. As we got closer the air was so thick with ash I had to keep the windshield wipers going on high and stop every ten miles to refill the washer tank with ditch water, we were using so much fluid. The freeway was solid traffic coming toward us but only a few cars going south. When we got off on the Spirit Lake Road, both lanes were coming at us and we had to bump along on the shoulder. The river was raging along at flood levels and full of uprooted trees. We kept bumping along dodging traffic and suffering the stares and yells of the fleeing traffic until we got to a little town where they had the road closed so we parked and started looking for a bite to eat. The sky was dark and people were throwing their worldly possessions into cars and others were battening down to wait it out.

There was a real end-of-the-world feeling in the air. I remember seeing one old lady whose only concern seemed to be to keep the ash-fall from covering her flowers and was standing out in the apocalyptic deluge with a water hose, spraying off her posies over and over. Amazingly, the café was still operating so we had a little break before turning around and heading home. We never saw the mountain because the visibility was so bad but we felt we'd got to the heart of the matter. Dawn took it all in and thanked me for giving her the experience of a lifetime. She was a good sport and I could have stood to see a lot more of her if events hadn't conspired otherwise.

With Howie and Donnie around I didn't have to worry about leaving the waterworks, they could run it as good as I could, so when I read that

Greyhound was rewarding Canadians for rescuing their Iranian diplomats in 1980 by offering a special deal, I decided to take them up on it. This was the deal where you could ride Greyhound buses for ninety-nine days for $99. Go anywhere you want in the US. I spent about a month on the road and had a fantastic trip. I finally got to see all the places my father told me about in the 1920s including the Brooklyn Bridge, which he walked across when it was newly opened. It's still a damned impressive structure.

Howie had made me promise that when I was in New York I'd look up a friend of his. This woman actually lived part of the year in Pender Harbour, where she had been married to a guy I knew well, a fisherman named John Daly. She was a big-name writer and I wasn't too keen about it but she'd lost John at almost the same time I'd lost Kay and I guess Howie figured that might give us something in common. I wasn't convinced, but when I got to New York I didn't have anything else to do so I called her up. Howie had been priming her apparently and she seemed excited to get the call. She wanted to know everything—where I'd been, where I was staying, how long I was staying, what I planned to do in New York, what I had been doing all my life, what I thought of Ronald Reagan and a lot of other things. I'd been afraid she'd be too highfalutin and I'd feel uncomfortable but that didn't seem to be an issue. I didn't know it then, but she had a world-class talent for putting people at ease and getting them to talk. She wouldn't have it but that I should come over to her apartment for lunch the very next day and I had no trouble agreeing.

Her name was Edith Iglauer.

Part 3

THE LUCKIEST GUY
IN
PENDER HARBOUR

FISHING
WITH JOHN

18

Hurricane Edie

So began the next chapter of my life, the final chapter.

I took a cab from the men's hostel where I was staying down in the Lower East Side to the address she gave me on the Upper East Side and found myself standing in front of what looked like a mansion confronted by a doorman who looked quite ready to give me the bum's rush until I gave him Edith's name. He took me over to the elevator which was one of the old ones with a lattice door and a big brass handle which he showed me how to use, saying it could be a bit cranky. There was some sort of problem not getting it to stop exactly even with the floor you were going to, in which case the steel lattice door wouldn't open. I told him I was an old donkey puncher and used to haywire equipment and he grinned and said, "That's cool man, maybe we git you to come here and fix it for us next time it git stuck fulla screamin old ladies."

Apart from the wonky elevator, which must have been original equipment, the place was palatial, with marble, Persian carpet and chandeliers everywhere. According to Edith it actually had been the mansion of the newspaper magnate Joseph Pulitzer and was now divided up into plush apartments that I thought must be costing her a fortune to rent but I later found out wasn't much more than a walk-up flat down in the cheap area where I was, due to some kind of rent control. I felt totally out of place and was wishing I hadn't listened to Howie and kept to my own low-rent part of town but once again, Edith greeted me like a long-lost

Edith Iglauer in the 1980s. She struck our coast like a hurricane and we were all better for it.

friend and soon had me so at ease I was telling her things about myself I'd never even told my kids. I don't suppose I could have told you after that first meeting what she looked like because her personality was so high-octane you didn't pay much attention to her looks, but she was very striking. She was small and curvaceous with a halo of luminous white hair and a good Jewish nose in a face that didn't seem like it should be attractive, but somehow was. Anyway, it was so mobile you didn't have much of a chance to study it.

She had worked off and on as a reporter and has the damndest talent for getting people to talk you ever saw. Her number one tactic is that she acts dumb. She doesn't mind pretending she's the only one in the room who doesn't understand what people are talking about. She feels comfortable in that role. It's her cover, and no matter how great her reputation, it's amazing how the utterance of one dumb question can get everybody trying to explain things to her. She doesn't let on what she might know about you but appears to want to know everything. She gives you the feeling that you and your personal story are the most interesting, amazing things she has ever come across. It's hard not to explain things to a sweet, dumb-seeming lady who appears in such desperate need of information only you have.

She has great personal warmth. Her personality surrounds you like a warm shower and makes you want to reveal your soul's intimate thoughts. Then next thing you're reading about your innermost thoughts in print and realizing you got worked over by a pro. She had recently filled half an issue of *The New Yorker* magazine with a long, intimate portrait of Canadian Prime Minister Pierre Elliott Trudeau, which revealed things about his private life other journalists are still feeding off. I felt reasonably safe from similar treatment.

Howie had given me quite a pep talk about New York. He said I should go all out and see all the sights and forget about the cost because it might be the only time I ever had the chance. The first time he went there he had cheaped out and then when he got back home he felt like a damn fool because he hadn't climbed the Statue of Liberty, he hadn't gone to the Museum of Natural History, he hadn't gone up the Empire State Building and it was like he hadn't been there at all. He said I should offer to take Edith to the Metropolitan Opera because she loved opera but never went on her own.

So when Edith asked me what I particularly wanted to see I said, "the opera." I had never been to the opera in my life and had only vague impressions of what it was, all bad. I'd never been much for listening to music and ever since Dr. Turnbull had switched me over to mono it all sounded a bit tinny. But Edith was delighted and started asking me all sorts of questions about which operas I liked the most. I had to admit I didn't know the first thing about it but claimed it had been one of my life's ambitions to go to New York and see an opera, possibly the most bald-faced lie I ever told. She swallowed it and has often been heard to say, "When I first met Frank, he was just desperate to go to the opera. He just loves opera!"

Actually, I was pleasantly surprised. I still can't tell you what opera we saw or who was in it but instead of hating it like I expected I thoroughly enjoyed it. I couldn't hear the words and have no idea what it was about but was quite blown away by the whole spectacle, the fancy staircase, the big chandelier, the ushers' uniforms, the curtain with its rippling colours, the spectacular sets, the soft seats, the fancy people in the crowd, the loud noise and just the fact of being there in New York, me, still going, still finding new things in this old world, as if my life itself was an opera. When we went out into the surging, roaring streets of the city it was snowing. I spread my arms and looked up at the falling flakes and the huge buildings disappearing out of sight with the music still going on in my head. The words of old Omar came to me:

Ah, fill the Cup—what means it to repeat
How Time is slipping underneath our feet

Unborn to-morrow, and dead yesterday
Why fret about them if to-day be sweet

"That's wonderful," she said. "I would never have guessed you knew Shakespeare."

I said that if she looked up and just concentrated on the falling flakes it would feel like she was floating up into the sky. Apparently she had never tried this, and we both stood there in front of the Lincoln Center with our arms spread out laughing and floating up into the sky. In New York, nobody cares what you do.

"All this, just for me," I said, having no idea why I said it but feeling about as good as I'd felt in fifty years.

She said I looked ecstatic. I think that was a good thing.

When we both found ourselves back in Pender Harbour, Edith started inviting me over to dinner. She had met John Daly in the course of doing a story for *The New Yorker* in 1968 and gave up her life in New York to marry him. Well, she didn't give it up completely. She kept her apartment

Edith at the Daly homestead in 1976.

and went back for the winter months. He hated big cities and hated "Ameriker" as he pronounced it and since he was away fishing from April to September they didn't actually see that much of each other. And they had only seven or eight years of this before he had a heart attack and died in 1978, only a few months before Kay died. The shortness of their time together didn't seem to in any way diminish her feeling of loss and she would mourn him with increasing devotion for the rest of her days. Not that she was a lonely widow stuck out in the wilds of Canada. She was a social dynamo who had made more friends during her short stay in Pender Harbour than I did over a lifetime. She felt things were slow if she didn't have company twice a week and didn't go out somewhere else on one or two of the remaining days. Her family called her Hurricane Edie, partly in recognition of her nonstop energy, partly in honour of something else I would come to know better—her force-ten personality.

Canadians—and Americans—got to experience the full blast of Hurricane Edie when the Seattle Yacht Club tried to expand its dock next to the John Daly homestead. In the post-war salad days when every truck driver in Vancouver was able to afford his own little day-cruiser, a lot of marinas sprang up in Pender Harbour since all the small boats needed shore facilities where they could get fuel and fresh food a day's cruising distance out of town. Every Pender Harbour fisherman and motel man with good waterfront was setting up in business as a marina, including the people that owned the dock next door to the Daly property.

Then Reaganism came in, truck drivers lost their disposable income as well as their leisure time, and only doctors, lawyers and stockbrokers could afford to go boating. Their boats were bigger, faster and better equipped and could make it up to Lund on their first day, so a lot of the marinas in Pender started to fold or go private. The one next door to Edith was sold to the Seattle Yacht Club for their members' private use as an outstation. When she was away for her annual New York stay one winter they expanded their dock system enormously, cutting off legal access to John Daly's old fishboat wharf, which no longer had any fishboat tied to it but which Edith saw as key to part of the fishing heritage she was there to protect.

Edith was outraged, and demanded local authorities do something.

Pender Harbour had no local authorities except the Chamber of Commerce, and they were all for the expanded yacht club. When she argued docking so many yachts in her confined bay would pollute the water (this was before holding tanks) the chamber's spokesman, Tom Barker, said something to the effect that a little poop in the water wouldn't hurt anybody. Edith seized on this, and the poor man had to suffer the rest of his days being referred to by her as "Poopy" Barker.

Most people around the Harbour sympathized with her problem but thought she might as well accept it as a done deal. The yacht club had put in heavy-duty concrete floats anchored by a forest of new creosote pilings, and the whole installation seemed as immovable as the Rock of Gibraltar. The Seattle Yacht Club had some of the wealthiest and most influential people in the US among its members and navigable waters were under the federal Coast Guard, which was known then and now as one of the most rock-ribbed bureaucracies in Canada. Edith battered down their defences enough to get at an official named Herb Adrian who tried to humour her by saying she shouldn't worry about the yacht club's water lease obstructing hers because leases were just "imaginary lines." I think he probably lived to regret saying that.

Seeing that government wasn't going to do its job, Hurricane Edie fired up her typewriter. Over the next four months, the yacht club and Coast Guard were buffeted with such a storm-surge of articles and letters and broadcasts and phone calls from worried cabinet ministers they didn't know what hit them. She used her old connections in the US media to bombard the yacht club on their home turf with headlines like "Expatriate American Ashamed of Her Country" and she saturated Canadian media with a barrage of stories screaming, "Canadian Government Sells Out Rights of Own Citizens to Foreign Interests." By fall Pender Harbour was witness to a spectacle never before seen in its history: that of perfectly good creosote pilings being rooted out and hauled away. The yacht club outstation was cut back to where it no longer encroached on the John Daly Memorial Water Lease and has never been allowed to expand beyond that in the years since. As for imaginary lines, Edith had Skinny Jimmy Dougan mark her lease boundary with a line of John's old fishing buoys, which those million-dollar yachts have been manoeuvring around and cursing ever since.

To this day officials up and down the West Coast snap to attention any time they hear the name Edith Iglauer. She simply says, "I thought I was being taken advantage of and I don't like being taken advantage of."

Edith's dinner invitations came thick and fast. If I tried to beg off she would demand to know why. Then she would press two or three more times, saying she really wanted to see me. So I'd go, but there would be five other people there, often including one or two other unattached males. You never knew who you would meet there. Sometimes it was an old fisherman or logger from Port Hardy. Other times it was some famous artist or politician you'd been reading about in the papers for years. Or a philosophy professor from Columbia University or a justice of the US federal court.

It took me a long time to figure out if I was anything special or just part of a team. All of these people would be introduced as Edith's dear, dear friends. She would frequently declare she "just loved" each and every one of them. She also frequently declared she "just loved" me but it was a distinction I had to share with every old boat bum and bush bunny who had ever been friends with her late husband John, not to mention my old tabby cat Lionel, so it was hard to know just what she meant by it. I found it hard to believe a woman with as much going on as she had would see anything in me—although she had been married to John Daly and he tied his glasses on with cod line, so that gave me hope.

For the first few years we went together I was still holding down my job at the waterworks but it was getting harder all the time. My knees were shot so I got them replaced but the doctors didn't do a proper job of it. They wanted to do one side at a time but that would have put me out of service for months so I said the hell with it, do them both at once and get it over with. I think that would have worked out okay except the surgeon did the port side himself then let his understudy try his hand at the starboard side and the apprentice didn't get the fit as tight as he should have. It left me knock-kneed.

I was relying on Donnie more and more to do the heavy stuff and having a tough time of it so one day we came up with the idea of contracting the job to Donnie's company, Indian Isle Construction, with me staying on as advisor. The board didn't like the idea of contracting to a company instead of a man but this gave them a way to get new young muscle without losing all the knowledge locked up in my ancient skull so they went for it. In truth Don was pretty well versed by this time and didn't need much help from me, so at age seventy-six I found myself waking up in the morning with no job to go to for the first time since I was twelve.

19

Around the World

Cindy had built a pretty good life for herself in Prince George with Ken Carling, her second husband—or partner, since they never got officially married—and they had been after me to go on a big trip around the world with them for some time. By 1982 I had run out of excuses, so off we went. They were expert travellers who went on a big trip somewhere every year, often to a scuba-diving destination. Prior to the Alaska trip with Donnie, my biggest trip had been to Washington State, first on our honeymoon then again in Howie Smith's Cadillac. I'd never been off the ground, except in a bush plane. I was a travel virgin.

We took off in mid-December and got back in mid-February. We did a couple days in London then flew to Nairobi, Kenya. We went on a bunch of safaris, spent a few days at the coast in Mombasa then went via the Seychelles to India then Thailand then Hong Kong, China and Japan. That first trip changed my thinking about a lot of things. Well, about the world mostly. It was both bigger and smaller than I thought. Smaller because here we were, we'd circumnavigated it in six weeks. You realize the actual distances are not that great, at least the way we travel today. But when you get out there you find worlds within worlds, huge cities you've never heard of, deserts and jungles so vast you couldn't cross them in a lifetime, ways of life so goddamn weird they boggle the mind. And yet on another level, people everywhere are the same. The sight of a baby makes them smile, a big butt makes them laugh, a favour makes them grateful, a bad turn makes them mad, exactly the same as in Pender Harbour.

Travelling with Ken and Cindy was a little trying on both sides. Ken was an accountant with the BC Buildings Corporation who'd been to every one of these places numerous times. He had very set ideas about what was worth doing and that mostly related to exotic restaurants and big tourist destinations like the Serengeti and the Taj Mahal. His main concern was getting proper treatment by officials, waiters and hotel staff and he was constantly arguing with them. He was forever haggling—with cabbies, with bellhops, and with souvenir sellers. He was a collector of African art and never went past a street stall without stopping to see what they had. Most of it he pronounced "garbage" and "fake" but if he saw anything half decent he'd start haggling to see how far he could beat these poor bastards down. He'd get them down almost to nothing and then walk away laughing.

Sometimes I'd buy something without haggling and he'd give me hell, saying I'd been played for a sucker. I didn't care, the damn stuff was so cheap anyway and you could see these poor bastards selling it were practically starving, but he cautioned me I should respect the local economic processes or it would throw everything out of whack, which somehow didn't prevent us from staying in fancy hotels and eating at expensive restaurants that charged more for one meal than a local family spent on food in a month. I overpaid and over-tipped every chance I got.

I was fascinated by everything I saw. Ken and Cindy slept on the plane and I was tired enough but I didn't want to miss anything. I sat in the window seat with my eyes glued to the scene unfolding below. I remember the thrill I felt when the Sahara began to spread under us and when Nile drainage or Mount Kilimanjaro hove into view. I couldn't believe I was finally seeing this stuff for real after ogling it for so many years in *National Geographic*.

I always woke up at six in the morning and knew Cindy and Ken wouldn't be up until 10:30 then we'd go out to see some sight. They booked various guided tours and sometimes we'd go out for days at a time. The goal was to see as many animals as you could and check them off a list the safari people handed out. Ken had a life list he was working on, trying to add to everything he'd seen on earlier trips. On one of our trips we spotted a small cheetah you could hardly make out sitting in a tree and that was the first time he'd ever seen a cheetah, my god, it made the whole trip for him. We'd see the odd giraffe or gazelle but they're not just standing around in big herds like in the films and we spent a lot of time banging along over dusty goat paths not seeing anything. Cindy was bound and determined to see elephants but that was one thing we never did see. I was intrigued just by the vegetation. Those big baobab trees are something to see. The older ones get hollow and they use them for homes and even barns.

We ventured into Tanzania on one multi-day trip and got stuck in a country hotel there that had hole-in-the-floor toilets, my god, you'd think it was the end of the world to hear Ken. They refused to stay there and we kept going dog-tired late into the night to find a slightly better place. I was pretty disgusted with them over that and decided to go on my own as much as possible, even though they didn't like to lose sight of me. We spent damn near three weeks there altogether and must have taken every safari going. We crisscrossed the Serengeti, got into the Ngorongoro Crater and in the end saw just about every type of African animal you ever heard of plus some I hadn't, although you didn't always see them very close or very clearly.

We went past Mount Kilimanjaro, reputedly the biggest free-standing mountain in the world although I had to wonder if the people who said that had ever been to Mount McKinley. Kilimanjaro is certainly a lot barer, with just the small crown of white on the very top. One of the high points for me was the Olduvai Gorge where the Leakeys discovered the first hominids and the Leakey Foundation still carries on research. I'd read about their work and found it very exciting to be there standing on the very ground where humanity was born. If you want to talk about a place that feels historic, there's nothing to touch that place. At least for me. When I thought about those little man-monkeys making the first tools

Because of the way it rears up out of the African plain with nothing else around, Mount Kilimanjaro dominates the view for miles in every direction. It reminded me of Mount McKinley that way.

and the Leakeys' long struggle to uncover their story, I got so choked up I could hardly speak, but the others I think found it boring, a dry gulch with an obscure science project in it. The more I travelled the more I came to realize what you get from a place depends on what you bring to it.

Back in Nairobi I got in the habit of going out early and walking the streets by myself until noon. I loved being able to just follow my own nose, check out anything that caught my eye. I'd go around and get talking to the guys working on the streets or the women bussing tables and see what I could find out. After our first short stay in Nairobi we went down to Mombasa on the coast. Ken had been crowing about this place the whole trip, saying there was no city like Mombasa but it was so damned hot I could hardly breathe. It was like a steam bath and my skin just crackled in that overproof tropical sun. I was relieved when they decided to go back to Nairobi, which was higher and cooler.

We were staying in a pretty fair hotel called the Fairview with a big swimming pool and I needed to get some laundry done so the hotel staff sent a girl up to my room and I got talking to her. She was from the Maasai tribe, tall, regal and jet black. I couldn't take my eyes off her, she was so strangely attractive and the weightless way she moved was like a cheetah or a lynx. I was only going to give her some underwear and socks but she looked at the clothes I was wearing and pointed out the food stains on the front and said I better give her that, too. I got out my pack and tried to find something better but she just laughed and took it all, leaving me one pair of shorts and a t-shirt. I was kind of worried, but a very short time later she was back with everything perfectly pressed and folded, and she put it all neatly away for me, laughing and teasing me about my messy habits. I was worried about what all this was going to cost, thinking about Ken and his warnings to always settle prices beforehand, but when she told me and I converted it in my head it came to about $1.50 Canadian. I gave her $10.

She didn't want to take it but I pressed her and we got talking. She and her mother supported themselves by doing washing by hand at their little back-street hovel, and paid most of what they earned to the concierge for access to the hotel patrons. They also took in business from their house so I fixed it up to bring more laundry to them directly so they wouldn't have to pay the hotel. I had seen Cindy setting out a big bag of stuff and took this over to them the next morning. Actually the girl—her name was Elizabeth— was waiting for me around the corner from the hotel and escorted me over. She whisked the laundry bag out of my arms and plopped it on top of her head and walked along with it balanced there. She could twist around other pedestrians, skip out of the way of traffic, hop over potholes and the thing never shifted. It was amazing, like it was glued there.

They had a little mud-walled apartment with a tin roof in the slum area and they welcomed me like royalty. Her mother grabbed the laundry and set in on it while Elizabeth plied me with spiced tea and conversation. Elizabeth's marital status was unclear—if she had a husband, he wasn't around. There were numerous children but it wasn't clear whose they were. Elizabeth wanted to save enough money to go to an English school so she could become a hairdresser, although she admitted the chances were not good. She grilled me about Canada, about my family and my work. She was bright and vivacious and charming and I couldn't help thinking if she did ever get to Canada she could pretty much write her own ticket.

They couldn't do enough for me. I had got quite a burn already and it was starting to peel and the mother brought over some kind of homemade ointment which Elizabeth carefully applied all over my face, laughing and giggling and making fun of my beet-red pate. Then she stood back and fanned me with a palm leaf.

I was in love.

They wanted to know what I was doing, where I was going next, and I told them I was kind of at loose ends because Ken and Cindy were heading back to Mombasa to soak up sun and do some scuba diving and I had no desire to spend a week waiting around in that terrible heat.

"Stay here with us! We will look after you and show you the real Nairobi!" Elizabeth said. So I spent a week living in a mud hut in Nairobi with two lovely Maasai princesses who couldn't do enough for me. It was kind of like those stories you read about old-time sailors who wash up on some tropical island where they worship white men, only this was Kibera, the largest urban slum in Africa. I guess most people would have been put off by the lack of first-class amenities and privacy, but you had to admire how clean it all was and what a well-ordered life they lived amid all that squalor. They bought water in jerry cans and bought food at the big outdoor market and cooked over charcoal. Plumbing was deluxe—you had your very own private bucket that was always empty and clean.

They prepared a feast every night, lots of fruit and meat, all done their way. I tried to give them a hundred shillings—about a single day's cost at the Fairview—and they were overwhelmed. They would only take ten, although I got Elizabeth to accept more when I left, for her education. In the daytime we went to all the parks and zoos in a hired rust bucket driven by a friend of theirs but for me the real show was Kibera, and the inside view I got of African life. At first you'd see all those shanties of rusty tin and mud and the open sewer and think, my god, this is the end of the earth, but it wasn't like a slum in our big cities, full of derelict people, it was a real going concern. The inhabitants were busy and full of life and doing most of the work of the city.

Everybody should have a few days of being treated like a god like I was for that week. Elizabeth was everything a man could dream of. She wanted me to marry her and bring her to Canada. "I love you until you die, White Man," she kept saying. "I take care of you when you old." I thought about it, too. I could just picture this six-foot Maasai princess carrying my groceries out of the Madeira Park IGA on her head. What would Granny Reid say? Or Edith Iglauer? Not that I was too worried about that. At that time I still didn't believe Edith had any real interest in me except as a member of the chorus. But I thought it would be unfair to Elizabeth to bring her to Canada and take advantage of her poverty, she'd be lost in a place like Pender Harbour. Or so I thought then. Now I am being pampered by a lovely Filipina girl whose situation isn't much different than Elizabeth's would have been, and she seems to be quite happy here. Things have changed a lot in thirty years. The Sunshine Coast was pretty white in those days and it was hard to imagine it ever changing.

After Africa we went to India. Bombay. Mumbai they call it now. I don't know why they keep changing all these names. In Bombay, English is the one language most people understand and when Indians were speaking English, they plainly said "Bombay." I bet millions of them still are.

Anyway, once we touched down in Bombay/Mumbai, Cindy and Ken as usual holed up in a good hotel and didn't get circulating until noon, then spent most of their time trying to decide where to go for dinner. I

Ken and Cindy in Bombay. I mean Mumbai.

got up at six and wandered the streets. Bombay was a lot bigger and wilder than Nairobi and you were set upon pretty well steady by people trying to sell you stuff or take you places. I would talk to them sometimes just to see what I could find out. They were an awful nuisance but they weren't at all threatening. There was this one fellow who wanted to clean your ears. He had a little gold spoon in a vial of bleach and he'd very delicately dig out your ear. I'd been meaning to get that done for years but nobody ever offered to tackle it back in Canada. It was a damn useful thing and only cost about five cents. There was every kind of a street performer. There was this one fellow who juggled babies. My god, he'd fling those kids around, it looked like their heads would fly off but they just giggled.

It was a real bugger to find your way around and there'd be a pedicab walla at every step offering to help. They were all such skinny, ragged, barefoot buggers I couldn't bear the thought of getting pedalled around by one of them, a guy as heavy as me, but I got so damn lost I had to hire one just to find my way back to the hotel. Oh Jesus, he'd duck in and out of traffic and go between buses, up on sidewalks, down stinking alleys, that was one of the scariest rides I ever took. I wondered if I'd ever be seen alive again, but he got me home in jig time. He was a chatty guy and wanted to sign up to be my regular ride so I made a deal with him to meet me the next morning. He was there bright and early and I hired him to show me the sights of Bombay. He was the best guide a man could ask for. He knew everything about the city, all the history, all the politics, all the seamy stuff and he was smart as a whip. And he called it Bombay, not Mumbai.

I still felt a bit guilty about sitting there like some fat rajah while this skinny bugger pedalled his guts out—he was no spring chicken, either, he looked to be in his fifties though it's hard to say, he might have only been in his thirties—so whenever he was having a hard pull I'd jump out and give him a push. He didn't know what to make of that at first and tried to talk me out of it, I think he thought it was a slight against his fitness, but once he got used to it he was happy as hell. I got him to take a break and have tea with me and he really opened up. If you'd seen a picture of this skinny little guy in his raggedy clothes and rubber-tire sandals you'd imagine some sort of wretch without the power of speech but I was amazed at what he knew. And not just about Bombay, or India. He knew all about

Canada. He admired our then-PM PierreTrudeau and was amused by his wife Margaret and her nutty antics with the Rolling Stones.

We became such good friends he invited me home to his place for dinner. That was quite an experience. He didn't even have a mud hovel. All he had was a piece of sidewalk. His wife and kids all wandered in from different directions and started setting up camp for the night on this eight-foot stretch of sidewalk. They had been there for years and everybody left it for them. They had mats and screens and bits of furniture all stashed in the surrounding neighbourhood and once they had it all set up it was surprisingly homey. They had some kind of a little barbecue burning cow dung or something—different members of the family brought different items they'd scrounged during the day and I'd given the man money to buy a chicken at the big market—a crazy place that was—and they turned out a damn fine meal. The man, I forget his name because it was too hard for me to say, Jawaharlal or some such thing, had a sideline going fixing other guys' pedicabs and guys started pulling up and leaving their machines to be repaired before the next day so I spent the evening helping him replace worn-out bearings with slightly less worn-out bearings, etc.

He was good, that guy. There wasn't a thing wrong with him or any of his family, either. They were very civilized, very intelligent people going through life and experiencing all the same ups and downs we do, living and dying on their little strip of sidewalk. I saw a boy from one of the other street families come over and start flirting with the daughter, and the same look came over the parents' faces that must have come over mine when I was worried about my daughters. The man could take a spoke wheel that was bent and smack it a few times and put all the spokes back in and tension them by hand until it was perfectly true, something it's damn hard to do even with the right instruments, and he'd do it all by eye as fast as you could watch. If I'd had a man like him working with me back at the gas station I might have made a go of it after all.

It was tough to say goodbye when Ken and Cindy decided to move on, and I left him a tip that he was embarrassed by and didn't want to accept, though it was only half a day's wages in Canada. I've been kicking myself ever since for being so damn cheap. I should have left him a month's wages and made a difference to their lives. I guess I was thinking about this when we were boarding our bus. As usual there were no end of crippled children and eyeless women begging that you were warned over and over again not to give anything to, except maybe the smallest denomination coin, so I reached in my pocket and slipped the blind woman a bill worth about $5. She thanked me and turned away while I went aboard and found Cindy and Ken.

I opened a window and looked out and it seemed to me there was something strange going on. There was a kind of rumble, and there were a lot more people around the bus than there had been a few minutes earlier. Soon the rumble became a roar, and there was a sea of people crushing around the bus, hollering and screaming and beating on the windows. I guess what had happened was the blind woman had shown somebody else the hundred rupees I'd given her and the word had spread like wildfire that there was some fool white man on this bus handing out huge amounts of money. Pretty soon they were rocking the bus and I thought my god, we are in real trouble here.

Luckily the blind woman couldn't identify me and nobody knew who the culprit was, but I shut the window and kept my head down just the same. It was scary. Ken was yelling, "Get this goddamn bus out of here!" but the driver couldn't move it without squashing bodies. There was real panic among the passengers. Next thing you know, there's a bunch of cops out there beating a path for the bus with billy clubs, smashing people over the head and kicking them out of the way. There was lots of blood. Eventually the bus was able to get free and we were safe. I didn't fess up, knowing what a dressing down I'd get from Ken, but I felt him eyeing me suspiciously, or imagined I did. That was one for his side of the argument.

Eventually we transferred to a train bound for Agra, 1,100 km inland. The main reason to go to Agra is to see India's number one tourist attraction, the Taj Mahal. It's a long, miserable train trip and I was wishing I'd begged off. I couldn't see going to all that trouble just to see another temple when there were fantastic, onion-roofed buildings covered in gold leaf everywhere you turned but I wasn't asked. Agra is just a sprawling village, although like a lot of Indian villages, it has over a million people. At least it was peaceful after the crush and noise of Bombay and as usual Ken and

Cindy booked us into a good hotel and disappeared into their room for the day. I was a big believer in pedicabs now and went out and found one right away the first morning. I picked one with an older driver and just like in Bombay, he turned out to be another top-notch guy. I liked to start the day by going to a McDonald's for coffee and an Egg McMuffin which drove Ken and Cindy crazy, they wouldn't be caught dead in a McDonald's in Canada let alone abroad, but there wasn't a McDonald's in Agra so the driver took me to a clean place where they served an English breakfast and let me buy him a cup of tea.

I told him I wanted to see the Taj Mahal and he shook his head. "Now is not the time," he said emphatically. "To see the Taj, it is best to go in thee early morning before thee sun rises and while thee mist is still rising from thee ground." He was so adamant about this I went along with him and let him take me to see the fort instead, which turned out to be quite an eyeful in its own right. That's one of the great things about a place like India. Everywhere you go, you're stumbling over some incredible sight you've never heard of before, and it gives it a kick you don't get from say, the Great Sphinx, which is only about twenty feet wide. If you stumbled across it in the woods you'd be impressed enough but you've heard so much about it being one of the wonders of the world you can't help feeling a bit underwhelmed by the size. Then there are other sights, that no matter how much you've heard about them or how many pictures you've seen, they are still so far beyond anything you imagined, seeing the real thing still blows your mind.

I arranged with my driver to meet before sunrise the next morning and sure enough, there he was waiting for me at the hotel entrance at 5:00 a.m. The bugger had slept there! He took me not to the Taj itself but to a hill nearby where he said I would have a good view of it, although it was foggy as well as being dark and I couldn't see a damn thing. He told me to sit and wait and he quietly moved off and left me alone.

I wondered what the hell kind of damn foolishness this was, but as the light began to increase I could see the spike on top of the dome sticking out of the mist. Then the points of the four minarets slowly emerged. The mist began to thin out and I could see the shadowy outline of the building. It shimmered and shifted as if in a dream, and it was a lot bigger than I

We had to take a train halfway across India to see the Taj Mahal and I wondered what all the fuss was about, but when I finally saw it emerge from the mist it took my breath away.

thought. Then slowly, slowly it began to get more solid and more real looking. I'm not much of a beauty guy, I'm more inclined to be impressed by engineering feats than artistic ones, but watching the Taj Mahal take shape in the morning mist was an experience on a whole different scale from anything I'd ever experienced. Just seeing that amazing structure materialize in the morning sunshine made a lump rise in your throat. Tears streamed down my face. I must have sat there for two hours, just shaking my head. Finally the driver came up to me. I realized he'd been standing back behind a tree, watching. He had tears on his face too.

"No matter how many times one views thee immortal splendour of the Taj, it never loses the power to move one," he said in the funny stiff way of talking they have there. I was almost afraid to go down for a closer look lest the spell be broken, but I needn't have worried. Every detail about that building seems better than you have any right to expect. The intricate carving and stonework inside is just unbelievable. There is some debate about how it all came to be, but the usual explanation is that it was built in 1648 by the Shah Jahan, the greatest of the Mogul emperors, as a memorial to his greatly beloved wife Mahal. Taj Mahal means Mahal's crown. Supposedly it took 20,000 workers twenty-two years to build but there are others who claim it was an existing Hindu palace Shah Jahan just reno'd. Seeing it, you can easily believe it was done out of love, especially the kind of love that hits a man after his wife has died.

Our next stop was Thailand. That was quite an eyeful too. Bangkok is like no other city. It's just go, go, go all the time. It's like Bombay that way but somehow even more frantic. It's just seething like a big anthill with motorbikes and Japanese cars scurrying around like bugs everywhere you look. It's all crisscrossed by canals which they call klongs and a lot of the traffic is by water—or was. They have been filling in the canals for a long time now as they convert from boats to cars but when we saw it there were still a lot in the poorer part of town. They had every type of watercraft you ever imagined, and lots you'd never think of. Tugs, barges, houseboats, water taxis, ferries, canoes.

Those big canoes were something to see. Some of them were actually dugouts I think but most of them were made of wide planks like an extra-long East Coast dory with kind of flat ends. For power they had the damndest setups, a regular car motor attached to a propeller and shaft but they hung it over the stern like a makeshift outboard and the skipper steered by swinging the whole assembly back and forth like a tiller. They call them longtails and some really flew along. Of course they didn't have mufflers so there was just this horrible din on these busy klongs, which were lined with old car tires for bumpers, just like the old-time BC fuel docks. In a lot of ways Thailand seemed more Western than the rest of Asia, kind of an East–West hybrid.

It's a Buddhist country but any thought you have of Buddhism being low-key and spiritual goes out the window pretty quick. They have one statue of the Buddha there made of solid gold—a big statue, weighing many tons. For sheer materialistic display the Buddhists put the Pope to shame. The temples are plastered with gold and jewels and the architecture is very swooping and garish, even compared to India, which is itself way more torqued-up than Western architecture. There didn't seem to be so many derelicts and down-and-outers begging at every turn. There were lots of people after you, but they all had something for you. It's like the whole city was one big bazaar. Food, sex, cigars, diamonds, booze, music, dancing.

Especially sex. Our hotel was overrun by tiny young girls eager to show foreign men the delights of the city. They were like little butterflies flitting around. They were doing most of their business with the Arabs. The hotel was full of big, boisterous boys in togas kicking up their heels, obviously happy to be a long way from home. One of them made Cindy's day by offering her forty dinars to go up to his room. After she'd expressed sufficient indignation and run the guy off, the only thing she wanted to know was how much a dinar was worth. "How much does that come to?" she said. "How much was he going to pay?" When she figured out it was only about $10 she was highly indignant.

"Why that cheap son of a bitch!" she fumed. "What did he take me for? I should have stomped on his toe!"

Poor Cyn.

After Thailand we went to Hong Kong, which was another surprise. It was a lot more Western even than Bangkok, so much so it wasn't like an Asian city at all. It's like Chicago or San Francisco had been picked up and dropped on a small island off the coast of China. It was completely and determinedly modern in a Western way. Of course this was fifteen years before the turnover, when it was still under British rule. Everybody there seemed to be more up to date than anybody in London or New York. You saw more of the latest gadgets and fashions for sale than in any Canadian city. Cindy said the level of spiffy dress made her feel so scruffy she went out and bought a new outfit, which made her look like a million bucks. I think she was still smarting at the low offer the Arab made her.

We stayed in a damn queer place, it wasn't a hotel really. It was hard to say what it was. It was called Chung King Mansions and it was this enormous complex covering four city blocks sixteen storeys high. It was like a little city unto itself. The bottom level was all shops, then there was a layer or two of offices, then up top there were apartments. We stayed in one of the apartments with an old lady who was running it as a bootleg B&B. You would see guys racing along the hallways in their pyjamas carrying a stack of video machines they were repairing in their bedroom, and a uniformed delivery man or two would be racing the other way and a wedding party would be getting into the elevator. Hustle and bustle everywhere. All the big Asian cities seemed to be on speed, and Hong Kong was the speediest of them all.

For me of course, Hong Kong was the place my brother Wesley died in a World War II POW camp and I spent some time trying to put together a picture of the World War II situation but there weren't many clues to go on. There were a few museums but they didn't really play up the war and the POW camps. Of course the places where the camps had been are all covered in high-rises now. What they have preserved are the cemeteries and I spent some time bumbling around in these but on that trip I didn't find the one where Wesley is, Sai Wan Military Cemetery. I did get there on a subsequent trip and the sight of his headstone completely undid me. I thought some day I would get over missing Wesley and hurting over his pointless death, but I guess it's not meant to be.

I wanted to get a look at mainland China and Cindy and Ken seemed to be content just to hang around Hong Kong so I bought a place on a three-day tour and set out on my own. I kind of thought China would be

Standing by my brother Wesley's grave in Hong Kong.

bright and colourful like India only more refined but it was the opposite. It was a tough place then, very colourless and grey and kind of brutal. After the flashy clothes in Hong Kong it was a real contrast to go to a place so close by where everybody was wearing denim coveralls. This was before the economic revolution that has since turned it into the new Japan and while it was still shaking off the after-effects of the Cultural Revolution. Travel was restricted to approved areas and you were accompanied everywhere by a guide-translator who was more concerned about keeping you from seeing things than the other way around.

A lot of the people on the tour were completely turned off and couldn't wait to get back to Hong Kong and have a decent meal. The food, like everything else, was bleak and basic. But you could see how hard they were trying, and how differently they were going at their recovery than India or Thailand. Everything had a plan and everything was being done for all the people and all of China—big dams, big highway systems, massive new infrastructure. The level of life was pretty low but everybody had a job and a basic income. And everywhere we went, the people would cluster around us and look at our clothing, our cameras, our stuff. They were very friendly and very eager to try out the few English words they'd been learning in night school.

One fellow came up with a big smile and said, "Hello!" We all said "hello" back. He grinned fit to bust, and tried it again, "Hello!" He followed us for half an hour, saying it over and over till we would have been happy to have our guide shoot him. But that was the spirit; they were just waking up to what the West was and what it had and they were all working on a master plan to get it. You could see this was going to be something to contend with in the pretty near future.

We made a short stopover in Japan on the way home, just enough to get a glimpse into what was going on there, which was a mixture of Asian vitality and Western technology brought to its highest peak; a country with all the frantic human swirl of India and Thailand but none of the disorganization, mess or poverty. It had the hottest economy on the planet at that time and was basically calling the tune in global finance, the ascendant power. You could feel it. It was similar to China in that every individual seemed to be dedicated to the country's success, but whereas in China it was enforced by top-down communist discipline, in Japan it was some sort of nationalistic zeal that was just there in the eyes of the people. Japan has since lost a lot of its momentum but you can never count it out because of that innate sense of national purpose it has.

Japan at that time was not very tourist friendly. It was entirely consumed with doing its own thing and nothing much was put on specially for foreigners. You felt in the way more than anything. At least that time. Edith and I went back ten years later and stayed with friends who showed us a different side.

After that first trip, I started going somewhere two or three times a year. I went so many places I can't remember them all. I went all over the US and Mexico, I went to Cuba twice with Cindy, I went to South America, I went back to Africa, all over Europe, across Siberia and through China and Japan but that first trip with Cindy and Ken made the strongest impression. It taught me once and for all what a small, isolated corner of the planet I had spent my life in and how much more there is to this world than the world we know in North America. And yet I came back convinced that even though there is more variety and difference than we ever dreamt of, there is really no such thing as "foreign." They're all just people like us under the skin. There's not one of those people in the slums of Nairobi or the streets of Bombay who couldn't come over here and within a few years be talking on an iPhone, wearing blue jeans, driving a big car, rooting for the Canucks and sending their kids to college, if given the chance.

And they all want the chance. Of course they do. To them this really is a place where the streets are paved with gold. It's better than that for them, it has plentiful food, freedom from disease, freedom from overwork and—freedom. That's the real thing I came back with. Just how much we have, without even realizing it. And how damned unfair that is. And how everybody knows it, except us. Once you've seen it, you know it's a situation that can't last. There will be a levelling, whether it's done the Japanese way, the Chinese way or the Al Qaeda way.

20

Septuagenarian Tomcat

I wasn't back in Pender an hour before Edith was on the phone wanting me over. She was back from her own winter stay in New York and was finding things in Garden Bay slow. I was a kind of fallback it seemed. Her other friends weren't always available, but I always was. She said she wanted to hear all about my trip but she got bored before we got halfway through my photos and took a break to phone her son Jay. Jay was in his thirties but often phoned several times a day and told her everything he was doing and they got into the most godawful red-faced arguments right there in front of you. It would go on for an hour and they'd hang up mad then ten minutes later they'd be back at it. She had a younger son who you seldom saw and was quite successful in the theatre back east but Jay at that time was drifting around trying to figure out what to do with himself.

Worrying about him took up a lot of Edith's time. He seemed lost to me but that didn't stop him from trying to set me straight every chance he got. If you told him you were going out to cut wood he'd say, "I certainly hope you're not going to cut down any trees. Trees are needed to purify the air we breathe. You do know that, don't you?" Jay did get his act together—eventually. He found a lovely English girl with similar beliefs to himself, raised a fine son, found his niche running a small theatre company in Vancouver and made his mother very happy.

Somehow we both decided to take a public speaking course in Sechelt and once a week we drove down together and put ourselves through this. She hadn't had to do much public speaking in the States where she wasn't a big name but since she moved to Canada she'd become quite a celebrity. Being connected to *The New Yorker* even in a part-time way was pretty heady stuff among Canadian book lovers and she was getting invited to do appearances at libraries and colleges the odd time, which scared the hell out of her. They say when you're born your brain is fully functioning and it keeps functioning every day of your life until you find yourself in front of a microphone. I had done a lot of standing up to talk at town hall meetings but I always made a damn bollocks of it. My thoughts would be clear until I stood up but then I just couldn't come out with the right words. I'd stammer and stutter and make a fool of myself while other guys who hadn't a clue would rattle off some phony nonsense and carry the day.

When I saw this course being offered I decided to see if I couldn't smarten up my delivery a little and Edith went for it too. So once a week we'd carpool at the Medical Clinic and drive the thirty miles to Sechelt together and go through this ordeal where we both struggled, but slowly got better. She was very encouraging. She's really wonderful that way, she goes all out to build up those around her. She thought my speech ideas were wonderful, though I'm not a bit sure they were. She did better than me, I think. She had this way of seeming vulnerable and little-girl inno-cent, it got the audience on her side every time. It was good fun in the end and it brought us closer together. Who is it that said love is 10 percent compatibility and 90 percent proximity? There's a lot to that.

It would be hard to imagine two less compatible people on the face of things. Her father had been a department store executive in Cleveland and she and her sister Jane used to be taken to school in a chauffeured limousine. They bribed the chauffeur to stop around the block so they could get out and appear to be walking to school like ordinary kids. She had gone to Wellesley, which I had only vaguely heard of but I now know is one of the top women's colleges in the US. Then she took her master's in journalism at Columbia University in New York and married another Columbia student, Phillip Hamburger. She became a war correspondent in the last days of World War II, where she and Phil were the first Western journalists in Yugoslavia after liberation.

Back in New York, Phil got hired on by *The New Yorker* magazine which was going great guns with James Thurber, E.B. White, A.J. Liebling, Harold Ross and that whole bunch, who Edith had over to their apartment for dinner and drinking sessions on a regular basis. I had managed to get through my life without ever picking up a copy of *The New Yorker* and had never heard of the Algonquin Round Table but since teaming up with Edith I've come to realize what a big deal it is for a lot of people. Edith was only a fringe member of the group, the wife of one of its lesser lights, but we have had people come rushing up to us in Tiananmen Square and go all gushy about her.

Actually she had a real hard time finding a place for herself on *The New Yorker*, which was a bit of an old boys' club—with some old girls too—and ended up sort of specializing in Canada by default because nobody else had any interest in it. She wrote some early articles about Eskimo art, a book about the Eskimo cooperative movement, a book about a guy who built early ice roads across the north, and the long article about Trudeau. Her total *New Yorker* output wasn't all that large—it fits into one book, *The Strangers Next Door*, which Howie and Mary published in later years. Most of what she wrote went over pretty big from what I can tell, but Phil got his nose out of joint every time she started to get serious attention and she figured he fixed things up behind the scenes so she didn't get very far up the ladder. She never did get on regular magazine staff.

The *New Yorker* bunch were all heavy boozers and Phil Hamburger developed a bad drinking problem that Edith finally got enough of, so one day around 1960 she flew down to Mexico and got a quickie divorce. She just walked into the courthouse, paid her money, and walked out single. I wouldn't have thought that could work, or why else would everybody go through all these godawful drawn-out lawsuits where the lawyers get half the money, but apparently it was legal and final and that's all there was to it. Maybe it only works if the other party doesn't contest it, I don't know. There's got to be some reason everybody doesn't just do it that way. Anyway, there she was in her mid-forties at loose ends on the face of the earth.

Most of her New York friends sided with Phil, who was still a name around town, and stopped asking her over so she started looking for a different place to live. She got the magazine to send her out to the West Coast, a part of Canada she hadn't written about previously, and she started doing the good reporter thing and going around meeting people. You'd have to see her in action to believe it. She bird-dogged every big name in Vancouver. After about a year, her list of friends read like a who's who of BC: Jack Shadbolt, Gordon Smith and Bill Reid the artists; Arthur Erickson the architect; Paul St. Pierre and Allan Fotheringham the writers; Gordon Gibson and Pat Carney the politicians; all sorts of millionaires and at least one billionaire—it was incredible. She just seemed to take it as normal to be with celebrities and start speaking as an equal and they welcomed her in places where I'd be sent around to the service entrance.

I couldn't do that in a million years and neither could anybody else I ever knew. I wouldn't expect to or want to. We like to think there's no class system in Canada but there is still damn little mixing between the top social level and the rest of us. You maybe don't think about it much until you run into someone like Edith who has that very unusual quality of being able to move back and forth and be completely at home in both camps. When she was among my kind of people she seemed one of us but when she was at a high-toned art opening with Vancouver's best she seemed one of them and I spent a lot of time trying to see how she did it.

It didn't hurt that she worked for the one of world's most influential magazines and was on familiar terms with the likes of Pierre Trudeau and Barbra Streisand—and wasn't shy about telling you, just in case you hadn't heard—but it was more than that, she just smelled right to these people. She could mention names. But the interesting thing about her is that she doesn't seem in any way class conscious. She is just as natural and interested talking to an Eskimo seal hunter or a barnacled old salmon troller as a prime minister. She started out on the West Coast by writing a great long article for *The New Yorker* on Erickson, who had burst onto the scene by designing Simon Fraser University in the mid-1960s and was by this time designing whole cities in the Middle East; then she followed that by doing an even longer piece on John Daly, the eccentric salmon fisherman nobody had ever heard of. And in the course of that she fell in love with

Daly and married him. Then he died and there she was, stranded on the beach in Garden Bay. And there I was, just across the bay in Madeira Park.

I kept filling in the slow times for her and after a while we just got so we were comfortable with each other. Although she's extremely discreet and avoids the steamy stuff in her writing, she's a very warm person physically who doesn't like sleeping alone any more than I do and eventually we figured out what to do about that. It just felt so good to have somebody to hug again. A nice soft bum to snuggle up against at night. The body warmth of another person, boy it feels good after you've gone without it for a few years. That's love in my book. For the first time in years I started getting a good night's sleep.

It's the dumb things you miss the most when you're alone and are sweetest when you get them back. Someone to share a morning coffee with. Someone to laugh at a morning fart with. Someone to share a really dumb joke with. Someone to discuss the most ordinary business of the day with, like going to the garbage dump, watering the garden, hosing seagull poop off the porch railing.

For the first five years or so she would make me park my car out of sight when I stayed over. She said she had her reputation to think of. All her regular circle in Pender Harbour knew we were kind of going together because I was always around but when she had outside company I faded into the shadows. I'd be introduced as "My friend Frank." Of course the locals probably knew I was spending nights there as soon as I started but didn't let on for a good while. Being on the sly was kind of weird at our age. In the worlds we'd both grown up in, a man couldn't dare live openly with a woman he wasn't married to, it would be an absolute scandal, but our kids had broken all that down and made it a pretty normal thing. Still, when it came to ourselves, it was hard to decide which era we belonged to. We had a foot in each and it took a while to iron things out. For the first fifteen years I kept my own house and went back there every day.

For a long stretch there, it was kind of awkward and we got in some fixes. Once when I was heading out in the morning there was a Jeep upside down in the ditch on Claydon Road right opposite Edith's driveway. The Jeep wasn't badly damaged but there was something about it that made me stop and take a look, and by god, here was a body inside it. This poor bastard had been rushing off for the early ferry, flipped his Jeep and broke his neck. Those damn Jeeps, it only takes a hard look to flip them over but the hotshots who get them have to find out the hard way.

It was tough on him but it also caused a bit of trouble for us. I had to wait for the cops and make a report and a few days later it was a big story in the local paper—fatal traffic accident discovered by Mr. Frank White who was driving along Claydon Road at 9:30 in the morning. Well, everybody who read that paper knew who lived on Claydon Road and we were out of the closet. There was a lot of tongue-clucking and teasing for the next few weeks. "Good work on that Jeep guy, Frank. Lucky thing you just happened to be out sightseeing on Claydon Road at 9:30 in the morning." "What was you doing out that time of morning anyway, Frank, huntin' rabbits?" It was embarrassing but it was also kind of a kick to be accused of tomcatting at my age.

When we were alone Edith had no problem showing how she felt. You could never accuse her of being cold. She would phone five times during the day telling me how much she missed me and urging me to hurry over to her place. I fixed up an automatic watering system for her window boxes and flower garden, and oh, it was like I'd invented the wheel. I was so brilliant, so creative . . . she'd really lay it on. "Where did you learn how do that?" she'd say. And she really wanted to know. She grilled me endlessly about my life and expressed admiration and amazement at the variety of things I'd done. A part of you always wondered if she meant it, but on the plus side a lot of her writing had been a celebration of the kind of work men like me did. She came from a white-collar background that left her unduly in awe of people who could do things with their hands. This went down pretty good after the beating my poor old ego had taken in the last few years with Kay. Sometimes I had to pinch myself.

It gave me pause sometimes when I caught myself uttering little intimacies that used to be reserved for Kay. I used to call Kay "Baby" and now I found myself calling Edith "Baby." I was a bit taken aback by my ability to just wipe the slate clean and start over with another person. You find yourself making the same moves and having the same feelings you had with your former partner and there is a bit of guilt at first but you get over it soon enough. The lizard brain takes charge and your body just goes ahead on its own like a train going down the track and soon that's the way it's always been. I guess evolution made us this way because in the old tribal days the attrition rate of mates was much higher and you couldn't have a bunch of grieving widows and widowers around wringing their hands and not doing the business of the tribe. But while they were in a couple, they had to be committed because that way the next generation would be produced and cared for. Edith had been over this road before and was quicker at shifting gears than I was.

On the other hand, she never quit worshipping John Daly. The whole damn place was a kind of shrine to John Daly. He had plastered the walls of his boat with sayings and clippings and before she sold it she had these carefully removed and mounted behind glass in the bathroom. There were yellowed old pieces of notepaper bearing scrawled notations like "The Indian lived in the world as an ecological participant rather than an economic competitor," "He saw the trees but never the whole wood," "He was every man's friend and never locked his cabin door," "Those friends thou hast, and their adoption tried,/Grapple them to thy soul with hoops of steel" and "Laughter is the original miracle drug for curing ill humour." I suspect there was a bit of censorship in selecting the quotes because there's none from Chairman Mao, one of John's main heroes.

John Daly, who I liked in real life, but whose ghost did a good job of haunting me.

There were browned clippings by a very hairy sixties columnist extolling some long-forgotten halfway house run by hippies and another one asking "Is Garlic the King of the Health Foods?" He saved corny cartoons, like one showing a skier looking back worried at his tracks passing on both sides of a tree and another of an overenthusiastic nurse chasing an undressed man with a menacing pair of shears while a doctor in the background says, "No, nurse, I said *slip* off his *spectacles.*" Every time I stood before the toilet I found myself facing this collected works, wondering what I could ever do or say to compete.

Bits of John's old fishing gear and boat lumber and an antique British Seagull outboard were kept in his old boat shed where nobody was allowed to get rid of them. She keeps herself listed as John and Edith Daly in the phone book to this day.

She would bring his name up fifty times a day. Everything reminded her of him. If I felt moved to recite a bit of Omar Khayyám, she'd say, "John used to quote Omar Khayyám." She kept in touch with John's oddball collection of friends and gave them the run of the place whenever they dropped around.

I knew John Daly a lot longer than she did and always thought of him as one of Pender Harbour's good guys, but all this worship made me start to hate him. Still, I could see there was no fighting it. It was clear from the start he was on a plane apart and neither I nor any other mortal man would ever displace him in Edith's heart. At least he was dead.

Her first husband, Phil Hamburger, was also present in our relationship and he was very much alive. He would phone her almost every day and since New York is three hours ahead of Pender Harbour he would usually catch us lounging in bed, cuddling and enjoying our morning coffee. They would often talk for over an hour. They'd still be yakking when I was dressed, fed and driving over to my place. Her favourite line about Phil was that he was the funniest man she ever met, which is strange because I never noticed her laughing during those phone calls. They mostly scared each other with stories about how bad things were in American politics. They were both FDR liberals who thought Reagan and the Bushes were agents of Satan.

Phil came out to visit a few times and we got along okay. He made me feel like he was peering down from a great height but I guess when you're living with a guy's former wife you have to cut him a bit of slack. None of Edith's other New York friends tried to pull rank. Bill Maxwell, the novelist and *The New Yorker* editor and his wife Emmy; Cecille Shawn, wife of *The New Yorker* editor Bill Shawn; Jacquie Bernstein, an MGM heiress; Jane Gunther, widow of the writer John Gunther whose "Inside" books I used to admire; Leigh Cauman, a Columbia logic professor; all of these I found the most regular folks you could want to meet and easy to talk to. In fact I had the impression they even admired me in some upside-down way.

There was a pair of federal court judges who came out quite a lot and we got to be the greatest friends. The woman would run up and give me a big kiss every time we met and I'd think, holy Christ, I've just been kissed by a judge! They were a great bunch once you got used to them. Like people anywhere I found if you could make them laugh, you were halfway home.

In October 1995 Edith and I went up to the Arctic and visited some of the places she had seen and written about some thirty years earlier. She wanted to update her first book, *Inuit Journey*, so she proposed a trip and I was happy to be invited along. I had been reading about the Arctic all my life and had always wanted to see it first-hand. When she first wrote the book there were some very dynamic changes taking place in the lifestyles of the Eskimo including the first moves toward running their own affairs. She had been invited to attend the first meetings of a government-sponsored plan to establish a system of co-operatives, owned and operated by the Natives, a plan being instituted by her friend Don Snowden, and this had been the subject of her book.

We left by way of Montreal for Kuujjuaq (formerly Fort Chimo), where we transferred to Air Inuit for the last leg of our flight. From the first sight of the Inuit-owned airline, the very expensive landing field (a benefit of the Cold War), the first-class roads and the comfortable homes in Kuujjuaq it was apparent my perception of life in the Arctic was very much out of date. The plane was a modern European make, piloted by an Inuit. It had room for sixty or seventy passengers, but half the seat area was blocked off to accommodate freight, mostly fresh milk, fruit and other foodstuffs.

We were shown about by an old acquaintance of Edith's named Neil. He drove us out into the wilderness. Although we were beyond the treeline there were a few stunted evergreens among the sparse growth of scrawny willow and birch. Scattered on some of the hills are the stone structures that look like human figures from a distance. I was told that they help in the caribou hunt somehow.

Wherever we went we could see people with their ATVs gathering the berries. We stayed overnight and in the morning were taken to the airport for a flight to Kangiqsualujjuaq, formerly George River, the village where the first co-op was started and where Edith had spent a lot of her time researching *Inuit Journey*. This plane was twenty-five or thirty seats, also with a Native pilot. It also carried considerable freight. The airfield was high above the town, blasted from a rocky hill, and seemed large enough for any aircraft. It seemed a surprisingly generous installation for a community of eight hundred people. The flight was met by a small crowd of people, somewhat like the gatherings that would meet the old Union Steamship boats on the coast.

Edith was greeted with such fondness you'd think she was a long-lost family member, and I was introduced all around. We were taken into town by her old friend Willie Emudluk, to his house where we were to stay three days. The house was nicely furnished, comfortable and clean, one storey with kitchen, living room and three or four bedrooms. Willie's wife Selima welcomed us and made us feel very much at home. It quickly became apparent that the fabled hospitality of the Inuit had not changed and throughout our stay we were treated as honoured guests.

In 1995 Edith and I took a spin up to Kangiqsualujjuaq (George River) to update her book *Inuit Journey*. We stayed with her old friend Willie Emudluk, who treated us royally.

The Emudluks were not young in years—I believe Willie was about seventy—but a spirit of youth filled the house. They had adopted a baby, he was about three and the joy of the family. A son of about eighteen was at home and it also seemed the married daughters and their children spent much of their time at Willie's. Many of Edith's old friends and acquaintances dropped in to renew their friendship, and I was once again impressed with her remarkable ability to make and keep friends wherever she went, among an astonishing range of different people.

After reading Edith's book, I had the impression the people were still largely itinerant hunters, living part of the year in tents or snow houses and the rest of the year in semi-permanent shacks with seal oil lamps. Her book captured the time when they were beginning to move from traditional self-reliance toward a dependence on southern supplies and paternalistic administration by Ottawa, their old culture beginning to crack under the stresses of modern ways but still mostly intact. Even then her depiction contrasted sharply with the image of proud Eskimo independence my old neighbour Bill White portrayed in his book *Mountie in Mukluks*, set in Cambridge Bay in the 1930s. In his telling the Inuit were still the masters of the land and the white policemen and traders were the helpless dependents.

As I was to find out, sixty years had brought some very dramatic changes and I spent the next few weeks adjusting my preconceptions to contemporary reality. Although fishing and hunting still occupy much of the Inuits' time during the season, technology—in the form of refrigeration, snowmobiles, high-powered outboards and first-class radio communication—has removed much of the old do-or-die aspect of the hunter's life. In Bill's time much of the hunter's day was spent finding food for the dogs which were so necessary for survival; today the snowmobile sits quietly by the side of the road until needed and the dogs lurk around the garbage dumps and are considered a nuisance.

One of the Emudluk daughters, Maggie, was mayor of George River. The mayor and council ran the affairs of the village just like any municipality in the south. The town was generally new and prosperous looking, a result of revenues received through the James Bay hydroelectric project. There was a large diesel-driven power generating plant and a first-class waterworks installation but the water was delivered daily by two men and a tanker truck. Each house was equipped with tanks to accommodate water and sewage. After the water truck made its delivery another tank truck pumped out the sewage. This operation seemed to be routine summer and winter. The streets were built up with crushed gravel to a very high standard and maintained by a civic crew well equipped with heavy machinery. The houses were all relatively new, well constructed and insulated, engineered for the extremes of weather in the north. Also there was a very nice arena for hockey, as well appointed as would be expected in a community many times larger in the south.

In the week before we arrived there had been a series of very tragic accidents at a friend of Edith's fishing camp. A man and his wife were out in the outboard-powered canoe setting a net; the man was in the bow when he asked his wife to start the motor. Somehow it started in gear with a jolt that knocked him overboard then ran over him, tangling him in the net and drowning him. In an attempt to rescue her husband the woman fell over and was seriously injured by the propeller as the boat circled back over her. She managed to get to shore where she was able to call the next camp on the radio and ask for help. A helicopter was brought in to medevac her out but things went from bad to worse: the helicopter crashed, killing all aboard. The funerals had just been held the day before we arrived.

Willie Emudluk had the Shell Oil agency for the area. Oil had become the key resource up there; it was needed for heating, transportation and power. Oil and gasoline were delivered once a year and stored till needed, a very expensive operation. Along with the fuel business, Willie operated a store stocked mostly with goods from the south for local consumption and some local crafts for sale to transients and has operated a camp for southern game hunters. I believe it is now run by one of his family.

Most of the shopping was done at the large and bright Northern Store, the successor to the Hudson's Bay. It was well stocked with all the goods that a community needed in the north. It offered a few local products for the occasional tourist but the volume of business was done in goods from the south, with durable goods delivered once or twice a year by boat and perishables flown in by regular air service.

Edith was disappointed with the state of the old co-op movement, which her friend Don Snowden had hoped would allow the people to achieve economic self-sufficiency by canning fish and caribou meat, producing lines of Native art for export and retaining profits from store and oil sales. Little of this spirit was apparent in the local co-op store, which was by this time on its last legs. Rumour had it that the growth of the co-op movement has been hindered by a top-down and somewhat self-indulgent management structure. In any case, by the time of our visit most of the town's trade was being done by others.

While walking through the town was I impressed by the number of children at the windows. It seemed that every house had a number of young, happy children and one is made to wonder if so many could have survived under the old way of life. It is true that much of the money behind the relative material comforts the George River people were enjoying flowed from the James Bay agreements as well as from the military spending during the Cold War, but I found it hard to imagine how this lifestyle could be maintained without almost total support from the south. I was dismayed to learn back in the south that those seemingly happy George River youngsters were fully involved in the gas sniffing, drug abuse and high suicide rates that afflict the modern Inuit all across the north. Whatever malaise it is that besets the modern Inuit soul, affluence doesn't seem to cure it.

That was our first extended trip together and we found we managed quite well together despite differences in style—Edith was a bit more like Cindy and Ken in liking a certain level of comfort when she could get it, while I liked roughing it. But Edith was a bit more like me in that she liked to get off the tourist track and mix with the natives, wherever we went. And she was good at that.

21

Living with a Legend

People always want to know how a fine lady like Edith got hooked up with a bush ape like me but really I consider myself quite a smoothie compared to the guy she was with before. John Daly was the real break with her past. After she'd been with that barnacled old fish-gutter marrying a nice gentleman logger like me was a step up, or at least sideways. I remember the rumours that started going around Pender Harbour when Edith first hooked up with John. Nobody could believe it. Not because the famous and well-connected *New Yorker* writer was courting a common fisherman—we didn't get *The New Yorker* in Pender Harbour and had never heard of her. We were amazed because John, who was one of the town's most confirmed and eccentric bachelors, was showing interest in a lady, and had apparently found a lady who was interested in him.

I knew John well and campaigned alongside him for years in local politics. We were two left-hand nuts in a town of right-threaded bolts and it made for a natural bond. But I was no match for him in bright ideas. I knew people who would carry an emergency stash of firewood in their car when they were making long winter trips up north, but John used to do that just for trips to the local post office. And he wouldn't start the car until he made sure everybody had their seat belt on, but if your route passed around the edge of Garden Bay Lake he'd order everybody to take their seat belts off again, because he'd heard some guy drowned when he couldn't get his seat belt off under water. John was thinking all the time.

John was one of these guys who came to every meeting with a petition to sign and made a long speech about everything under the sun from pollution to American corporations taking over Canada to shrinking salmon runs to that wonderful man Mao Tse-tung to dogs swimming in the local water reservoir. Everything under the sun except the thing that was actually on the agenda. We had other long talkers like Steve Dediluke or Frankie Lee you didn't mind as much because they were entertaining, but John delivered his broadsides in a lecturing drone, as if it was going to do us no end of good to spend twenty minutes exposed to his uplifting thoughts. And if you met him outside the meeting he would start the whole process all over again, ignoring everything you did to signal you were overdue for a visit to the outhouse.

He was one of those people who seemed only set to broadcast, never to receive. We all thought it was because he had been a bachelor too long and spent too much time out alone on his fishboat. He had quite a squint that got worse the longer his harangues went on, which contributed to the opinion his nonstop talking must be some kind of a condition.

He had been married once, back in the 1940s, and had somehow managed to get matched up with one of the most lively women ever to hit the coast—a woman known as Pixie. Their common ground was the outdoors. One of the many things that marked John as different from the average local was he sometimes went outdoors when he didn't have to. Your authentic old-time Pender Harbourite was forced to spend so much of his life outdoors in pursuit of necessities, the idea of doing it voluntarily on days off was looked upon as extreme eccentricity. John didn't care. He'd spend days rambling around on top of the Caren Range just picking blueberries and exclaiming about the mountain air. And he'd often disappear for a couple of weeks in the winter to ski—a waste of good beer-drinking time to most of us then. This all went back to his genteel upbringing and his early years in Vancouver when he was in a group of outdoor nuts that built a ski hut on top of Hollyburn Mountain and spent the weekends partying and skiing.

It was there he met Pixie, who was an equal fresh air fiend. Her real name was Mary but nobody knew that, they only ever called her Pixie. John and Pixie stayed together long enough to beget two sons before she departed on a round of adventures that gave Penderites of even the most dubious virtue occasion to wax righteous.

I always liked Pixie. She became the secretary of the hospital when it was still in Garden Bay and stayed with it when it moved to Sechelt. She kept that position for years and became such a mainstay that when she retired one of the doctors said he didn't know how they were going to carry on without her. He was right, the place has never been the same since.

What you remember about Pixie is that she was always bright and alive and on the lookout for a bit of excitement. That wasn't the most popular way to be around Pender Harbour, which was always kind of a grumpy place, but the longer I live the more I appreciate people who cast a little light in the gloom.

John kept the boys and raised them pretty much on his own, and even those who thought he was a dangerous radical or else a harmless nut had to admit he was a wonderful father. He had quite a struggle raising those boys what with spending half the year fishing but he did a great job of it. There is a scrawled note on the bathroom wall that provides a glimpse of his parenting style.

I guess he was leaving early to go out for the day, he was always a very busy guy, so he wrote a note for the boys to find when they got up. It's not dated but it must be after they were big enough to be left on their own, probably in the early 1950s, and he wanted to make sure they did their chores.

The page is divided into two columns, one for Sean and one for Dick. John's compositions, even his innumerable letters to the editor, often looked more like diagrams, with cryptic messages overflowing the page and afterthoughts running down the sides, all in his barely readable scrawl. The column under Sean's name read:

Wood into house
Wood from garden
Clear dish rack
Lay table
Make bed & tidy room

Dick's list was:

Kindling
Lamps
Lunches
Oil
Make bed
Wood from garden

There is pay for this work, calculated by how eagerly they go about it. For Sean it's fifty cents "Dragging" or seventy-five cents "Willing." Dick, the senior man, gets seventy-five cents "Dragging" or a dollar "Willing." Across the bottom is a joint message to "D & S": "Put vegetables on if I am late for supper lay table & any other jobs to make life happier." John believed in the redeeming qualities of work and instilled self-reliance into his kids from an early age. It had good effect. Both boys graduated from university and went on to distinguished careers, Sean as a geologist and Dick as a writer with a PhD in anthropology.

There was a lot to admire about John, if you looked past the goofy stuff. He served on every worthy cause in sight including the school board. He helped start a local credit union and a fisherman's insurance co-op. And being a diehard socialist didn't prevent him from salting away a healthy estate, all carefully invested and drawn up to provide for Edith as long as she lived. I have to remind myself, the real John Daly was a lot easier to like than the myth.

When the word got out that John was back with a woman after thirty-odd years, everybody was breaking their necks to get a look at her and were amazed to discover not only that was she sound of limb and in possession of all her faculties, she was quite a dame. It was generally assumed it would only last until she found out what an odd duck he was, but when it kept on and led to marriage people had to give their heads a shake.

I've never been able to figure out if Edith actually discovered depths of genius in old John that the rest of us had all missed or whether she was just discovering the fine qualities of your typical West Coast man and giving him all the credit. Certainly he never sounded better than she makes him sound in *Fishing with John*, the book she wrote about their life together, although I have to admit I find it hard to read because she captured just enough of his way of talking that I glaze over after a few pages. And like I say, a lot of the amazing feats she credits him with are pretty standard fare for any West Coast fisherman. As I get it from guys who fished around him, John wasn't one of the high-liners but he had stuck with it and become a steady producer over years of setbacks and that gave him solid respect around the Harbour despite his eccentric personal habits. Well, actually, eccentric personal habits didn't rate much notice in Pender Harbour in those days.

John loved being a West Coast fisherman. He had been raised by blue-stockings who taught him to look down on common folk and sent him to English boarding schools and he spent the rest of his life trying to overcome it. I first met him when I was on the milk haul in the 1930s and he was working for BC Electric in Vancouver. I remember him as a tall, gawky Englishman who seemed lost. When I ran into him again up here, he looked and sounded more like an old-time fisherman than those who were born to it. The other guys left their fishing garb on the boat but John wore his to town, showing off the fish scales proudly. It was like he'd finally found his place and he was making the most of it.

He had a convert's devotion to the old-time ways of the coast and this caused friction when he and Edith got together. Whereas I was mostly willing to go along with her agenda, John wasn't. He fought to make her adapt to his lifestyle and it led to some dandy battles. He liked to wash his feet in the sink, he was built like a heron and could just lift his leg up and plop it into the washbasin, and she had some citified upper-class objection to this. She couldn't live without a dishwasher and he thought dishwashers were a consumerist abomination. And of course the big one was John treated his ex-wife Pixie as a member of the household, allowing her to walk in without knocking whenever she felt like it. There was a battle royal over that.

People think Edith and I are an unlikely pair but for me the real mystery is how in hell did her and John ever get paired up? I think one answer is right there in her book—she went out on his boat. Just being out on the water on this coast for any length of time can be a life-changing experience. The landscape is so overpowering it casts a kind of spell that makes daily cares seem trivial. I had a taste of it here and there, first when Kay and I started exploring the islands around Nanoose Bay in the 1940s, and it was always one of my big aims to go back and get a better dose of it. That was what was really behind my decision to build the *Flash* aka *Marilyn Kay,* which I hoped to someday use making long leisurely visits to some of these places I'd got glimpses of in my working life. John made sure Edith got a good eyeful of the coast and she was fully captured by its spell. But it wasn't just the scenery.

I don't know if she realized what she was getting into or not when she went out fishing with him. In her mind she was probably just a professional writer doing research, like she'd done when she went out with the truckers building their ice road across the tundra or when she shadowed construction workers building the World Trade Center. She didn't accept limits on where she could go or what she could write about just because she was a woman. An interviewer asked her once if she was a feminist because of all these intrepid woman reporter capers she pulled but she said no, she didn't think of herself as a feminist, she was just curious about how the world worked and didn't see why she shouldn't follow her nose wherever it took her.

It wasn't so much she broke down barriers as she seemed to not notice them, and when it came to crewing on John Daly's old troller to research commercial fishing, she just jumped aboard. But the way coast people thought back in those days a woman didn't go out on a man's fishboat unless they were a couple or were planning to be one in short order. Nowadays apparently there are lots of lady deckhands who don't sleep with the captain, much as cynical old-timers like me find that hard to believe. If you went out on a guy's boat for more than a trip across the harbour, that was the same as shacking up with him the way old-timers saw it. I'm sure John was aware of that, because every time he got a call on the radiophone his buddies would ask "How's the little woman?"

"She's not a little woman, she's a New York reporter and she's going to blow the lid off the corruption in this industry!"

Edith and John while out fishing on the *More Kelp*. People thought Edith and I were an unlikely match, but the real break with her old New York life came when she married John.

"Whatever you say, John. Say, is that a pair of panties flapping from your port stay, or some kind of new socialist flag?"

He made her take her underwear down and dry it inside. He also made her hide her car when she stayed over at his place before they were married, saying, "I have a good reputation in this town!" Edith was amused that John thought it was his reputation that would get the worst of it. Later on when I was overnighting on the sly, she made me hide my car using almost the same words, but I could see her point there.

There was no such thing as privacy on those old one-man trollers and John's *More Kelp* didn't even have a toilet. He was still using a deck bucket. That was typical. A plumbed-in head was a waste of money and space to him. John must have been the last guy on the coast who still didn't have one. It wouldn't have been that big a deal to have Jimmy Reid pop one in when the boat was on the ways for its annual bottom cleaning but to John's way of thinking that would be selling out to Madison Avenue or something. The deck bucket was a terror to Edith, but he just told her to get used to it, it was part of the authentic fishboat experience she was supposed to be documenting. In his way he was a bit of a poo scholar—back home he used to crouch in some kind of contraption that replicated the posture of Australian aborigines or something, which was supposed to make taking a dump more healthy and fulfilling.

His belief in the special powers of the deck bucket became quite a cause of friction between Edith and him. A man of course can take a leak over the side anytime he wants, but for a woman it's out with the bucket ten times a day. It was a damned ordeal. Even after she got used to having no privacy, she was always afraid the bucket would tip over if there was a bit of a sea. And the rim of the bucket bites into your ass, you can't really sit, you have to hover over it. It was a big concession when John finally bought a seat to go on the bucket—he phoned her in New York in the middle of the night to offer it to her along with his marriage proposal. That was her engagement ring—a toilet seat. What she saw in that old cod walloper beats me but she saw a lot more than anybody else.

I have to shake my head when I think what it took for her to accept John's offer. It was such a break with the kind of life she'd always followed. And she cared about that old life. She kept going back to it, she'd spend four or five months a year back east chumming with her old crowd. She kept her apartment in New York for years. And John was no part of that. He went to New York once but refused to go back. The mystery to me is why they didn't spend more time together.

After that first year when she spent most of the fishing season on the boat, she never went back for more than a few trips so they didn't see much of each other during the trolling season, which in those days ran from April to September. John fished one of the longest seasons of anybody. Lots of guys, when they got older, cut back to just the good part of the season in mid-summer, or just day-fished the gulf, but he kept on fishing pretty much the maximum time allowed, putting in months up north when he barely covered cost and putting a hell of a strain on his bad heart, which had already blown up once on the fishing grounds.

He had a big sign over his basement door saying "Faith in Humanity not $$$." It got him a lot of good publicity but you have to wonder why he didn't pay more attention to it himself. He could have said, "Hell, I've got a few bucks in the bank and I don't know how much time I've got left with my bum ticker and all—why don't I cut back and spend a few extra months with my lovely lady?" But no, he kept chasing $$$ to the last day of the trolling season most years. And she didn't do much to make up for it. Come winter, off to New York she goes and doesn't come back till spring. This only left them a short stretch after he got back from fishing and another one after she got back from New York, when they went on some trips together. They were on one of these in March 1978 when John fell dead from a heart attack.

I've asked her why they didn't spend more time together and she says they didn't realize how little time they had. To me, that doesn't quite answer the question. Who says to herself, "I worship the ground this man stands on but I think I'll spend most of my time away from him for the next five years, even though his bad heart could go at any moment?" As for myself, I couldn't be away from her for an hour but she started phoning everybody in Pender Harbour looking for me. I wasn't paying attention at the time she and John were married so I don't know what kind of relationship they had but I do find it strange the way they used their time together, considering she spent the next forty years worshipping his memory. But then people are strange and nothing they do really surprises me anymore.

22

Friends

Learning to live with Edith was one of the hardest things I ever did, and having to take second place to the ghost of John Daly was only part of it. I don't mean to say it wasn't great—if it hadn't been I couldn't have kept on with it. She was very loving and good to cuddle and she was lots of fun. I have seen a whole new side of life on account of her. There was always something happening around her, and if there wasn't she would make it happen. That had its upside and its downside. Sometimes you just wanted a quiet day, but there weren't many quiet days around her. A quiet day was a wasted day to her. She was allergic to quiet. If she saw a Friday night coming up without a dinner guest she would start phoning and keep phoning until we had somebody, often two or three people. There was a houseguest often as not.

Edith wasn't in the Harbour very long before she had twice as many friends as me, and the friends I did have quickly became closer to her than they ever were to me. Joe Harrison who I had worked with for years on the Ratepayers Association but had never sat down to dinner with, became a regular dinner guest along with his wife Solveigh, who I'd seen grow from a little girl but hardly ever spoke to. Ray Phillips is a local fisherman Edith kept in touch with because he was one of John's friends and I knew from crossing paths over the years but there again, because of Edith I came to know him and his wife Doris and their whole family much better than I would have on my own. Ray wrote a couple books of his own, one on

Kleindale and one on Jervis Inlet, that are among the best anybody has written on this area.

The local doctor John Farrer who I'd been taking my lumbago and ingrown toenails to for years but never saw outside the clinic, became a regular at evening dos, along with his partner Jane McOuat, who, again, had taught my grandkids but I'd never got to know personally. Farrer was an interesting specimen. For a doctor he was unusually unassuming and down to earth but it turned out that he was heir to one of the big estates in the north of England, with its own village, manor house and tenant farms. When his father died he had to pack up and move back to England to become lord of the manor, with Jane as his lady. He didn't care for it and escaped back to the Sunshine Coast every chance he got, but I think Jane found it kind of a kick.

Our constant fallback was our next-door neighbour, Anne Clemence. Anne was born and raised in England, where she trained to be a nurse. She wanted to see the world and started taking nursing jobs in different places, ending up at the little mission hospital in Garden Bay sometime in the 1960s. That was the end of her world tour. She fell in love with a local character named Sam Lamont—a log salvager, but one of the more respectable ones—and soon became his deckhand, learning to run his powerful tug in howling southeasters while he ran around on the beach hooking up logs. Some people took to calling her Tugboat Annie but it didn't really fit—she always remained the well-mannered English lady. Sam died not many years after John Daly and Edith formed a bond with Anne that continues to this day. She is a bit younger than us and as we have become more decrepit she has helped out with rides to events and done much in her unobtrusive way to keep our experiment in independent living manageable.

Thank you, Anne.

One of the locals who came around a lot was a guy named Ben Dlin, a psychiatrist who had grown up in Alberta then moved to Philadelphia. He semi-retired and bought a big waterfront place on Francis Peninsula sometime in the 1990s, got himself a $40,000 Boston Whaler, did the heavy-duty sports fishing thing, grew a big garden, carved Indian masks, played golf, got to know everybody, he was a real dynamo.

The unsinkable Anne Clemence, English nurse turned BC coast log salvager, unveiling one of her baking masterpieces at my ninety-fifth birthday. That's Marilyn on the left and my niece Heather on the right.

He gave us to understand he had made quite a mark in US psychiatry circles. He had scholarly papers coming out his ears. He had all kinds of patients who were geniuses and millionaires and had these terrible screw-ups he fixed just like I fixed cars in my garage. Once he was called in to analyze the whole Philadelphia Phillies baseball team and took credit for helping them win the World Series. Or was it for helping them to recover from winning the World Series? Anyway, he aced it, according to him.

Now, old Ben was just as direct as a bolt of lightning. He believed all the problems that throw us off the track are the result of a bunged-up childhood, from the way we were treated by our parents. He figured you just had to get psychoanalyzed and go back and see where you went off the rails, straighten that out, then you'd be fine. Simple as that. One patient I remember him describing was a woman who had seven personalities. She was some bright egg who was a successful lawyer or executive or something but she had this helluva problem that buggered everything up and Ben said he got her down on his couch and found out she had these seven different personalities at war inside her like mad cats in a gunny sack and one after the other he exorcised them or whatever and got her back to her one real self.

To hear him tell it, it was straightforward as clearing squirrels out of the attic. I did notice however that that particular patient still needed quite a bit of help because once when I was over to visit she called up in a hell of a state and he had to excuse himself while he went and talked to her for half an hour. This was after she'd already been seeing him for twenty years or so, and I remember thinking, those damn squirrels must keep coming back. I also remember thinking, wow, twenty years at $200 an hour or whatever—it's lucky this woman was making money with one of her personalities because no poor person would ever have been able to afford Ben's cure.

Ben was always hinting he'd like to get me down on his couch and analyze me—he said getting analyzed was good for you even if you didn't think you had anything haywire, like preventative maintenance—but I couldn't quite buy the whole deal. For one thing, Ben had the most screwed-up personal life of anybody I ever met.

He had this wife Lorna, who as far as I could see was a real nice person. But only if you met her on her own, without Ben around. If he was in the house, she would just go after him and he would go after her. They were the Bickersons on jet fuel. They would just stand there in a room full of company peeling hide off each other like a couple of mad fishwives. They couldn't stop themselves. The first couple of times we went to dinner there we thought it must have been some sort of exceptional crisis, but then we realized this was every day, all the time. We, and I think most of their friends, avoided going to visit if they were both home. They kept their place in Philadelphia and most of the year Lorna stayed there and let Ben come out and fish by himself, which was a relief to us all.

But it was just hard to believe a guy who couldn't stop trashing his wife in front of company had all the answers to human behaviour.

I guess he was a pretty good doctor. I was laid up one time with quite an infection in my foot. I wasn't taking it too seriously because it was just from an ingrown toenail but it was damn sore and taking a long time to go away. I went up to the clinic and they gave me some pills and told me to stay off it, so I was laying low.

Ben came by and said, "What the hell's wrong with you? Let me see that." Well, he just hauled me up to the clinic and told them to put me on an antibiotic drip. They thought the pills would do but he insisted on the heavy artillery and he bullied them into it. He claimed I was almost dead. My regular doctor didn't seem to think it was all that terrible, but to Ben the local doctors were mostly just slackers and quacks. He said there was a red line crawling halfway up my leg and if it got to my groin it would be lights out. I used to hear that about blood poisoning when I was a kid—if the red line reached your heart you'd die—but came to think of it as folklore until Ben said it was true after all.

The local doctors went along with him and sure enough the infection went away. After that Ben never missed a chance to remind me how he'd saved my life and if it wasn't for him I'd be dead and buried. Maybe he was right, I don't know, but I didn't like the way he crowbarred me with it and that didn't make me any keener to let him get me on his couch and try to pry all my hidden screw-ups out of my unconscious. I could see myself twenty years later, still on that couch, still talking and the meter still running.

Ben was good company mostly, like a friendly pit bull, but he made me a little uncomfortable. He liked to speak out about things most people liked to keep quiet about, especially sex. He loved to tell dirty jokes in mixed company and he gave regular hints that he was quite the bedroom warrior. He made passes at several of Edith's friends although she always insisted he never made one at her. Still, he got very close to her and came around a lot when I was away and I have to admit I was suspicious of his intentions. He hosted any Jewish celebrations that came up while he was in town and pressed Edith to attend, even though she wasn't religious and didn't usually observe them. Anyway, she usually went and it made me feel like her and Ben had something between them I could never be part of.

I also didn't like the way he treated Cindy. He wrote a book about his life growing up in a small, tough cow town in rural Alberta and having to fight all the way to school and back every day because of all the anti-Semites. First he tried to get Howie to publish it by saying how he had saved my life and all, but Howie, the bugger, he sloughed it off on Cindy. He said it was more her thing since Ben was from up north. I don't think she wanted to do it, but Ben went to work on her about how he'd saved my life and got her talked into it. So she put out a pretty good-looking book called *Country Doctor* and it had some good parts about life in the small town and about his early years as a doctor on horseback but according to Ben he won every fight he was ever in, was the first Jew admitted to the Alberta school of medicine, made a miraculous cure in virtually every case and it was all a bit too much to swallow.

Well, as soon as the book came out he proceeded to make Cindy's life miserable, basically because she failed to turn this little book full of professional boasting into an international bestseller. He phoned her morning, noon and night complaining that it wasn't reviewed in this paper or that paper or on sale in some drugstore in Poughkeepsie—completely unrealistic expectations from this small publisher who had really only taken him on as a favour in the first place.

It's strange what happened to Ben. One summer when he was over to visit, I thought I noticed something not quite right. He was talking even more than usual, but his thoughts were skittering all over the place. He wasn't his usual razor-sharp self. Then somebody else told me they'd seen him stopping cars on the road and talking the ear off complete strangers. I remember saying to Edith, "We might not see Ben again." I don't know what made me say that because another friend who had Alzheimer's just sank slowly for about ten years. I just had a flash of intuition, which is rare for me. Edith didn't credit it but sure enough, when Ben went back to Philadelphia that winter his family put him into hospital and he sank like a rock. He had Alzheimer's all right, but it must have been a very fast-moving kind and it killed him before a year was out. I kind of missed him after he was gone, and felt bad about holding out against him. Most people's flame kind of smoulders, but Ben's roared like a blowtorch.

Edith always had quite a stream of visitors from out of town, some from New York or Cleveland, many from Vancouver. Her own family isn't very big but I was amazed how often they made the trip out from the eastern US just for her birthday or mine. She just had the one sister, Jane, who would come at least twice a year, but Jane had two daughters, Betsy and Anne, and they would come regularly as well. Even Anne's daughter Claire would regularly make it out to spend a few days with her great-aunt,

One of our trips east to visit Edith's sister Jane (right) and Jane's daughter Betsy, a jewellery maker.

often bringing her own young family. And Edith would return the favour by trekking halfway across the world to attend their birthdays and graduations and play openings.

I once accompanied her to her grandson Nicholas's bar mitzvah in Dallas, which I found very moving. I thought it would be religious, but it wasn't all that much, in fact young Nicholas announced in his speech that he didn't believe in God, a pretty nervy thing for a young guy surrounded by rabbis to do. The whole show seemed to be mostly about family, the immediate Hamburger-Iglauer one, the greater family of the Jews and the even greater one of humanity. It made me think a lot about family and ritual. The Jews have used that ritualistic tradition to hold their great family together for thousands of years while my crowd, whatever you want to call us, lapsed Christians or whatever, we have no glue holding us together and lose our connections after a single generation. I don't even know who my grandmother was, or didn't until Irene Carmichael looked it up on the internet. I had always steered clear of any kind of ritual or formality in my own life because I thought that kind of thing was empty and meaningless. Kay and I observed Christmas and that was about it. We didn't even give the kids birthday presents after about age five. We tried to raise the kids to be just naturally decent and considerate in an ordinary, every day way and to treat all people the same as you would treat family. I still think that's not such a bad thing to shoot for.

Family only made up a small part of the company we regularly put up at our little beach shack in Garden Bay. There were quite few close friends of Edith's who would come several times a year. The Shadbolts were regulars. Jack and Doris. The women would go off together and I would be left to keep the old guy company. We found quite a bit to talk about—the old Vancouver gas works with its landmark tower; Frederick Ducharme, the flasher who really had something to flash; the Alcazar Hotel where he'd painted the murals and I'd drunk a lot of beer—but he was more of a lecturer than a talker and he'd get off on these goddamned philosophical monologues where I had no idea what he was talking about, and I'm not sure he did either. I wouldn't have taken him for an artist if I didn't know it beforehand. He never did anything artistic while he was around and didn't seem the artist type somehow. He seemed more like an absent-minded philosophy professor.

Bill Reid was different. He'd bring his paintings with him and work on them while he was talking to you and even in a restaurant he'd be doodling on the napkin. He talked a lot about the Haida way of doing things but he wasn't like any Indian I'd ever met. He was more like some kind of very well-travelled professional who had learned about Indians from studying them. But he lived and breathed art and was always tied up in knots over various big projects he was working on where the foundry wasn't doing its job or his crews weren't showing up for work and weren't following his instructions when they did or some such thing. His wife Martine was a beautiful Parisian aristocrat who became another really close friend of Edith's and I became very attached to as well. At times she had a pretty rough go with Bill, who was falling apart from Parkinson's disease and didn't always act like a saint.

He could be sweet as anything one day and an arrogant boor the next. You never knew what you were going to get. But most of the time I got the good side. He and Edith had a rougher time. She had done the big profile of Arthur Erickson in *The New Yorker* that must have been worth millions to him in terms of international commissions and I think maybe

Bill hoped she would do the same for him. She tried, but her famous method didn't work on Bill. The dumb questions made him testy and she didn't get the good stuff. Bill Shawn, her editor in New York, wouldn't take the article and she had to print it in Canada with *Saturday Night*. I don't think Bill was too impressed by that.

Erickson came up to visit a time or two but never stayed for more than a few hours. He always brought an entourage and once even came in a stretch limousine that idled with its lights on the whole time. I don't think he and I exchanged three words. He seemed self-conscious about his celebrity status, as if being found in an old fisherman's shack talking to an old truck driver might somehow damage it. The young gigolo type he had with him was even more that way, treating me as if I didn't exist and saying stuff like "Oh, Arthur, you must check out the bathroom! It's tooooo priceless!" Edith's house is crammed with art which I had always assumed was highly valuable but I saw Erickson give it the once-over and kind of frown, except one small picture over the sofa that looked like the king of spades seen through one of those bathroom windows that makes everything blurry.

"Is that Rouault print signed?" he asked. It wasn't.

"Too bad!" he said.

Edith had some really top flight Eskimo prints and carvings that later went to the National Art Gallery and they sort of glommed on to that, as if amazed to find such rare stuff in such a crummy place. The young guy kept whining like a little kid about getting back to town for some do so off they went in their limousine. Generally I found with Edith's friends, the bigger fish they were the less airs they put on. Erickson struck me as a guy who was in over his head. I wasn't too surprised when I heard his wheels fell off and he lost everything a few years later. But Edith never quit saying he was a genius and I'm willing to take her word for it.

I couldn't help thinking about the first time I'd ever heard of Erickson and that was back in the fifties when Kay and I were building the house on Francis Peninsula Road. She was studying up on house designs and one she just fell in love with was one by this young architect that had won all sorts of prizes over on Vancouver Island. She got me to take her over to have a look at it. I was surprised to find it had been built for Bob Filberg, the head of Comox Logging, who I knew from my contract log hauling days.

This new house was a crazy thing I thought, all picture windows and plaster arches and nothing much I could see working into our old cookhouse, but it actually did give me a few ideas. It had a pretty much open floor plan with the kitchen, dining room and living room all running together and a big free-standing fireplace in the middle. Open floor plans are standard now but I hadn't seen it much up to that time. Back home, I took the power saw to the wall separating the kitchen and living room and bricked up a free-standing brick fireplace in there that was open on two sides. Erickson had some kind of a shiny gold-plated hood hanging down for his but I didn't have one of those handy so I stuck in a forty-five-gallon gas drum. I figured the effect would be about the same, and the barrel was probably a damn sight more efficient. Once the paint burned off and you could breathe, it heated that house for the next fifty years. So thanks to Arthur Erickson for that.

But just joining up those dots gives me pause. There was poor Kay, reading about this Erickson and so inflamed by the idea of this fancy architect and all the fine things in life people like that represented to her. Just eating her heart out, and me standing back shaking my head, secure in my conviction this was all some silly fantasy of the kind women are subject to. Then thirty years later, here I am breaking bread with this same architect and living a life that is pretty much pure leisure, art talk, travel and generally savouring the finer things in life seven days a week.

Kay would have given her eye teeth for one day of this kind of existence, and yet here I am who wouldn't have given you two cents for it, floating in it, stuffed with it, marinated in it. There's no justice. And now I can see what Kay was pining for. It wasn't just a pipe dream. This kind of life does exist, is attainable by mere mortals. She was right to go looking for it and I was wrong to think she was off her rocker. But at the same time, I'm not sure this lives up to the dream she had. The feast on the table never tastes as good to the eaters as it does in the minds of the hungry folk pressing their noses to the window.

I don't have any friends left alive except my kids. All our friends are basically Edith's. She has this ability to make friends and keep them. When we went across the US in my RV towing a U-Haul full of her furniture one time I got an idea of just how many friends she really had. No matter what backwater town we found ourselves in, she would say, "I think I know somebody here." And she'd go look in the phone book and say, "Here they are, let's call them up."

These would be some people she had bumped into somewhere for a few hours forty years before but they would remember her and greet her like a sister and throw their home open to us. Sometimes it would be a guide from one of the boys' summer camps; other times it would be somebody famous she'd written about but they'd all be equally delighted to see her and throw their arms around her. In Escondido we called on a famous artist named Harry Sternberg who had done murals all across the country during Roosevelt's New Deal, a great old guy who insisted on selling me one of his paintings for whatever I felt like paying. I think I gave him fifty bucks for a little painting of some flowers, the only work of art I ever owned.

I had to wonder at all these friends, and why Edith had so many and I had so few.

It's a class thing partly, I came to think. A working guy doesn't really work at making friends. You end up knowing a lot of people because you

Almost anywhere we stopped on our various road trips around the US Edith would end up knowing someone. In Escondido it was famed painter Harry Sternberg and his wife.

work with a lot of people and you often get to know them pretty well because you see how they handle pain and danger and isolation. Working people also tend to be more open in the way they live. A worker who's having trouble at home will get drunk and spill his guts where a middle-class guy will keep it all under wraps. Also, workers don't have as many ways of explaining what happens to them. There's no passive-aggressive syndromes in the bunkhouse. You're just being an effing a-hole and if one of your mates doesn't pop you one, you at least get told off straight. It's all a lot more down to earth.

The friendships are all a lot more down to earth, too. You don't go out of your way to "make" a friend, you know these guys are going to be getting in your face in the course of the job and it's more a question of avoiding getting involved than going out looking for it. And the friendships you allow to happen tend to be deep, guys you've really gone through the mill with and have your back. On the job, a guy who goes out of his way to "make" friends is likely to be avoided. It's supposed to be a natural process, where only people who pass the test of being good buddies are admitted.

That's the kind of friend-making I was used to and in the course of my life I only had a few—Rendell McKinnon early on, Les McGarva, Dutch Parberry, Jack Spence, Sam Hately, Jim Tyner, Bill White, Bill Milligan. And a lot of those friendships didn't last. We had fallings out. This happens when a friendship involves going into business together, getting drunk together, chasing girls together, buying property together, etc.

Sam was one of my longest-lasting friends but at a certain point he went off the rails and I had to get him help. He had been up Jervis Inlet on one of his marathon falling contracts and got convinced he'd discovered a race of giants. He loaded his old boat with all these pointy boulders he figured were ancient spearheads, some of them two hundred pounds. "Can you imagine the size of the guy who chucked that spear?" he'd say. He was raging twenty-four hours a day so his wife Merle came running over and asked me to do something. I called Dr. Swan, who knew Sam well, and between us we got him packed off to a treatment place for a spell.

He never forgave me for that, although they got him calmed down in pretty short order and pretty soon it was as if nothing had happened. He told me all the trouble had been caused by a broken muffler on one of his saws that gave him carbon monoxide poisoning. Maybe so, or maybe it was just from being in the bush too long but Sam had an excitable nature at the best of times. He'd get ranting so wildly sometimes it was kind of scary, because he was built like a moose and he'd been a commando in the war. It could be he had a touch of this giddyup-whoa disorder.

Most of my friends had a screw loose when you got right down to it. Jim Tyner, who was a paraplegic and walked with crutches, used to get drunk and make a fool of himself by boasting about what a lady killer he was in his secret life. Then he'd feel guilty the next day since he was the unofficial mayor of Pender Harbour and supposedly respectable and we'd both avoid each other for a while. I have to say most of our race are kind of flawed up close and if you get to know them too well you risk being put off. To me the only ones you could call a true friend would be the ones you went through the wars with and still admire, who are damn few and far between. And even those I would hesitate to say I actually "loved."

Love to me is something you really only have for your children, your wife (on good days) and maybe one or two other very close relatives. I loved Wesley, and after she died I realized how much I had loved Kay. When Edith started turning up with literally dozens she called "dear, dear friends" whom she "absolutely loved" I thought, holy smokes, how did she have time to find all those nuggets in the gravel of life? It took me a while to understand that in the circles she came from, friendship was a quite different animal than the one I knew.

These hundreds of friends she has she doesn't really know at all and they don't know her—by my standards. It would not be considered the basis for a true friendship in the average bunkhouse. But middle-class people seem to have this thing where they can form relationships quickly, then maintain that link over years with little rituals like exchanging birthday gifts and Christmas cards—and visiting. Edith had a stack of little books crammed with names and addresses of people she sent presents to, listing all the presents she's sent over the years. There are hundreds of names in these books and she had to keep notes because there were so many she couldn't remember and might have sent someone the same gift twice. This is just beyond my comprehension.

To an outsider it's a curious process, this middle-class friend collecting.

Why do they do it? For social advantage? To get ahead in their careers? A little of both probably, but it is also pleasant to have all these people you can meet with and do things like have dinners, card games and attend art openings without having to make a pact in blood. They keep their friends at arm's-length and go through a careful ritual. They don't get naked and go to the mat like workies do. This way you can fit in a lot more "friends" into one life.

A working guy spends hours every week with his best buddies, there's not room in the day for more than a few. But a middle-class friendship can start with an initial contact of a few hours and be kept up for years with minimal effort. If you work at it there's no reason you can't have a few hundred. Edith did have some close friends, like Jacquie Bernstein in New York and after she came here, Doris Shadbolt, but they weren't many and even at that they weren't the every day kind of friends.

There's also a part I haven't mentioned here, and that's sense of team. Edith was accepted at sight into Vancouver society because she came bearing the right credentials from *The New Yorker*, Pierre Trudeau, and a dozen other important names only the in-crowd know. So there was a feeling right away, she's one of us, part of our team, she has the secret handshake. The working guy doesn't have anything to match this. Oh, I can go up to a bunch of hardhats on a construction site and say, "You can't make any money sitting down!" in a tone of voice that tells them I've been in their spot, but it's not the same.

Maybe this is all bullshit, I don't know. I've got nothing left to do but sit and think about things and I end up thinking in circles. I had a good idea when I started out but I can't remember what it was now.

The longer I lasted, the more I'd get invited to say a few words here and there, mostly at funerals of my old friends and acquaintances as their ranks inexorably thinned. I got to give so many eulogies I started to feel like Billy Graham. I couldn't believe some of these guys I came out to bury. I lived to see my old competitor Wilf Harper pack it in and even saw his son Alfie go over the hill. I forget if I spoke at Wilf's funeral but I know they asked me to do Alfie's, which surprised me. I knew Alfie from the time he was a little boy riding around in his dad's gravel truck but I don't think we spoke ten words in his entire life. Still, I was honoured to be asked and didn't find it difficult at all to say some good things about Alfie. I sent off Frank Campbell, who had given me fits when he came to work for me in Green Bay but spent some of his last years boarding with me in my old house:

I first met Frank when he came to set chokers for me in Green Bay. He was about nineteen or twenty. He thought I was an old man then. Well, that's fair enough, because I thought he was just a kid. Forty years have gone by and I never stopped thinking of Frank as a young fella. Now here we are today at Frank's funeral. It's hard for me to realize it, but I saw his whole adult life go by. I saw him start out as a green kid, I saw him become a man, a good man, a decent man, I saw him become a father, I saw him become a grandfather, I saw him become an old-timer just like me. Now I have seen him die. I feel like a part of me has died with him.

23

Travels with Edith

can't remember now all the trips Edith and I took but we were burning up the globe for a few years there. We made numerous trips back and forth across North America, driving through the US and Canada. We did a tour of the Maritime provinces where she got very impatient with me for spending too much time in graveyards trying to find traces of Grandma Carmichael's people, variously known as Belyeas or Bulliers. She'd often fly out to New York for her winter visit then I'd drive out to bring her back.

Once she decided to take her old furniture out of storage and bring it back to Garden Bay so I drove out pulling a U-Haul trailer with the old camperized minivan I had then. We loaded it up with all her old heirlooms and set out for home but along the way we got thinking it would lessen the monotony if we got off the usual route so we turned south and began exploring new territory. Well, I dragged that trailer through the Carolinas, Georgia, Alabama, Mississippi, New Orleans, Texas, New Mexico and half the continental US. It was a great trip, and everywhere we went Edith seemed to be able to scare up a few old acquaintances who would drop what they were doing and show us around.

The most ambitious trip was one we took with Edith's stepson Dick Daly in 1993. Sometime in late January or early February Edith told me that Dick's wife Liv, who lives in Norway, had said that she was thinking of inviting a few friends to take a trip on the Trans-Siberian Railroad on the occasion of her husband's fiftieth birthday, the tenth of April. The idea sounded a little off the wall and unlikely to ever come to much. I suggested it would be a great adventure but gave it little consideration till sometime later Edith showed me a prospective itinerary and a tentative price around $1,800. She wanted to know what I thought of it now.

I was interested. Siberia had never been high on my list of places to visit but I knew the Trans-Siberian Railroad was the longest railway in the world and thought it would be an adventure. Edith was lukewarm. She still had a healthy American dislike of Russia and had never heard a thing about Siberia that made her want to go there, but she was very devoted to John Daly's eldest son and liked the fact the group would muster in Oslo. She had been working on an article on fish farming for *The New Yorker* and wanted to see a man in Norway who had information she needed. As the project developed we found that we would need visas for Mongolia and China and the easiest way to get them would be to send the passports to Norway and have Liv get them all processed together. So we hit Norway in early April and on April 8 left for Moscow where we would begin our

That worried look is one I had a lot on our 1993 trip on the Trans-Siberian railway. Russia was in chaos and every official seemed to want a different piece of paper. Also didn't want their picture taken.

10,000-mile, two-week train ride to Beijing via Mongolia on the world's longest railroad.

I can find hardly any photos from that trip, particularly the Siberia leg. We were stuck on the train with little opportunity to explore most of the time, but more than that, I seldom saw anything worth pointing a camera at. Siberia as we saw it was just a bunch of bush. It wasn't even very good quality bush. The trees were runty little things nobody would bother cutting in Canada, except maybe for pulp. The little we did see of the people gave the impression of a hardscrabble existence.

There were cities but we didn't see much of them. The railway had apparently been laid out in such a manner as to miss most of the cities so the developers would save the cost of expensive rights-of-way. Most of what we went through wasn't as far north as I expected, generally somewhere on the same latitude as Edmonton, though of course Siberia extends right to the Arctic. We had our hopes built up for Lake Baikal which we heard intriguing things about, but we skirted by its shore for only a short distance and got little sense of it except that it's very big—wider than the Georgia Strait to judge by the glimpse we had.

The train itself was as bleak as the countryside. The seats were worn and hard, the bunks narrow and the heat uncertain. Each car had its own coal stove that frequently ran out of coal and kept us coated with a fine skein of coal dust for the entire trip. Being filthy and unable to wash is what Edith remembers most about that trip. Food supply was equally tenuous. The train's cook would get out on the platform with his basket and try to scrounge up the makings of a meal from whatever hawkers happened to be selling—little pastries, rutabagas, a duck if we were lucky. This was just after the fall of the Soviet Union and everything was in chaos, nobody knew whose responsibility it was to look after the train's needs or what the new rules were going to be for visas or anything else.

The best thing about taking the Trans-Siberian Railway was being able to say you'd done it later. It's a great conversation starter anywhere you go. People are immediately in awe and want to know all about it. We should have all been issued T-shirts saying "I survived the Trans-Siberian Railway 1993." Unfortunately there is not much to say about it other than the fact you did it. It was an epic of boredom.

Things didn't start to look up until we finally got out of Siberia and into Mongolia. I didn't know what to expect from Mongolia and crossing the cold wasteland of the Gobi Desert didn't seem too promising at first but the warmth and friendliness of the people was a contrast to the dour, depressing Siberians.

The next memorable experience for me was when our train reached the Chinese border and we had to disembark while they jacked the whole thing up and switched the wheels for the narrower-gauge Chinese rails. They lifted each car individually on a hoist and removed the Russian trucks—sets of four wheels, springs and axles—wheeled them down the track, and wheeled narrower Chinese trucks back in. It took hours. Just an incredible amount of work, and they had to do this on every trip, coming and going. Why they did it this way instead of using the adjustable-gauge trucks like they have in many parts of Europe would be hard to say.

We ran across the Great Wall of China in several places but I am sorry to say it was a bit of a letdown. First, it's not very big. It varies in height from about that of a tall man to about that of a two-storey building. It doesn't tower up before you like the Edinburgh castle, or even the wall of a large fort like Fort Adams in Rhode Island. It's more like a city wall around a small medieval town. I had always heard it was the only man-made structure visible from space, but that has to be bullshit, since it is nowhere near as wide as the average freeway. Looking down at it from space would be like looking down at a water hose from a plane a mile up in the air.

Its entire claim to greatness is based on its length, which is about 5,000 miles on the main trunk and over 10,000 miles including all the branches. The main wall would stretch right across the Canada–US border with 1,000 miles left over. But since you can't see more than a mile or so in any one chunk in most places, you just have to take all that length on faith. And of course, it is no longer all there. Some of it was built of stone and brick but most was made of packed dirt that has long since collapsed. The stone parts have been cannibalized by builders who for hundreds of years treated it as a handy local rock quarry. The impressive-looking sections with battlements and guardhouses you see on postcards are mostly relatively short stretches that have been reconstructed as tourist attractions near big cities. Which is not to deny it was one of the wonders of the

Inspecting the Great Wall with Edith, Dick Daly, his wife Liv (front) and two of their friends in 1993.

ancient world. It might be the most wonderful one of all, but its greatness doesn't knock your eyes off like the Taj Mahal or those big Mexican ruins.

Beijing itself was interesting. The big tourist attraction is the Forbidden City which is not forbidden and not a city but a palace about the size of the West Edmonton Mall containing 9,999 rooms formerly used by the emperors and their hangers-on. The present structures were mostly built in the 1700s and used right into the twentieth century so the whole thing is in mint condition. A couple of the main buildings are a pretty fair size, but most of them are not all that huge. The thing that got me was that they were built out of wood and some of the roof beams would hold their own in a BC coast longhouse. They must have had some serious timber in old-time China and it must have been long gone by the nineteenth

At the Forbidden City in Beijing I spent all day trying to find where they used the big Douglas fir timbers we sent over from BC, but it wasn't obvious.

century because when they were renovating the palace in 1884 they had to come to BC to find timbers big enough to replace the original beams. That was a little before my time in the BC woods but I do remember stories of this special order for knot-free timbers two feet square and 120 feet long that had to be carefully babied out of the bush somewhere on what is now the UBC Endowment Lands in Vancouver. Normally trees that big would be bucked into short lengths and moving them in one piece must have been quite the operation with bull teams. I kept an eye peeled for any BC Douglas fir but it was hard to say the way they carved it all up.

Edith had picked up a cold somewhere along the way and just got sicker and sicker for the whole rest of the trip. We eventually parted from the Siberia crew and spent another two weeks sightseeing in China and Japan by ourselves. We both got damn sick and China was still a pretty uncomfortable place to be in 1993 so the rest of our time there kind of blurs. We ducked into Hong Kong again and this time I had the right information to visit Wesley's grave at Sai Wan cemetery, which fulfilled a life mission.

We were booked for a week in Japan and we were both so beat we just wished we could be home but fortunately we decided to look up an old college friend of Howie's named Dave Jack, who had become a magazine publisher in Kobe. Dave grew up in London but came to Canada to attend university before moving to Japan. He had apparently stayed at our place in the Harbour back in the 1960s but I couldn't even remember and wouldn't have had the nerve to bother him except Edith was all for it.

Dave and his Japanese wife Sachiko turned out to be the kindest people Edith or I met in the whole of Asia. They welcomed us like royalty and took us out to their little farm in Sasayama, which they were restoring along traditional Japanese lines with a thatched roof and all the old-timey touches, including special shoes you had to slip into each time you went from one room to another. If you got up in the night to take a pee, you had to go through about four changes of footwear on your dash to the can, and Edith could never get it right. Dave and Sachiko, mostly Sachiko, sensed how beat we were and basically just pampered us for the whole time we were there, and we just relaxed and let them do it.

I pottered around in the little backyard garden they had there and helped Dave lay out some stone pathways. He was such a blur of activity,

Edith and I in New Brunswick sometime in the 1990s.

tossing around a few shovelfuls of soil, dashing off to his office, picking at this and pecking at that, I could never figure out quite what he was up to. Their magazine, which they operated together, was a kind of events calendar for the Kansai region (Kobe-Osaka-Kyoto) for English-language readers and was quite a successful operation. But Dave had all kinds of other irons in the fire—a dormitory for schoolgirls in Bangladesh, an ecological preserve in Hong Kong, a folklore centre in Scotland, an artist's loft in Vancouver—and he seemed to spend all his time moving between these projects trying to make good things happen like a small-scale Jimmy Carter. I don't think he has any great fortune to spend on it, he just seems to want to use what he has to make a difference, even a small difference. I couldn't help thinking that if more people did like him it would be a lot better world.

Dave managed to spare plenty of time to show Edith and I around and take us out to some fabulous sites and restaurants we would never have been able to find (or afford) on our own. Typically, Edith and Sachiko became fast friends and have been visiting and exchanging gifts ever since. By the time we were ready to take our flight home we were almost feeling human again. We hadn't quite racked up the miles I had with Cindy and Ken in 1982 but these were harder miles, and I was ten years older. My old brown house at Lagoon and Francis Peninsula Roads had never been such a welcome sight.

Edith and I continued to take a trip or two each year up until a "Great Cities of Europe" tour in 2004 that was a flaming disaster because of her sore back. We never should have gone and I couldn't tell you to this day how we came to do such a dumb thing. I would say it was all Edith's idea, except I don't want to risk restarting the argument. She has this way of twisting your arm until you agree to do something, then it becomes something that's all your doing and she has to put up with it. We argued for months—

"I thought you said you wanted to see Belfast where your father came from, I thought you wanted to see Scotland where your mother's people came from . . . "

"Well, I kind of do I guess . . . "

"All right then, let's book it before it's too late . . . "

"Okay . . . "

"I'm just doing this for you, you know. I've seen all these places."

"But I don't need to see them right now. We could wait until your back is better . . . "

"Do you want to go or not? I have to know because my travel agent is waiting for me to call."

"Well, I guess I can stand it if you can . . . "

"I can stand it if I know it's what you want. I've seen it all before so it's not for me."

There was no way I could dislodge the idea from her head, so eventually we found ourselves on this bus bouncing all over Europe and the British Isles with the goddamndest collection of neurotics and nitwits you ever met in your life. It would have been a disaster even if we were both in good shape but Edith's back was giving her such agony I fully expected she'd end up in the emergency ward before we were done. She couldn't sit, she couldn't sleep, she didn't feel like eating and every time I suggested we drop out and spend a few days resting in some nice hotel she'd gasp, "No, we have to keep on because I know how much you want to see these goddamned places. It doesn't matter to me because I've seen them all before."

That's my baby.

24

The Greatest Show on Earth

That was our last expedition overseas. Our next big escapade was the summer of 2005, which we spent in New York getting Edith's back fixed. All her Canadian doctors told her she shouldn't do it because she was too old to go through five hours of surgery and given her advanced osteoporosis it was doubtful an operation would succeed but she just ignored them and went for it. We spent the whole summer in New York, recovering in hospital for about three weeks then another month or so in her friend Leigh Cauman's sprawling old apartment on Riverside Drive.

She had got addicted to morphine in the hospital and went through cold-turkey withdrawal at Leigh's which caused her to grow big horns and long fangs and terrorize everyone within shouting distance. We tried to hire caregivers but she fired them as fast as we hired them. Jay was there part of the time, just as stressed out as she was, bouncing off the walls and adding to the commotion. I don't think we could have made it through without my grandson Patrick, who was attending Columbia University at that time and also rooming with Leigh, along with his beautiful future wife Ariel.

Patrick hadn't had much of an idea what he wanted to be growing up in Pender Harbour except maybe a hockey player but at university he had started chasing a girl who worked on the student newspaper and got interested in Edith's old profession. Edith jumped all over this and convinced him the only thing to do was go to her old journalism school in New York, where she not only helped him get accepted, she arranged for cheap board with her childhood friend Leigh, who had been a Columbia professor and owned this big ramshackle place across the street. That made the whole thing affordable but proved to be a mixed blessing because he ended up being Leigh's personal caregiver.

He had his hands full waiting upon her even before we showed up and he must have felt like the lone orderly on duty during full moon at the nuthouse but he is a very smooth operator whose cool competence I came to admire through that ordeal. I would put my life in that guy's hands any day. Eventually Edith got well enough to fly back to Garden Bay and once she got straightened around, the operation was a complete success. While many of her friends who listened to their doctors went on to battle their spinal stenosis by spending their eighties and nineties bombed on morphine, Edith got another ten years of quality living. Chalk up another one for Hurricane Edie.

Cindy always came down from Prince George for Christmas and after Kay died she took me on several vacations abroad, sometimes with Ken and sometimes just the two of us. Although she and Ken never married they seemed to have a pretty good thing together. His whole focus was high living—gourmet dining, pricey cognac, exotic vacations, collecting Native art. They hit the booze pretty steady but at first it didn't seem to be a problem. Then in about 2000 Ken retired and the bloody guy, he just sat down and drank himself to death. He lost all interest in travel, business, food and did nothing but sit at home and pound back vodka all day long.

Cindy was beside herself and phoned me up once saying, "I've got to get a break. Ken's driving me nuts. I just can't sit here any longer and watch him kill himself. Let's go to Cuba." She left Ken in the care of a nurse. So we spent ten days or so banging around Cuba and while we were there Ken died at home in his bed with his forty-pounder of vodka at his side. It was quite a jolt to her naturally, but everybody knew it was coming so we figured she could handle it. And she seemed to, for a while.

She'd had such a battle with Ken trying to get him to stop drinking I thought it would at least serve as a lesson to her about her own drinking, but that would be too logical. She had been completely fed up with Ken before he finally went down for the third time, but now she was doing the standard survivor thing of going all mushy about what a fine person he'd been and beating herself up about how she hadn't done enough to help him. Bizarrely, instead of swearing off booze herself, she dove in deeper than ever.

In the winter of 2005 she slipped on the ice outside her door and got banged up pretty good. She was probably a little tipsy at the time but you didn't have to be, up there. I had taken a header myself and pulverized what was left of my kneecap when I was up visiting. Anyway, she decided the time had come to get away from the rough northern winters and move back to the coast where she could be close to the family. I ought to have been happy about this, but we all knew what a problem she'd be bringing with her so we couldn't help feeling a little uneasy about it. Still, with family around her she might pull herself together.

She set up her publishing office in Halfmoon Bay and we were seeing a lot of her but her behaviour continued to be a worry. She was never without a wineglass in her hand and even when she wasn't obviously drunk her conversation was confused. She looked bloated and her colour wasn't good.

Cindy never stopped smiling.

I remembered Les McGarva going the same way before he died and it worried the hell out of me, but she was just as stubborn as ever and wouldn't let you even bring up the subject of drinking. Then one day, Friday, May 13, 2005, to be exact, Edith phoned her up and invited her to go to dinner and a show with us in Sechelt.

I pulled into her yard and thought it was funny she didn't come to the door. I knocked but no answer. I opened the door and her dog just about took my arm off. She had a rotten goddamned pit bull that terrorized everybody

everywhere she went but it was just another one of Cindy's things—
nobody was going to tell her she couldn't have this vicious dog, which she
insisted was sweet and wonderful once you got to know it. I booted the
mutt out of the way and got a better look. Cindy was lying on the floor in
a pool of blood. At first I thought the dog had attacked her. I bent down
and took her pulse and thought I could feel something. I started giving her
mouth-to-mouth while Edith called the ambulance, then Howie and Don.
I kept doing mouth-to-mouth until the ambulance got there but found
out she'd been dead the whole time.

The grim, hard-faced doctor at the hospital told us bluntly that there
was no use doing an autopsy because it would only prove what she was
already sure of, and that was that Cindy died from a gastrointestinal
haemorrhage. The doctor said even if she'd been in the hospital when it
happened there was nothing they could have done to save her. A haemorrhage can happen to anyone at any time but in the doctor's opinion
Cindy's was likely linked to alcohol abuse.

Everybody complimented me on how well I handled the whole thing
but the truth was I was completely numb. I was running on autopilot. You
wish you could cry or yell or get drunk like I would have done in the old
days, but you get to a point in your life where your feelings just can't rise
to the occasion anymore. It feels like your heart has turned to stone, which
is worse than the sharpest pain. I have never to this day completely come
to grips with it, except to say, "Poor little Cyn."

She had an uphill battle all the way.

You could blame booze but of course it's not only the booze. Alcohol is
just a chemical. There has to be a susceptibility in the person to create the
drinking problem. But if that weakness is there—and I think it's there in
damn near everybody, given the right conditions—booze is just the thing
to throw gas on the embers.

It's no big news to say alcohol does more damage to life and limb and
costs more in broken lives, lost jobs, health care and every other social
indicator than any other drug. Just look at the impact it's had on my own
story here—and I haven't told the half of it. I bet if I added it up, half
the people from my close circle died with a bottle in their hands, decades

before their time and with their lives in shambles, most of them. Les McGarva, Jack Spence, Frank Campbell, two of my sisters' husbands, Ken Carling, Cindy—I could go on. And I don't think that's one bit unusual. Everybody thinks their own experience with alcohol is an exception where really it's the norm.

For most of my life I was just as big an apologist for alcohol as anybody. But the longer I live and the more devastation I see it cause the more I wonder if shrugging it off is really the best we can do. Someday hopefully we will wake up and start treating alcohol addiction like we've learned to treat nicotine addiction. Stop pushing it at every chance and provide some properly funded treatment services instead of leaving it to overworked volunteers like AA and MADD. Educate people. I think that's the main thing. Pull back the veil of silence and shine light on the problem. I think that was the biggest thing in the battle against smoking—the scientific research and public education.

In the meantime we have to deal with the problem on an individual level in our own families. You have to fight back, I see now. If Kay hadn't made such a goddamn scene about my drinking back when we were first married, I would have ended up just like Les McGarva. I was in love with drinking, but that brave young woman forced me to choose. It took me years to appreciate what she'd done for me. Not that I quit completely, but I cut back to occasional binges and tapered down to a rare beer as I got older. Edith took a stand too, in her own life. She divorced Phillip Hamburger over his boozing, and it saved him, too. He quit drinking and got his life back on track. I can think of other cases where people got their spouses off the bottle by forcing them to choose. It's easier just to go along saying, "He has to make up his own mind," but that is a cop-out. If you truly care about a person, you have to take a stand.

So here I am, fed, washed and warm. The kids all did great, except poor Cyn. Marilyn had the two boys who went into the computer business and Howie's two boys both turned out fine too. Silas is a publisher and public administrator and Patrick is a reporter with the *Globe and Mail* newspaper, both married with children. Don married Crystal Cummings, whose family went back to a famous BC pioneer named Portuguese Joe

Silvey who had married into the Sechelt nation, so we finally acquired some serious local roots. Crystal is a wonderful girl and gave us two fine twins, Daniel and Kathleen. So far there's eight great-grandchildren, all healthy and beautiful. Not one bad apple in the bunch. Not even one as bad as me. This is everything a man could hope for. But do you think I can just sit back and enjoy it?

Every day that goes by I have this empty feeling, thinking I should have done something that I didn't get to. I couldn't name what it even was most of the time. I used to wake up worrying about getting the trucks out on the road ready to put in a full day's hauling. Or about getting the logging crew all organized and putting logs in the water. Or getting the Narrows Road subdivision finished by the July 1 deadline. A thousand things to be done, ordering in the blasters, refilling the fuel tanks on all the machines, finding a new cat operator, replacing the bad rollers on the loader and on and on.

Now it's fixing the automatic sprinkler for Edith's window boxes, something I've been avoiding since last year. Or writing a single email congratulating my grandson Patrick on his wedding, which I put off until it was too late. Now instead of R and R'ing the rear end of the gravel truck, my day's big challenge is getting dressed and getting out to the breakfast table—and it isn't a bit less daunting. Coping with extreme old age is some of the hardest work I've ever done.

It's okay, I'd be ungrateful to complain, knowing how much worse a lot of my old pals ended up, most of them dead with burst livers thirty years ago and others like Jack Spence faded away to shadows in institutions, alone and forgotten. But it occurs to me—and maybe here's the great insight I've been looking for—it occurs to me we are nuts to spend all our lives preparing for this. Work hard all your life and postpone enjoying life so you can do it in your old age. Well, I worked hard all my life and didn't lay away a nickel for my old age but it didn't matter, I still ended up living like a goddamn rajah. Hell, with my old age pension, CPP and a bit of rental income from a mouldy old house trailer I bought ten years ago, I've got more money in the bank than at any time in my life. And I've had thirty years of retirement to do all the things most guys only dream of— travel the world, win the love of a fancy dame, go to endless parties with the rich and famous, watch my seed spread and multiply, achieve honour in my own town—but I have to keep reminding myself about that.

Most times, when I think about my life, these last thirty years don't even enter into my thoughts. They seem to have gone by in the blink of an eye. The only things that I remember vividly are things that happened in my younger years. There could be a lesson there. Maybe we should stop placing our younger years at the service of our later years and spending all the time we're going to remember butting our heads against various walls so when we're old we can be like me and sit around remembering all that head-butting. But then, what the hell else is a guy going to do? Spend your whole life gadding about like a playboy?

What was so memorable about my early years in the twenties and thirties and my prime years in the forties and fifties is that everything was very real. I didn't have time to stop and think if I was doing what I wanted to do because I was doing what I had to do. There is a hell of a difference between doing what you have to do and what you choose to do. In fact, that's probably the biggest difference between the kind of people I spent the first part of my life among and the kind of people I spent the last part among. And you know, this may seem crazy, but I wouldn't trade the life of civilized amusement I led in the last thirty years for the life of toil and hard knocks I lived before.

I can't think of a better way to put it than to say that early life was more real. The fears and worries were heavier but the laughs and victories were better. I'm not sure you'd get that if you were always doing something you didn't really have to do but just picked it from a list of lifestyle options. I didn't retire until I was almost eighty, but when I did I found the sudden lack of purpose to my days unbearable. So there, I don't have any big solution after all. Life is life. It's not under our control and it doesn't follow any script. It just is. And as someone said, it's the greatest show on earth because it's the only show on earth so you might as well just wade in and make the most of it.

The Moving Finger writes; and, having writ,
Moves on: nor all thy Piety nor Wit
Shall lure it back to cancel half a Line,
Nor all thy Tears wash out a Word of it.

I guess the biggest adjustment I had to make living with Edith and the biggest injustice to Kay, was getting used to sitting in the passenger seat and letting the woman do the driving. Not literally—Edith always liked me to drive and egged me on by telling me what a great driver I was even after I started dragging one wheel in the ditch but we went where she wanted to go. She would deny this of course, but if I am allowed to call witnesses I am confident I can eliminate all doubt.

I didn't mind this. There was a time I would have found it hard to have a woman bossing me around (or a man, for that matter) but I learned it's okay to consent to be led if you reserve the right to withdraw your consent, which I did whenever things got too crazy. And she accepted that, so it worked. We were retired and I really didn't know how to play all day, all week, all year. It was a foreign concept to me and she had much more experience at it.

I also lived in her house, John Daly's old house, now owned by his sons but where she had lifetime occupancy. I would rather have lived in my own perfectly good house, the one I built with my own hands and which has our old Green Bay cookhouse still lodged somewhere in its heart, but she wouldn't consider coming over to my side. She must watch over the John Daly Memorial Shrine. There was just never any doubt about that. So I paid the taxes and lights on my house while it sat empty and also paid my share of running her place. I didn't complain. I consider myself the luckiest man in Pender Harbour. We have a great life together. We've been at it now for thirty-three years if you go back to the Metropolitan Opera in 1981. That's only six years less than I was with Kay. I think it's longer than Edith was with Phil.

Howie says he was worried about us getting too serious at first because he was afraid she would chew me up and spit me out, and I guess he wasn't the only one but they should have had more faith. I am a pretty gristly old bastard and make for pretty tough chewing. She tried, in her Hurricane Edie way, and I gave her lots to chew on but if she ever drew blood I would growl and she would back off.

We didn't officially get married until 2006. We had never talked about it and as far as I knew it wasn't on the agenda. We had everything we wanted and

there was the problem of separate estates—more on her side than mine—
and we didn't want to deal with any more legalities than necessary. But one
day she just came out with the idea that we ought to get married so I could
go to New York and get a back operation on her US medical plan.

I wasn't sure she was serious, so I let it pass and waited to see if it came
up again. The same doctor who did her in 2005 had examined me and
offered to fix me up for the minor consideration of about $140,000 cash
money. We went home to think about it and the next year she came up
with this plan that we get married so I could get coverage under her *New
Yorker* medical plan and get the operation. The only trouble was, it wasn't a
bit clear the plan would cover me since I was a foreigner, my condition was
pre-existing and several other hard things. It even turned out that Edith
didn't get her own operation fully covered. She still had to pay $40,000
or so. But once Edith gets an idea, she doesn't let minor obstacles stand in
the way. She decided we were getting married—just for medical reasons,
mind you. I was fine with it. She was my eighty-nine-year-old baby. I
would marry her any day of the week, whatever the reason. But, boy, she
was in a hurry.

I got mixed up in some of the damndest things tagging around with Edith. Here I am on a movie
set chumming it up with one of Charlie's Angels. L to R: director Lee Rose, Jaclyn Smith, me,
Edith signing a book, Tim Matheson. They were filming *Fishing with John*.

Howie and Mary were on holiday in Cuba but we couldn't wait for them to return. The only thing that she would allow to hold us up was the pre-nup. She had a brother-in-law lawyer who advised her on all important matters and they decided the one and only thing that could delay the course of true love was getting a pre-nuptial agreement so neither of us ended up getting our mitts on the other's dough. I had nothing—I'd taken care of things by gifting my property to the kids years earlier.

I don't to this day know what Edith has in her estate. She is very secretive about that. She will only say that she is "comfortable" but I know she considered buying the Daly property which sits on three acres of prime waterfront so I reckon she's not going to have to resort to eating pet food any time soon. There was a great flurry of emails, faxes and special deliveries as various lawyers were reached off-hours and by god if she didn't produce a great long pre-nuptial document for me to sign. I signed without even looking at it. If anybody wants my orthopaedic shoes and leftover Depends, they're welcome to them. With that out of the way she phoned up a marriage commissioner who had married some friends of ours and arranged a date at the commissioner's home in West Vancouver. At first the only guests were going to be her son Jay and his partner Atty, but my son Don and his wife Crystal heard about it and they told my daughter Marilyn so we had a handful after all.

It ended up my back pain died down to a dull roar on its own and we never did do anything with Edith's medical but we didn't regret for a minute getting married. We realized immediately it was the right thing to do, even if we'd done it for the wrong reason. We had been dragging along with that sort of half-assed, "this is my dear friend Frank" stuff too long. It was worth it just in terms of simplified wording.

But it was more than that. I had long since quit hiding my car in the bushes, but there was still a mental hangover of that, of having only one foot in the door and the other out. For both of us. Now we had come in and closed the door. It was only symbolic and we were old enough to be above all the official hocus-pocus, but it was surprising the difference it made in the way we felt. We were like a couple of teenaged lovebirds. As far as financial benefits, they turned out to be all negative. With Edith's extra income added to mine I lost my Canada pension supplement, which has set me back at least $40,000 to date. To the end though, Edith would tell people, "We only got married so I could get Frank on my medical." That's my girl.

So here I sit in my lift-chair, Edith across the room working on a jigsaw puzzle she has been working on contentedly for three weeks, not making any progress as far as I can tell. I think this will be her last jigsaw puzzle. At ninety-seven she looks just as good as ever, at least to me, and she is just as much fun to be around as ever but her memory is pretty much gone. Just before Christmas 2009 she slipped and broke her femur. They put her under a general anaesthetic and she came back confused.

She'd been pretty confused after her back operation in 2005 so I didn't get too worried but after a few months I noticed she wasn't bouncing back all the way this time. She was forgetting our doctor's appointments and Aquafit times. This was unlike her. She'd always had a mind like a steel trap and supported it with a good note-taking habit. Now she was taking more notes than ever, but she'd make the same note five times and still forget it. I could see I was going to have to try to take up the slack but it wasn't going to be easy. If I told Edith she'd forgot something she would be mad as hell and we'd have a big argument. Then by the time it was clear I'd been right she would have forgotten entirely and I would get no credit.

We'd get to dinnertime and there would be nothing on the table or even in the fridge. Don got in a young Filipina woman to live in the spare bedroom and cook for us and make sure we took our pills and she was wonderful. At first it was only supposed to last while Edith was recovering but it was so damned handy we kept her on. Edith didn't like having a stranger in the house and especially didn't like the fact she hadn't been the one who chose the caregiver and she'd complain about her within her hearing. But the girl just kept smiling and doing such a wonderful job of cooking, cleaning, driving Edith back and forth to her physio, shopping for groceries and keeping our meds in order we couldn't face life without her. She has since moved on but now we have Digna and Mina, who are cut from the same cloth and look after our every need. I joke with them that it's worth getting old and broken down just to have a couple of angels waiting at my elbow looking after my every desire.

Of course, that's true and not true. This slow dance into extreme old age is a scary business. Every time you think you've finally adjusted, it throws a new curve at you. Dropping things you never dropped before. Dropping food on your shirt (something I was none too swift about at the best of times). At first you think you're just getting careless and you tell yourself, "I'm going to have to be more careful." But—surprise surprise!—you're soon dropping more stuff than a two-year-old. In fact this is what is happening to you—you are being reintroduced to your inner infant. Same rubber legs. Same leaky gaskets. Same wobbly chin and weepy eyes. Same gappy memory. Same tiny attention span. Only this big blob is not nearly as cute as he used to be, and this time instead of getting better every day he's getting worse.

I spent a lot of time worrying about losing my mind when I was much younger and think I probably wasted a lot of doctors' time whining about it over the years. I think they probably started explaining to me that I was simply getting older way back in my forties but I was convinced that what was happening to me was much more serious than that. At every new stage of the great downward slide I would get worried all over again and run off demanding to be tested, sure I had brain cancer or something.

I was the first person I knew to have their brain scanned. The results were not encouraging. The doctors wanted to know if I had been dropped on my head a lot. It must have been quite a mess in there because one of the doctors, a guy named Estey, got my kids aside and told them I had thinning of the cerebral cortex and wouldn't be able to be on my own much longer. Estey was good that way, he always seemed to make an effort to satisfy your worst fears. It kind of made up for all the other doctors who spent their time trying to tell you you were just imagining it. Anyway that shut me up for a while and for a long time there I was walking around quite grateful I could still find the doorknob and know which way to turn it.

That must have been forty years ago. I was still working. I have explored the world, had a whole new life and written two books since then. If only I knew it, I had the mind of a rocket scientist then compared to what I have now. So my message to all you middle-aged folks who think you're losing your mind because you can't remember that phone number is, yes, losing your mind is exactly what's happening. But the good news is, it's going to go on for a hell of a long time.

I guess aging is necessary or there would be no place to stand by now, or we'd still be hanging by our tails, since generational succession is necessary for evolution to happen. But some of the tricks the gods of aging play on us poor victims seem just plain mean. Just as you get so clumsy you're bumping and scraping on everything, your skin gets as thin as tissue paper so every scratch bleeds. Just as you lose the ability to bend down to cut your toenails, they start growing faster and more jagged. Ladies' bosoms, which they no longer have any use for, swell up like zucchinis, while the male appendage, which still has a job to do, shrinks out of sight. I know a lot of young bucks just getting into their seventies are not going to want to hear this, but that shrinkage you are beginning to notice keeps right on going until you have an innie instead of an outie. When you go to pee, you can't even tell which flap it's hiding under.

You live in denial for a long time and develop all kinds of ways of cheating, writing notes to yourself and sticking them under the windshield wiper: "Get bread. Get milk. Get pads. Take wallet." You relearn the art of holding things with two hands. With the help of your physio, you learn the proper way to get out of a chair and wonder how it is you never figured that out in all the years you've been doing it.

You learn the roll and crawl method for getting up if you do fall down. That is, for *when* you fall down. On one of our last trips to Vancouver by ourselves Edith and I were staying at our favourite hotel, the Sylvia, and I took a swan dive through the doorway. I was having a hard time doing the roll because my big butt was stuck in the doorway so Edith bent over to give me lift and fell down on top of me. We were both stuck in the doorway then, wriggling around like a couple of beached seals. It took me twenty minutes to wriggle out from under her and seal-hump over to a chair I could pull myself up on. It would have gone quicker if we'd been able to stop laughing.

Doors keep closing. I kept driving until I was ninety-six and would have kept on except one day my legs stopped working. I'd been getting pretty tippy but I kept exercising on the stationary bike and thought I was going to keep my legs, but one day I just found I no longer had the strength to stand. It happened so quick I thought it must be a temporary disorder of some kind so I went to the doctor.

"What do you think is wrong, John?"

He laughed. "What's wrong is you're ninety-six! Most guys your age have been off their feet for ten years already! In fact most guys your age have been pushing up daisies for ten years already!"

Thanks a lot.

I kept driving a little but it wasn't much use because when I got anywhere I couldn't get out of the car. Howie and Don had taken away my old blue pickup and given me a nice little purple Honda that I could handle easier. I loved that little car and felt bad whenever I put a new dent in it. After I had it six months it had so many dents it looked like it had been in one of those storms with baseball-sized hail they have on the prairies. It didn't bother me so much if I could look at a dent and remember where I'd got it. When there started to be big long scrapes and I couldn't remember where I'd got them, I had to admit that wasn't good. Still, I figured it couldn't be too serious as long as there weren't any bits of scalp stuck to it. I'd get static from local busybodies who thought I was a menace to public safety but I didn't figure my tame little jaunts to the medical clinic were much of a threat in a town where you could barely sleep at night for the sound of drugged-up punks burning rubber on the main drag. I'd driven a million miles and those little paint scrapes were the most damage I ever did do.

I'd been driving since I was thirteen and it was hard to give up, especially in a place where you're fifteen miles from the grocery store, but I found you don't have to worry too much about deciding which things to stop doing because you're so old. Just give it a bit more time and the decision will make itself. I wheeled out to the carport in my wheelchair one day and struggled into the driver's seat but when I went to push my foot down on the accelerator I couldn't do it. I didn't have the strength. I could start the engine but I couldn't get the revs up high enough to turn the wheels. That was the end of the great driving career.

People are making quite a big deal over my getting to a hundred but it's really not so special these days. I read somewhere there are 6,000 centenarians drawing breath in Canada right now and it's one of the fastest-growing age cohorts, percentage-wise. Someone is predicting that fully half of the kids born today will live to a hundred or more. Of course, when they say that they're making several brave assumptions I wouldn't want to make about society being able to keep rolling smoothly ahead with no bumps in the road caused by global warming, food shortages, economic collapses, etc. I'm afraid my little great-grandchildren are going to have a fun time of it, but I try not to worry too much about that. It's only us old farts who waste their time grieving over the great days that are gone. Kids take the world as they find it and make the most of it. Like I say, I lived through the some of the worst disasters in history and I think I've had an easy go of it.

People ask me what I owe my long life to and I say, "Medicare." It's sure not clean living. I smoked and drank, never met a sausage I didn't like, breathed noxious fumes without a respirator and took on so much stress I went forty years without getting a good night's sleep. If I was ever held up as an example of how to live it would cause a national health crisis.

Without affordable modern medicine I wouldn't have lived as long as my old man, who died at sixty-four. I got a bone infection in my forties that would have stopped me if not for antibiotics. The tic douloureux would have finished me in my fifties if not for Dr. Turnbull and his handy cranium cutter. And I would have been off my feet in my seventies if not for joint replacements. For a while there I was getting so many operations and getting so many bionic parts my son-in-law Dave Wilson joked about expecting to see bolts sticking out the sides of my head. I don't feel like it but I guess I'm the forerunner of a new trend, a working man kept alive far past his time by universal health care. They say if this trend continues by 3014 there will be 25 million people my age in North America. I'm sure glad I won't be around to witness that.

When I peer into the battered old gas drum these days it's clear I'm running on fumes. Living this long is like returning from a very long journey revisiting landmarks you never expected to see again—oh, here's where I learned how to drive—now I'm unlearning that; here's where I unlearn how to walk; here's where I unlearn how to eat; here's where I unlearn my name. It's the great undoing. I seem to remember uttering some brave talk not so very many years ago about how I hoped somebody would shoot me before I got to the stage I'm at now but once you're here you find yourself kind of hanging on. The next step in the great undoing is so close you can smell it and there seems no need to rush. Living this way may not be great, but it's something. And when you're this close to the great blackout you can see that it is just a whole bunch of nothing.

Of course it's different for everybody and Edith and I are a bit unusual in that we still have each other. Our individual ages are not that special but our combined age (197) probably puts us near the top of the list for couples still living together in their own home. Having companionship at this final stage of the journey is such a gift I can't imagine being without it.

When Edith looks at me with my breakfast all over my bib she just laughs. She doesn't spill her food all down her front or need help in the bathroom like I do but she does now have to ask me who John Daly was.

"He was one of your many husbands."

"How many husbands did I have?"

"Only three that I know of. But there's still time."

When she laughs it sounds just as good to me as it did when I first heard it all those years ago in New York.

"You're the only man for me. I love you to pieces," she says.

I tell her it was worth waiting a hundred years for that.

And I mean it.

Index

Page numbers in **bold** refer to photographs